I0335932

ALSO BY THE AUTHORS

***Joy Jots: Exercises for a Happy Heart* by Dr. Tamara Gray**

Now in its second edition, *Joy Jots* is a collection of fifty-two weekly essays that take the reader through a year of seasons, blessings, and joyful spiritual growth. The reader goes on a journey from lessons learned to lessons lived, from talking about joy to feeling joy, and from the limitation of misery to the freedom of joy.

A joy jot is a phrase coined around mindful thankfulness. As the reader works through the reflection prompts and practical projects at the end of each essay, she will find herself collecting joy jots—happy moments or points of deep thankfulness to God. As the habit of joy develops, the reader will begin to know herself better, draw closer to her fellow human beings, and set herself firmly upon the path that leads to real, all-encompassing joy—in this life and the next.

Every day should have a joy jot!

***A Compendium of the Sources on the Prophetic Narrative* by Samira al-Zayid, translated by Susan Imady, Tamara Gray, and Randa Mardini**

This multiple award-winning, comprehensive compilation of narrations and details of the life of Prophet Muhammad ﷺ has never before been available in English! Internationally acclaimed as "the most authoritative resource" on the *sīra*, this two-volume translation is revolutionary in bringing his ﷺ life to vivid reality for everyone who opens its beautiful pages. The original volumes have won the approval and praise of numerous scholars. Now, it is at last available as a treasured English text for your personal or educational development.

***Sophia's Journal* by Najiyah Diana Maxfield**

Her cell phone is dead and she has no idea where she is.

After a bad fall in the river, sixteen-year-old Sophia suddenly finds herself in nineteenth-century Kansas. She struggles to adjust to new food, new entertainment, and a new family. She is still a twenty-first century Muslim girl, though, so slavery is intolerable and the way Native Americans are treated is unacceptable. Sophia copes the best she can as she tries to understand how she got there, how she can help those she's met, and if she will ever get back.

Sophia's Journal is a fresh take on a pivotal moment in American history. Filled with adventure, romance, and self-discovery, it offers a glimpse into a world half-forgotten, from a vantage point like no other.

PROJECT LINA

Bringing Our Whole Selves to Islam

PROJECT LINA

Bringing Our Whole Selves to Islam

Dr. Tamara Gray & Najiyah Diana Maxfield

DAYBREAK PRESS
Minneapolis
2020

Project Lina: Bringing Our Whole Selves to Islam

Published by:

Daybreak Press | 3533 Lexington Ave N.| Arden HIlls, MN. 55126

Online: www.rabata.org/daybreakpress/ | Email: daybreakpress@rabata.org

ISBN: 978-0-9992990-5-0

Library of Congress Control Number: 2020936249

Cover design by Reyhana Ismail: www.reyoflightdesign.com

Design and typesetting by www.scholarlytype.com

Keep Calm and Muslim On cartoons by Mya Lixian Gosling

www.goodticklebrain.com/keepcalmandmuslimon

Printed in the United States of America

بسم الله الرحمن الرحيم

In the Name of God, Most Gracious, Most Merciful

To our beloved sisters, friends, and family members who have chosen to walk the path of faith—we dedicate this book to you in hopes that it will be a welling spring of love, warmth, and hope in a world that often seems a desert.

To our teachers who have nourished us and helped us bring our whole selves to Islam, given us strong spines plated in knowledge, and pushed us to tend our own relationship ties—we dedicate this book to you in hopes that it will be a continuous reward and a continuation of your blessings in our lives and the lives of others.

To our beloved Messenger, Muhammad son of Abdullah, peace and blessings be upon him, the fountainhead of joy, knowledge, and goodness—we dedicate this book to you as we dedicate our lives to your example, light, and love.

CONTENTS

Lina 1

Acknowledgements 2

Foreword: Turning Toward Islam and Why *Feeling* Muslim Matters 3

Project Lina Becomes a Book: An Introduction 19

Module One: Know Yourself 23

Will the Real Me Please Stand Up? 25

Part One: What's in the Self? 27

Part Two: What's in a Name? 58

Part Three: What's in a Culture? 76

Module Two: Declare Independence 89

Independent Thinking 91

Part One: Know the Terms 94

Part Two: Know the Belief 129

Part Three: Know the Tools 154

Module Three: Tend Your Ties 173

Musical Webs 175

Part One: Parents, Family, and Other People Who Didn't Buy a Ticket to Your Conversion 176

Part Two: Friends 201

Part Three: Wed Wisely 212

Conclusion 228

Appendix A: Questions for a Potential Suitor 231

Appendix B: Resources 242

Appendix C: Salat and *Duʿā*'s for Parents 245

Notes 250

LINA

The Arabic word *līna* means "palm tree" in English. A palm tree is a fascinating tree in that it is uniquely adapted to draw its sustenance from deep within the earth, using those nutrients to produce highly beneficial fruit. Building on this metaphor, *Project Lina: Bringing Our Whole Selves to Islam* offers Muslims the necessary steps to grow as a palm tree grows—digging deep roots into the soil of knowledge and faith and spreading wide branches that become heavy with the fruit of Islamic work and good deeds.

ACKNOWLEDGEMENTS

The foundation of this book was built over many conversations, tears of pain, and smiles of delight. We have both worked with converts for years, nascent and veteran, and the topics, stories, and types of support found here are a direct result of their goodness, openness, and sometimes, their failures and tragedies.

We thank everyone we have worked with during the Project Lina workshops, those we have learned from on the Muslim Women Convert Circle Facebook page, and every convert we have met and loved across the globe.

This book is enriched by Karla Kovacik, whose research in the lived experiences of convert Muslim women has been succinctly and beautifully summarized in a special foreword.

We are also indebted to Jennifer Crooker (tailsoffaithandlove.com) and Mya Lixian Gosling (goodticklebrain.com/keepcalmandmuslimon) for their generous contributions of original material to this book. Andrea Cluck, may God have mercy on her soul, also contributed her original list of questions to ask a suitor, which is found in Appendix A, and we (and everyone who finds a good husband as a result!) are very grateful. We have also used Andrea's 99 names of God chart in the book and pray that her reward is continuous.

The entire team at Rabata—and especially Raghad al Syed, Afshan Malik, and Eamaan Rabbat—supported us, encouraged us, and picked up our slack to make sure this book saw the light of day. We are grateful and pray that their blessings are numerous and their reward is sparkly as a result.

We were able to dig in and write the first draft of *Project Lina* because of a generous grant from the Minnesota Educational Trust Fund. We are grateful to them for their belief in this project.

FOREWORD

Turning Toward Islam and Why *Feeling* Muslim Matters

Karla Kovacik

The turning away from the familiar and known territory of one's family upbringing and the turning toward the unfamiliar and unknown territory of a new religious tradition—a new way of life—is a complex process. Even more complex is understanding how our identities shift and change and grow as a result of this turning and whether there are factors that can affect these changes and if so, what they are. This line of questioning grew out of my own experiences as an American female convert to Islam, as well as from listening to the experiences of so many of my convert friends. I wondered how many others were experiencing challenges in their conversion, such as religious discrimination and prejudice, not only from strangers but also from friends and family and even from other Muslims. I wondered how many other converts felt locked out of religious knowledge or were feeling alienated and lonely in their newfound religion.

Questions Become Research

These questions kept me up at night and became the topic of many discussions with friends—discussions which would ultimately lead me to design and conduct a mixed-methods study of US women converts to Islam, and as of today, it remains the largest study of its kind. I remember the afternoon when I began playing around with the term "feeling Muslim."[1] I wondered how many other converts did not *feel* Muslim—and I also wondered what it means to feel Muslim. Through my study, Feeling Muslim: An Intimate Portrait of Identity Cultivation among American Female Converts to Islam, which was conducted in 2014, and the writing of my 2015 MA thesis, "Feeling Muslim: Prolegomena to the Study of American Female Converts to Islam," I began to understand the complex and varied answers to those questions.

In 2014, 459 American women converts from all over the world answered the call to participate in the Feeling Muslim study. Of the 459 women who completed the quantitative section, 257 of them also completed the qualitative questions in the study, which were challenging and required a great deal of introspection as well as honesty regarding their personal and private experiences.

It is from the answers of these 257 women that I was able to glean the most information.

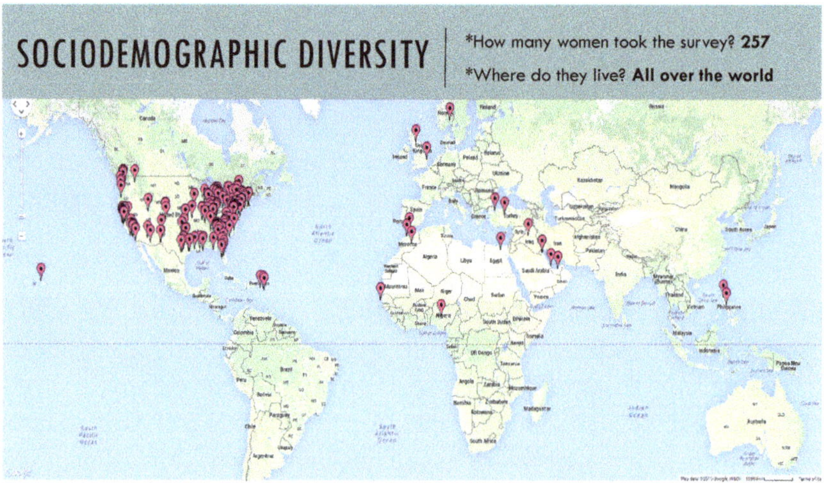

Educational Background

Based on the sample, Muslim women converts are highly educated. One hundred percent either graduated high school or completed a GED, and a whopping 95%

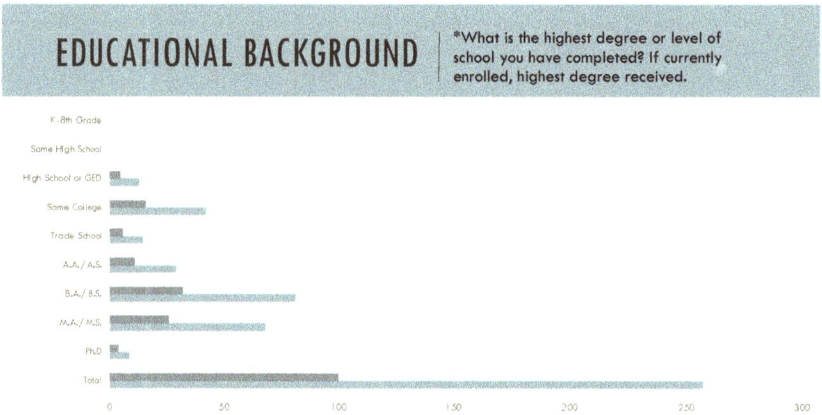

	Total	Ph.D	M.A./M.S.	B.A./B.S.	A.A./A.S.	Trade School	Some College	High School or GED	Some High School	K-8th Grade
Percentage	100	4	26	32	11	6	16	5	0	0
Number of Responses	257	9	68	81	29	15	42	13	0	0

attended college. Of the 95%, 6% attended trade school, 11% have an associate's degree, 32% have a bachelor's degree, 26% have a master's, and 4% have a PhD. Basically, we are smart, there are a lot of us, and we are all over the place.

Race and Ethnicity

In addition to being smart, American women converts to Islam are an incredibly racially diverse group. Of the women who completed the study, 2% are Asian, 7% are Latina, 14% belong to two or more races, 20% are African American, and 53% are Caucasian (the remaining 4% identified as other). We are literally a snapshot of the world, all in one group!

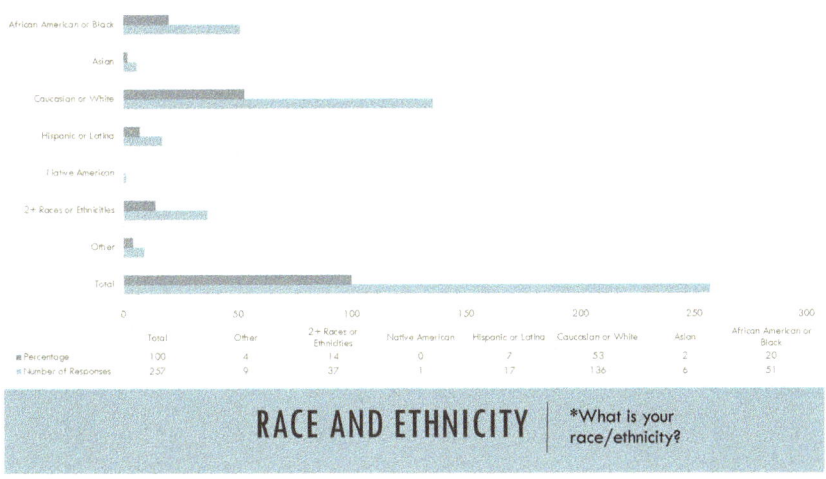

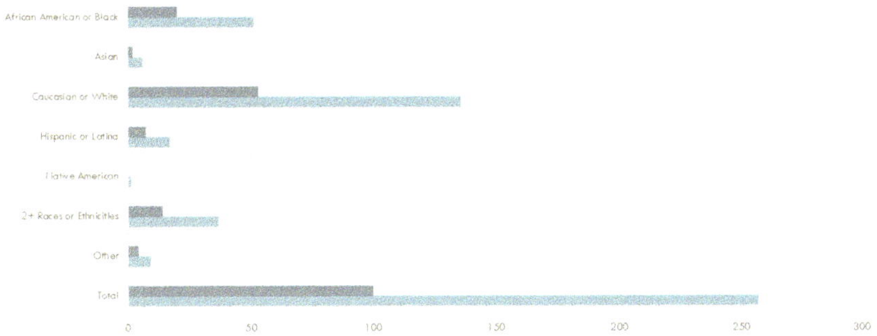

	Total	Other	2+ Races or Ethnicities	Native American	Hispanic or Latina	Caucasian or White	Asian	African American or Black
Percentage	100	4	14	0	7	53	2	20
Number of Responses	257	9	37	1	17	136	6	51

RACE AND ETHNICITY | *What is your race/ethnicity?

How Old Were We When We Converted?

American female converts to Islam choose to convert at many different ages. In the study, 63% of the women were twenty to thirty-four years old at the time of conversion, and 18% were thirty-five years old and older. Additionally, 16% reported being between the ages of sixteen and nineteen at the time of conversion, and 2% reported they were less than sixteen years old, proving that Islam is a religion for all people, in all times, in all places.

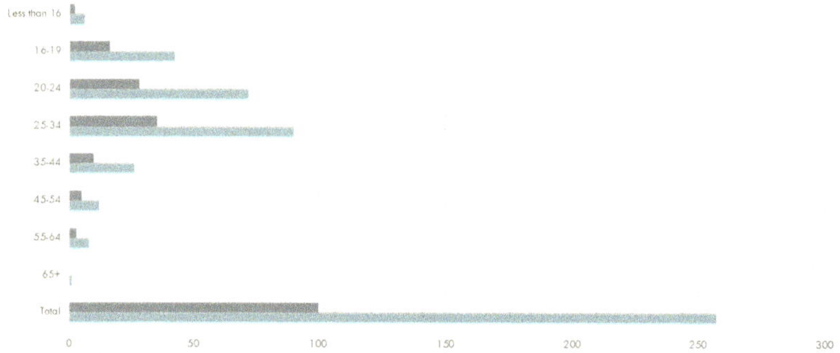

	Total	65+	55-64	45-54	35-44	25-34	20-24	16-19	Less than 16
Percentage	100	0	3	5	10	35	28	16	2
Number of Responses	257	1	8	12	26	90	72	42	6

AGE AT THE TIME OF CONVERSION TO ISLAM | *What was your age at the time of your conversion to Islam?

Converting to Islam from . . . ?

What else? Well, we also held diverse beliefs prior to conversion. A majority of the women were Protestant or Catholic prior to conversion, with others converting from agnosticism, atheism, Buddhism, Judaism, no religious background, or other. Okay. So we're all over the place, we're educated, we're racially and ethnically diverse, and our former beliefs are diverse as well.

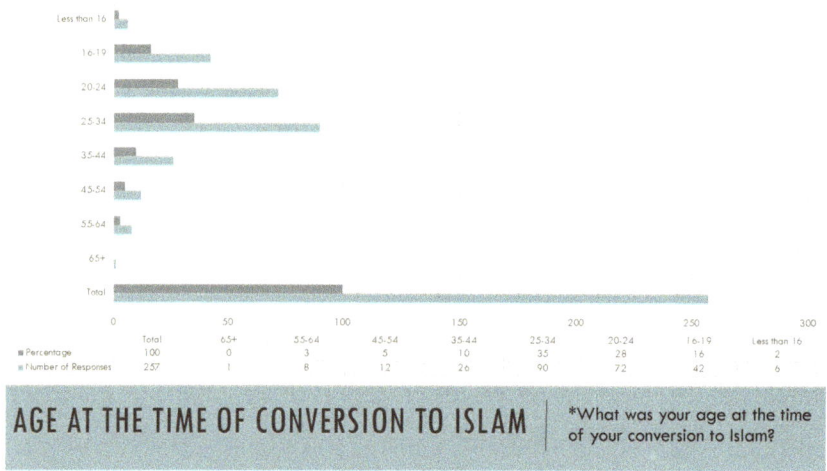

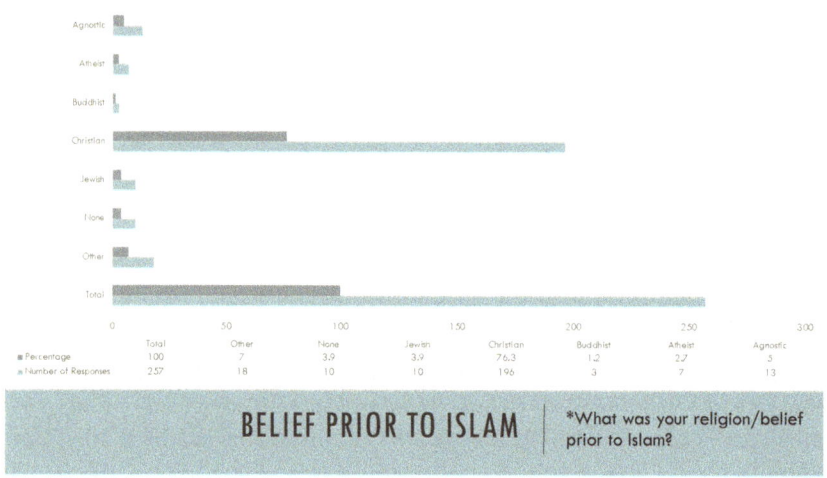

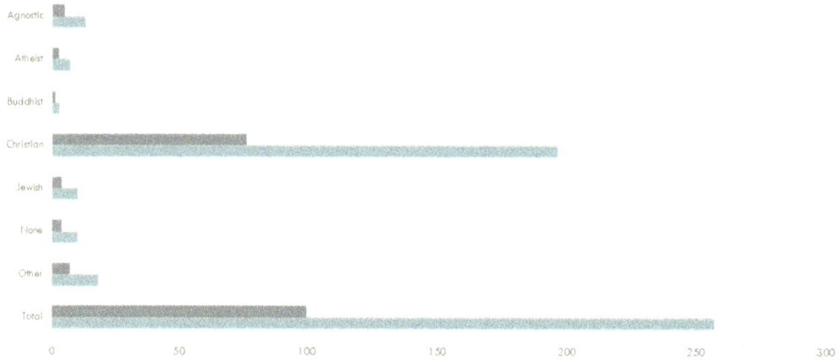

	Total	Other	None	Jewish	Christian	Buddhist	Atheist	Agnostic
Percentage	100	7	3.9	3.9	76.3	1.2	2.7	5
Number of Responses	257	18	10	10	196	3	7	13

BELIEF PRIOR TO ISLAM | *What was your religion/belief prior to Islam?

All Converts Are Married, Right? No!

Let's talk about relationship status. Most American female converts to Islam are (*drumroll*) single in some form at the time of conversion. A whopping 80% of the women were single, divorced, or separated at the time of conversion, with only 20% reporting they were married or engaged. The single status changed for many after conversion to Islam, with 61% of the women reporting their current status (at the time of participation in the study) as married or engaged and 39% as either single, divorced, separated, or widowed. But these statistics certainly debunk the myth that a woman converts for her spouse. While some women did report dating or being friends with a Muslim man before conversion or marrying a Muslim man and then converting, these responses were not the majority and are not representative of the experiences of most American women converts.

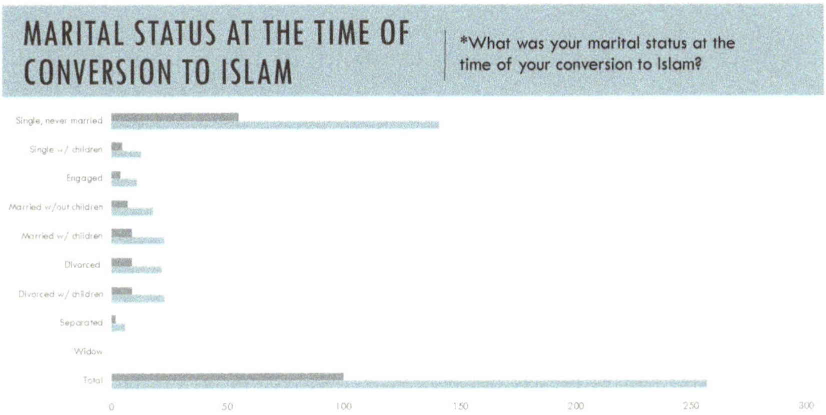

	Total	Widow	Separated	Divorced w/ children	Divorced	Married w/ children	Married w/out children	Engaged	Single w/ children	Single, never married
Percentage	100	0	2	9	9	9	7	4	5	55
Number of Responses	257	0	6	23	22	23	18	11	13	141

How Long Had They Been Muslim?

I was elated to find so much variation in the length of time the women had been Muslim. It was interesting to think about their conversions through a historical lens—thinking about what was happening in the United States and the world more than twenty years ago all the way up to the last three years. I kicked myself, wishing I had added more ranges to choose from after realizing that many of the participants had come into Islam through the Nation of Islam and shifted to Sunni Islam with Malcolm X and/or Warith Deen Muhammad in the 1960s and the 1970s. It is also interesting to look at these numbers in terms of pre- and post-9/11 conversions. The study was conducted in 2014, thirteen years after 9/11. If this sample is any indication, it seems that there was a rapid increase in conversion post-9/11, with 60% of the women reporting that they converted between 2003 and 2014.

LENGTH OF TIME AS MUSLIM | *How long have you been Muslim?

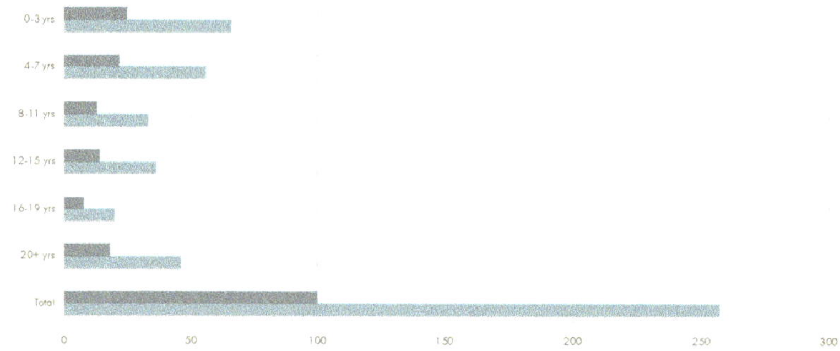

	Total	20+ yrs	16-19 yrs	12-15 yrs	8-11 yrs	4-7 yrs	0-3 yrs
Percentages	100	18	8	14	13	22	25
Number of Responses	257	46	20	36	33	56	66

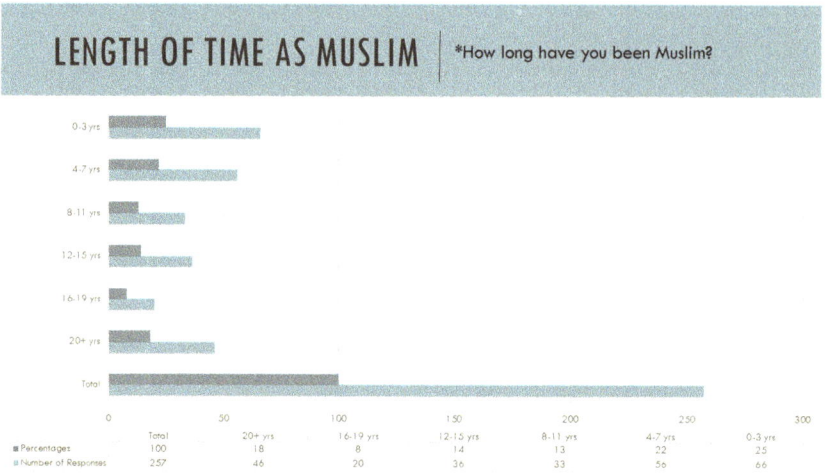

How Do Converts Self-Identify Regarding Branches of Islam?

Yet another interesting statistic came from the varied responses about which branch(es) of Islam the women chose. The largest percentage of the women, 52%, identify solely as Sunni, with the next largest group, 13%, identifying as other, and 11% identifying as both Sunni and Sufi. There were also respondents who identified as solely Sufi, Shi'a, or Nation of Islam, in addition to other branches and combinations of branches. Overall, what I found in these statistics is that American women converts to Islam are not a monolith. We are diverse in many ways. But although we have our differences, the thread that unites us all is that we made the decision to turn away from the territory of the familiar and known and turn toward a new way of thinking, a new way of living, a new way of being: Islam.

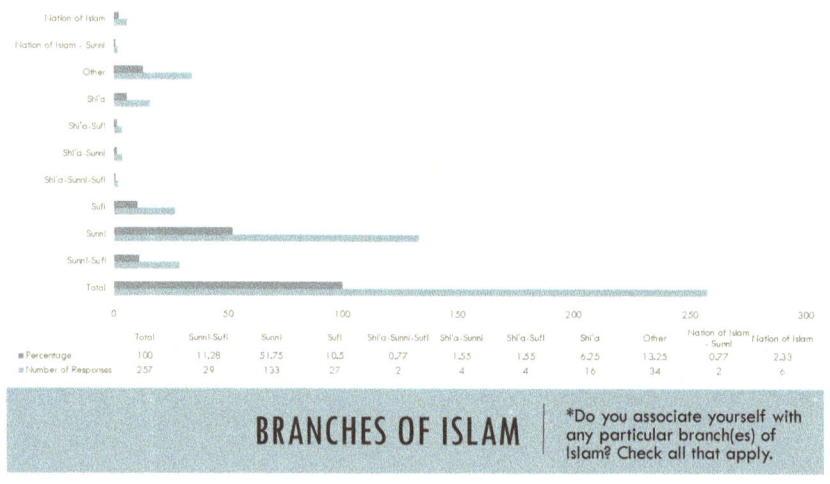

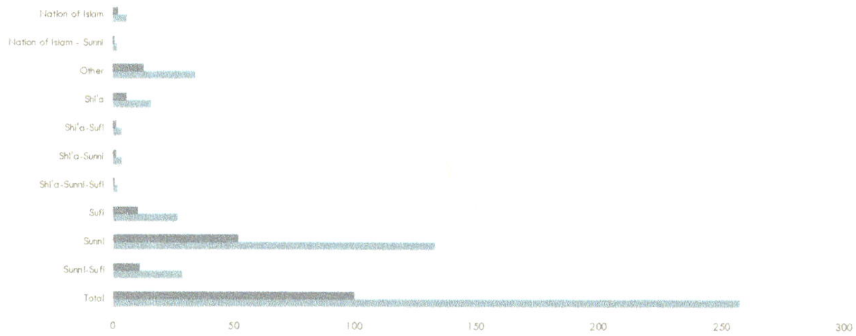

	Total	Sunni-Sufi	Sunni	Sufi	Shi'a-Sunni-Sufi	Shi'a-Sunni	Shi'a-Sufi	Shi'a	Other	Nation of Islam - Sunni	Nation of Islam
Percentage	100	11.28	51.75	10.5	0.77	1.55	1.55	6.25	13.25	0.77	2.33
Number of Responses	257	29	133	27	2	4	4	16	34	2	6

BRANCHES OF ISLAM | *Do you associate yourself with any particular branch(es) of Islam? Check all that apply.

Feeling Muslim

Once I worked my way through the sociodemographic data and got an overall picture of just who American women converts to Islam are, it was time to start reading the written responses of these women—and did they ever write! The outpouring of soul and emotion was incredible. The responses were both beautiful and heart-wrenching. There were days when my data analyst and editor, Barbara (who converted at the age of sixty-two), and I had to take long breaks and talk through things, processing how certain responses made us feel. And that's really what this is all about: feelings, and in particular, *feeling* Muslim and why it matters.

The question the entire study hinged on was, "For you, is there a difference between becoming Muslim by taking the *shahāda* and *feeling* Muslim?" An overwhelming 73% responded that for them there was indeed a difference between becoming Muslim by taking the *shahāda* and *feeling* Muslim. Barbara's and my small circle of friends was not alone in feeling that there was something beyond taking the *shahāda*—that thing that you can't quite put your finger on, but you know it's there: *feeling* Muslim, which I believe is key to the development and formation of a strong Muslim identity, a strong sense of Muslimness.

How We Accomplish *Feeling* Muslim

How the women defined *feeling* Muslim—what it means to *feel* Muslim, when it happens, how it happens, whether it happens at all, and most of all, whether there were outside influences that nurtured or hindered feelings of Muslimness—drove the continuation of my inquiry.

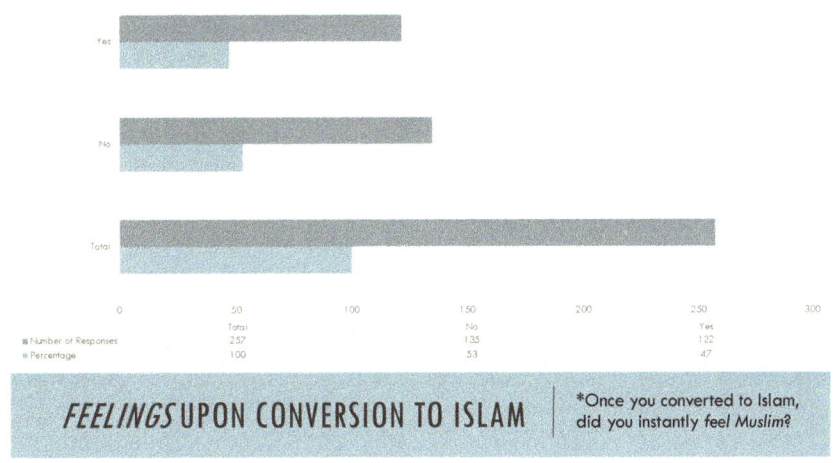

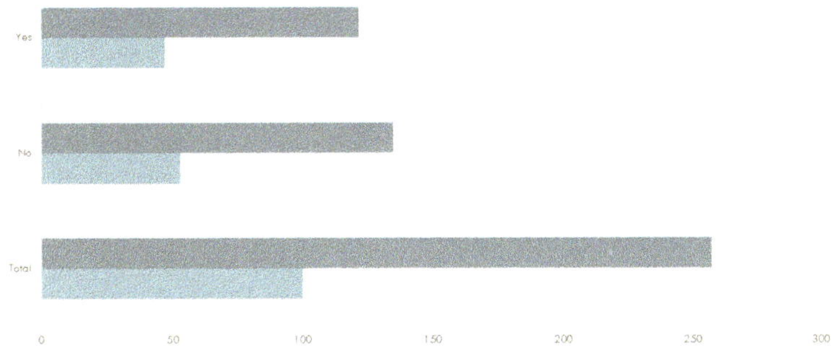

	Total	No	Yes
Number of Responses	257	135	122
Percentage	100	53	47

FEELINGS **UPON CONVERSION TO ISLAM** | *Once you converted to Islam, did you instantly *feel Muslim*?

Did You Feel Muslim Instantly upon Conversion?

Interestingly, 53% of the women said they did not instantly *feel* Muslim upon conversion, while 47% said that they did. No one chose to opt out of this question by choosing NA (not applicable), which is important because it shows that every woman clearly identified either *feeling* Muslim instantly at the time of conversion or not. This told me that these feelings of Muslimness are not static; they can change, for better or worse. And while we are not our emotions, our feelings of Muslimness are more than just fleeting feelings; they are often the foundational building blocks of our Muslim identities—and the foundation they form can be built up by nurturing them, and thus strengthening our Muslim identities, or torn down by hindering them, and thus weakening our Muslim identities.

What Exactly Does It Mean to Feel Muslim?

Several strong themes emerged around the definition of feeling Muslim: feeling Muslim in relation to identity, in relation to community, and in a relationship with the divine. The women also spoke of feeling Muslim as being a process. Here, I'll explore each of these themes using the answers given to me by the women in my study (whose names have been changed to preserve their anonymity).

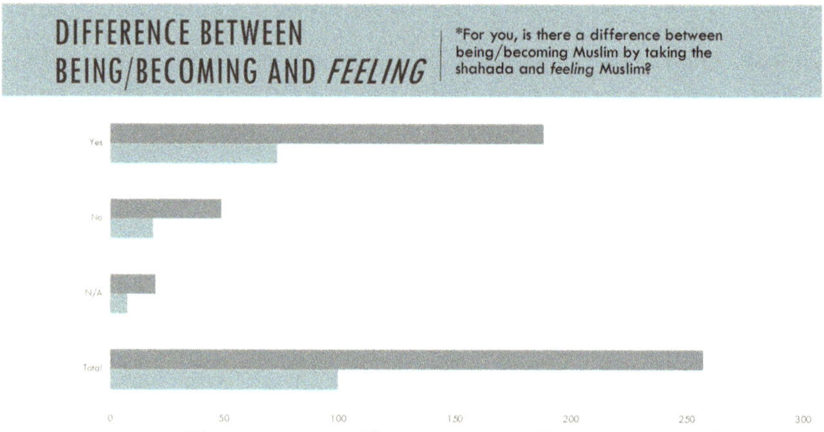

	Total	N/A	No	Yes
Number of Responses	257	20	49	188
Percentage	100	7.78	19.07	73.15

Identity

Regarding the theme of identity and feeling Muslim, Susan said, "Feeling Muslim is more of an internalization of an identity that transcends spiritual beliefs. It's also about culture. It's the feeling you get when Ramadan approaches. It's the feeling you get when you're around non-Muslims. It's a feeling when you hear the *adhān*." Penny also discussed identity and feeling Muslim and said, "This is wrapped up in the question of identity. I identify as Muslim in many ways. Although it's not the only portion of my identity, it is a large portion because it makes up the greater portion of my values and guides my everyday choices. But feeling Muslim would entail feeling I belong as well. That of which I don't always feel. (sic) It's hard to connect to Muslims often." These two responses closely mirror the responses of many of the women who described feeling Muslim as feeling that Muslimness becomes a large guiding portion of their identities, even if not the only part. This also suggests that the development and formation of our Muslim identities is a process that happens gradually, over time, and that it is an extension of the process of religious conversion, which itself consists of stages.[2]

Community

For the theme of feeling Muslim and community, Sumayyah stated, "I feel Muslim because I have a community where we all actively try our best to help each other out and bring each other up, while learning together more about Islam and encouraging more learning and to hang in there through the tougher times, having people that we have so many things in common with, not feeling alone." Ashley said, "The main part of feeling Muslim is spirituality. As an American and Caucasian and not upper class, I don't feel as if the community is or has been welcoming. This makes it difficult to strengthen my *īmān* since I must use the internet or books to learn. To be a part of the Islamic community and to pray with other Muslims and be welcome inside the masjid would help me feel more Muslim. I can pray at home and know I am Muslim based on my

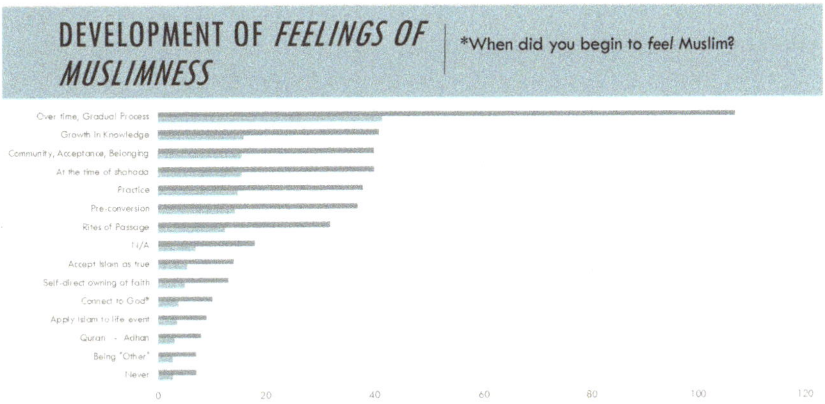

	Never	Being "Other"	Quran - Adhan	Apply Islam to life event	Connect to God*	Self-direct owning of faith	Accept Islam as true	N/A	Rites of Passage	Pre-conversion	Practice	At the time of shahada	Community, Acceptance, Belonging	Growth in Knowledge	Over time, Gradual Process
257	7	7	8	9	10	13	14	18	32	37	38	40	40	41	107
100.00	2.72	2.72	3.11	3.5	3.89	5.06	5.45	7	12.45	14.4	14.79	15.56	15.56	15.95	41.63

beliefs. But to be surrounded by a community of Muslims and practicing our faith in groups and being able to participate in Islamic activities with other Muslims, such as visiting the sick or praying with other Muslims and being able to strengthen my faith and feeding off the positive energy of other Muslims is something that would make me feel Muslim, and this is nonexistent for me in my community."

Ashley's experience of her Muslim community as unwelcoming, making her feel as though she does not belong and stifling her ability to learn and grow in her religion is, unfortunately, a common theme among American women converts to Islam. Her assertion that community support would help her feel Muslim is corroborated by Sumayyah's experience of community support and encouragement.

The Divine

Definitions of feeling Muslim in relation to the divine were varied and described a shift in worldview, a change in outlook on life, outward identification as Muslim, and trust in Allah. Tanya explained, "I think when you 'feel Muslim,' you see the world differently. You see the beauty of Allah's creations. You see how something others might perceive as 'bad' (losing a job, divorce, etc.) is actually something good because Allah intends good for us. You feel like a stranger, not only because of your dress but your outlook on life." Constance seemed to agree with Tanya, saying, "When I can openly show my faith to Allah and to others is when I feel Muslim. It is nothing that is seen with the eyes or made clear by other people but a feeling that the world is whole, and we are here for a purpose that only Allah knows. Once we can truly put all our trust in Allah, we feel Muslim." Both Tanya and Constance described changes in their worldview as their trust in Allah grew. They seemed to tie their outward appearance as Muslims to feelings of Muslimness.

A Process

The theme of feeling Muslim as a process is interesting; many of the women describe the processes they have experienced or are experiencing. Noura said, "I think becoming Muslim is a process, and the regular rules that define Muslims don't always apply to new Muslims, unless they begin with a lot of knowledge. It's a process. The more one learns, the more one is able to become." Sharon seemed to agree with Noura and stated that feeling Muslim is "just a state of being, an acceptance of how things are in the world metaphysically and physically. It's been an evolving process though; sincerity in a wide range of beliefs didn't come all at once but progressed over time." Another respondent, Sara, very clearly articulated that "feeling Muslim means I am secure in my belief in God, in my faith and practice, and in the major tenets of Islam. That I do not need to look to others for validation or religious or cultural authenticity." These three responses represent what many of the women expressed, that feeling Muslim is a process; it is something that happens gradually, over time. It is taking ownership of one's Islam, and it is in this gradual process that we can begin to identify phases in the formation and cultivation of our Muslim identities, identifying key events and factors that aid the process, hinder it, or stop it completely.

How Can We Develop Feelings of Being Muslim?

What all these women have done is provide precisely the kind of information that Muslim communities around the world can use to help American converts to Islam *feel* Muslim, thus increasing the likelihood they will remain in the fold of Islam and not just survive but thrive.

Forty-two percent of the women experienced feeling Muslim as a gradual process that happens over time. Nearly the same percentage began to feel Muslim with a growth in their Islamic knowledge and practice, community acceptance, and a sense of belonging. Many women also reported beginning to feel Muslim prior to conversion when they were part of a community and participated in rites of passage, such as fasting Ramadan for the first time, celebrating ʿEid, going for *ʿumrah* or hajj, or learning to read the Quran in Arabic. The emergence of these themes reiterated that feelings of Muslimness are fluid—they are constantly changing and growing, strengthening or weakening—and they can be affected by outside influences, for better or worse. And sometimes the worse results in our convert brothers and sisters leaving Islam.

What Nurtures and Hinders the Feeling of Being Muslim?

I asked the question, "Were there any outside influences that nurtured or hindered your feelings of Muslimness?" From my own experiences and those of friends, I already knew the answer was a hard "yes."

However, it was an overwhelmingly beautiful and meaningful experience to have it corroborated statistically when 80.54% of the women responded with a resounding "yes" and went on to describe their experiences in great detail. Reading about the experiences of my convert sisters the world over was profound, and it was the kind of experience that spurs one to action.

Nurturing Influences

Let's start with the influences that nurtured converts' feelings of Muslimness. Lakisha said, "My feelings of being a Muslim happened the first time I attended the prayer. I was so afraid that I would mess up and I'd get lectured from people, lol. But I was welcomed with such warmth and friendliness. Also, attending classes for new Muslims helped nurture the feelings." Andrea also experienced nurturing and said, "I was nurtured by friends, especially older sisters who took me under their wing." Another sister learned to nurture herself and explained this by stating that "My 'feelings of Muslimness' come and go with what I put emphasis on in my life. When I remember to give my cares to Allah and ask Him for help, I feel very Muslim." Along the same lines, Sophia replied, "My feelings of Muslimness evolved as I slowly explored, learned about, and truly understood Islam and adopted its practices. Friends helped me learn about this and alerted me to behaviors and community culture I had previously not been exposed to, but the main source of Muslimness was the extent of my knowledge and adherence to what I learned." Another sister, Lena, enthusiastically responded, "The convert sisters I became friends with through a class nurtured my feelings of Muslimness just by saying 'Let's go pray Maghrib,' by talking about the Quran and Allah, and by understanding when discussing what it's like dealing with non-Muslim family members who just don't 'get' why we'd want to be Muslim."

Responses like these help us peek into the lives of convert women and understand what helps them feel Muslim and what doesn't.

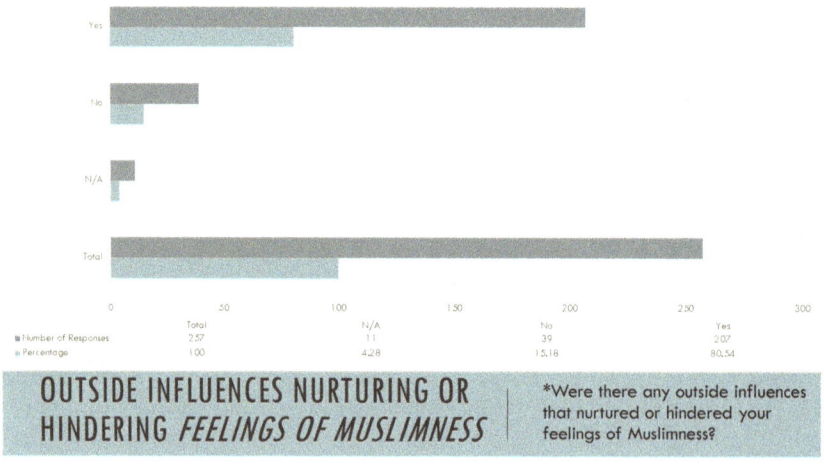

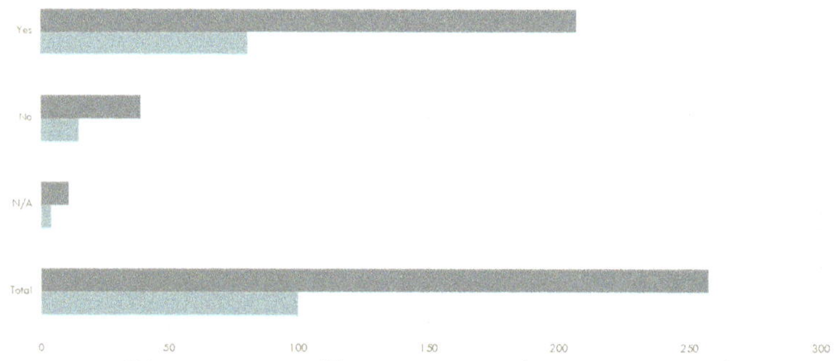

	Total	N/A	No	Yes
Number of Responses	257	11	39	207
Percentage	100	4.28	15.18	80.54

OUTSIDE INFLUENCES NURTURING OR HINDERING *FEELINGS OF MUSLIMNESS*

*Were there any outside influences that nurtured or hindered your feelings of Muslimness?

Hindering Influences

Regarding outside influences that hindered feelings of Muslimness, Angela related, "I felt less Muslim when I saw women constantly leaving the mosque due to mistreatment or being divorced by their husbands when they would not endure the mistreatment that came with being a part of the community. I felt less Muslim when it became clear that I was only asked to come to the mosque for financial purposes." Nicole described feeling hindered due to "the fact that the born-Muslims on campus considered me a joke. They kept waiting for me to leave Islam. I was the outsider." Another sister, Carrie, said, "I think that I started to feel not Muslim when I noticed the differential treatment I received in the mosque. All of the advice regarding nail polish, shaving, length of skirts, pants, shirtsleeves. It became very depressing because I felt as though I didn't measure up and wasn't being seen as an equal. I was being judged. Also, the fact that I was still married and hadn't gotten my husband to visit the mosque or be introduced to any of my Muslim friends. I felt like the Muslim community was beginning to reject me even more for being married to a non-Muslim." (Carrie did add though, that her Muslimness "was affirmed by my convert friends.")

Anna was frustrated and stated that "one hindrance is cultural. It can feel alienating to be a Muslim in a culture that equates Islam to terrorist extremism."

The clear thematic pattern demonstrates that outside influences can and do nurture and/or hinder feelings of Muslimness. There are positive and practical things that American Muslim communities can do to help the Muslim *feeling* blossom, and, equally important, there are things communities must stop doing to prevent those feelings from withering and dying.

When Hindrance Becomes Heartbreak

The severity of the problems American women converts are facing is absolutely heartbreaking and damaging to a person's feelings of Muslimness (a person's very identity as a Muslim) to such a degree that many have thought of leaving Islam. Thirty percent of the women said yes, they had thought about leaving Islam. And of the almost 70% of women who wrote "no," that they had not thought about leaving Islam, a majority answered with a hard "no" and did not go further. However, a significant percentage of that same group answered, "No, but . . . " and went on to express that the thought had, in fact, entered their minds before, which changed the overall statistic drastically. Instead of 30% of American women converts saying they had thought about leaving Islam, it was now 42.8%—a truly devastating statistic. This is where the importance of feelings of Muslimness and the effects of outside influences nurturing or hindering the development of Muslim identity really show in a tangible way: with many of our convert sisters either thinking about leaving Islam or actually taking that drastic step.

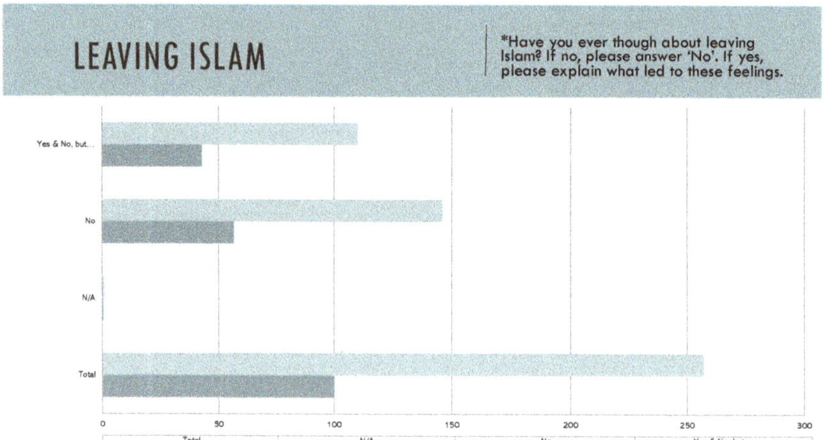

	Total	N/A	No	Yes & No, but...
Number of Responses	257	1	146	110
Percentage	100	0.39	56.81	42.80

Where We Stand

The information garnered through my research can both give converts some general guidelines that will help them cultivate their Muslim identities and also enable the American Muslim community to develop curricula and outreach programs that will be beneficial for converts based on their own feedback rather than what born-Muslims believe is best for them. This does not mean that all curricula and outreach by born-Muslims is bad; it means there is a lot of room for improvement, that converts should be involved in the design of these programs, and that the work needs to begin right now.

Dr. Ihsan Bagby conducted a brilliant three-part study of the American Muslim community, "The American Mosque 2011: Activities, Administration and Vitality of the American Mosque," which resulted in the documentary *Unmosqued*. In his study, Dr. Bagby revealed that 85% of full-time paid imams in the US were born outside the United States, which makes it extremely unlikely that they would be able to identify the unique needs of American converts to Islam, much less identify their needs as a primary concern. This is corroborated by another finding of Dr. Bagby's study, which showed that only 3% of mosques in the United States consider classes for converts to Islam a top priority. Wow! This information makes it abundantly clear that many mosques in the American Muslim community are not the best place for American converts to learn about Islam and grow their feelings of Muslimness (or even for the children and grandchildren of immigrants who more closely identify with converts, but we'll save that for another day). Quite simply, most mosques were not built with us in mind and heart; the programming does not reflect the needs of the convert community at all, and it is in many instances detrimental to our growth. However, that can change.

Where We Need to Be

Four things are absolutely essential for any curricula or programming for converts to be successful: hiring qualified American convert imams (there are a lot), listening to converts in order to understand the unique convert experience, including converts in the planning of events and religious holidays, and letting converts lead convert outreach programs without constant interference from mosque boards. The importance of curricula, outreach, and programming *by* American converts and *for* American converts cannot be overstated. This is one of many reasons convert-led organizations such as Rabata are so important. Rabata has several amazing projects that are beneficial for the growth and development of American women converts to Islam and Muslim women in general:

1. **Ribaat:** a four-level online academic program, providing Muslim women all over the world with a solid foundation in the Islamic sciences, Arabic, and Quran
2. **Daybreak Press:** a non-profit press publishing dynamic women authors whose books are promoting positive cultural change
3. **Muslim Women Convert Circle:** an incredible Facebook group for Muslim women converts to ask questions and seek fellowship
4. **Project Lina:** a groundbreaking nine-session workshop just for female converts to Islam, which is an incredible tool for the retention of American female converts to Islam, as it is designed by women with Islamic knowledge, convert experience, and an understanding of Western culture and ways of learning. In other words, it *is* designed with our needs in mind and heart.

In writing this book, *Project Lina*, Dr. Tamara Gray and Najiyah Maxfield have drawn an intricate map to lovingly guide Muslim women converts, whether new or veteran, as we traverse this unfamiliar territory, while simultaneously rooting us in the foundations of our religion and strengthening our roots by providing us with the tools we need to take ownership of our Islam, ultimately leading to *feeling* Muslim.

PROJECT LINA BECOMES A BOOK: AN INTRODUCTION

In 2012, I (Tamara) sat in my daughter's car in a snowy parking lot in St. Cloud, Minnesota and cried. I cried for Syria, and I cried for a dear friend of mine who had been slowly losing her religion and (it seemed) had recently sealed the deal. I was in every kind of grief. I was grieving the state of the country I had lived and learned and loved in, and I was grieving my dear friend, whom I had raised my children with. I was also selfishly grieving my own failures. "I am a *dāʿiya!*" I said to myself. "How does my best friend lose her religion? What in the world is wrong with me?" My heart was shattered. I was cold in the most complete of ways.

As I cried, I realized that there was nothing, nothing at all, that I could do about the situation in my beloved Syria, but maybe, just maybe, I could help prevent the midlife convert catastrophe my friend had experienced from happening to others. I dug an old receipt out from a pocket, found a pen, and began to plan out what would become Project Lina. I pray and beg Allah that the blessings that have come from this project worldwide will manifest themselves in goodness for her and that she will be brought back to light and love.

When I decided to turn the workshop into a book, I invited Najiyah Maxfield to join me in writing it, knowing that her experiences would enrich and improve the manuscript.

The Metaphor

As I mapped out Project Lina, I thought about the literal meaning of *līna* (palm tree), and I knew this metaphor was key. A palm tree could survive a hurricane! A drought in a desert! And a palm tree is an evergreen, so it stays green and fresh year-round. Further research informed me that there are over 2,600 species of palm trees, so they are diverse, just like converts. And perhaps most importantly, palm trees bear fruit. Fruit that was beloved by the Beloved ﷺ.

So how to grow deep roots, a strong trunk, and beautiful greenery plus luscious dates? We need to bring our whole selves to Islam, develop deep *ʿaqīda*, and tend our relationship ties. Hence the modules were born.

Module One: *Know Yourself*

Muslim converts are just like everyone else: complicated. We have backgrounds, personalities, and cultures that influence who we are, how we feel about ourselves, and how we practice Islam. This module pushes the pause button on our lives and asks us to extend compassion to ourselves. We think about our deep sense of self, our names and how they influence us, and different things that have made us who we are today. Then we consider how we might ensure that our whole selves are enveloped in the loving embrace of Islam.

Module Two: *Declare Independence*

Converts face a unique challenge; suddenly being the person who doesn't know the answer can be really difficult for women (and men) who are confident and in-the-know in other areas of their lives. This section offers a strong foundation in basic Islamic knowledge that will fill learning gaps and provide direction for continuous growth. We hope that it will give convert women the ability to stand firmly on a solid foundation whenever they hear something wonky. We deal with some terms that may be challenging, so that we can have a common language. Many converts remain in a Swiss cheese state of knowledge, regardless of the number of years they have been Muslim. Most readers will know much of what is presented in this section, but each of us has our own holes to plug up. Finally, we offer tools that can be used to stay strong and healthy as we walk forward in our spiritual journey.

Module Three: *Tend Your Ties*

Many, many converts complain of feeling isolated and lonely. This can be the result of strained family relations, a cross-cultural marriage, and/or the loss of friends. In this section we talk about all of these relationships and more. Our hope is that we can all be proactive in preventing isolation and loneliness and work to create community in all of our relationships. In the first section we talk about the family we grew up with—our parents and siblings—and how to re-establish, heal, and/or build these relationships. We then move on to our new families and address wedding wisely and raising children as good Muslims when we ourselves were not raised as Muslims. Finally, we talk about friends, old and new, and reach out in compassion as we realize the very real challenges of making friends as adults.

The Palm Tree Metaphor

Palm trees have a fibrous root system that shoots out hundreds of roots into the surrounding soil. The roots are not the long deep tap roots of other trees, but thin roots that grow out horizontally from the base. They stabilize and anchor the tree, allowing it to find nutrients and moisture. The taller the tree, the wider the root base.

We see these roots in the three modules of this book. As converts, we naturally do not have roots in Islam or Muslim culture. But we do have the opportunity to appreciate the beautiful roots of family, faith, and good character that we brought with us to Islam, grow roots of knowledge and certainty, and expand our roots of family and friends. With a secure root base, we will be able to grow tall and strong, extending our fronds as long arms of love to embrace this life with positive energy and influence. A healthy palm tree is a healthy soul, and it is of the healthy soul that Allah speaks in the verse, ﴾ *O contented soul—return to your Lord, pleased and pleasing* ﴿ (Q. 89:27–28). We pray that we will all meet together on the Last Day and be invited into Paradise together.

MODULE ONE

KNOW YOURSELF

1

WILL THE REAL ME PLEASE STAND UP?

Tamara Circa 1985

Dressed in black from head to toe and gossiping with rice in the crook of my fingers—such was my pitiful self a few short months after I converted to Islam in January 1985. My preconvert self had been an artsy dresser who used a fork for everything but sandwiches, pizza, and ice-cream cones and talked politics and religion. What had happened to *me?*

The Cultural Conversion

Muslims around the world are a proud people. Many majority Muslim countries have been traumatized by colonialism, postcolonial dictatorships, wars, imperial scooping of resources, and other economic and political obstacles. To survive, they have held closely to their cultures, each feeling a bit superior to the other in an amusing my-food-is-better-than-your-food sort of way. For converts entering the Muslim community, this pride of culture can be both exciting and overwhelming. For me in 1985, a slightly confused combination of Gulf Arab culture, Malaysian habits, and Salafi influences had overcome me and brought me to a place where I did not recognize myself anymore.

In some countries up to 70% of converts eventually leave Islam—not because of a change in belief, but because they could not find space for themselves in the community. We believe they could not hold on to themselves in the community. Anyone who walks across the bridge and enters Islam has gone through a rigorous struggle of belief and landed in a place of decision; so what happens? We all know women who spent years wearing hijab, fasting, and praying, only to walk away fifteen years later without any real explanation. It mimics a bad marriage: a long period of negativity, a lack of authenticity, and a pattern of missed connectivity, which add up to giving up.

We have all experienced microaggressions, like being asked, "Do you still eat the food of the *kuffār*—hamburgers and pizza?" or being told not to visit or get close to our family because they are "*kuffār*." We have been told that we laugh "too loud" and asked a dozen times if we "know the Fatiha."

Sometimes as converts we want to fit in somewhere but can no longer find anywhere we feel we really belong, so we add on a second conversion (to a culture) and begin living in ways that slowly pull us away from ourselves.

A Caveat

It is important to pause here and recognize that a religious life is not meant to be comfortable or easy. Walking a spiritual path is about effort, discomfort, struggle, and hard work. It is about thinking about others before yourself and making real sacrifices for the pleasure of God.

What we are suggesting here is that one cannot follow this path without her whole self. Inevitably, a crisis will occur (because this is the nature of life) that will challenge us to the core, and at this point we need our deepest selves to be rooted in faith. We need to have roots in our relationship with God and our love of Prophet Muhammad ﷺ. We need to be a palm tree. The palm tree withstands great tribulation—when cut, it can grow back, and its fronds, when pulled out, can be shoved into the ground and will grow. It has broad roots and a flexible trunk that bends instead of breaking when stormy winds set upon it.

But in order to be this extraordinary tree, we need to know ourselves, so that we can bring ourselves—our bettered selves—to Islam, where we can grow, and, in bearing fruit, help to make the world a place of joy, faith, and goodness.

PART ONE: WHAT'S IN THE SELF?

﴾ *We shall show them our signs in the horizons and within themselves so that it will become evident to them that it is the Truth.* ﴿ (Q. 41:53)

Knowing Ourselves

The signs that are within us cannot be seen or known if we do not first know ourselves. It is because of these signs that it has been said, "Those who know themselves know God."

Imam al-Ghazali described this knowing as knowing the truth about ourselves. He criticized the one who defines this knowing as the knowledge of wants and desires; he compared the person who knows what they want to eat or knows that they need sexual satisfaction to a farm animal, and the person who knows what wealth and power they want to a predatory animal. Instead, true knowing, for Imam al-Ghazali, is to know the true nature of one's heart. It is the heart, or soul, or spirit—that which can only be seen with the inner eye—that is the true essence of the self. In order to know this self, we must be free of the grip of desire, fear, and anger.[3]

Ibn al-Qayyim al-Jawziyya says there are three ways to understand the importance of knowing ourselves. First, knowing ourselves will help us to see the greatness of God. We see our weakness and know God's strength. We see our ignorance and know God's knowledge of all things. The further we go on this path of truly knowing ourselves, the more we glorify God and realize Allahu Akbar in its true meaning. Second, knowing our good qualities—whether in generosity, mercy, or love—brings about the realization that the One who created us has far more generosity, mercy, or love than what we find within ourselves. Third, Ibn al-Qayyim marvels at the one who does not know herself—the very closest of relationships. No one is more accessible for us to know than our own selves, so if we do not know who we are, then how will we know God?[4]

Sibghatullah

There is a very beautiful verse in Surat al-Baqara that describes the process of coming closer and closer to God. In a rough (but literal) translation it says, ﴾ *The dye of God, and what is better than the dye of God?* ﴿ (Q. 2:138). This verse has been discussed and wondered about by students and scholars of *tafsīr*. I (Tamara) remember sitting with one of my teachers when she suddenly looked at me, quoted this verse, and asked, "*Sibghatullah*—do you know what that means?" I nodded but was afraid that if this was a pop quiz, I would not be able to explain the nuances of *tafsīr* embedded in this verse. She smiled and laughed saying, "Women get their hair dyed all the time. The dye seeps in but the nature of the hair does not change—it stays hair."

And so to walk this path is not to change the nature of our created selves—but rather to color ourselves with the dye of God, usually said to be the *way* of God. We must know ourselves in order to dye ourselves. Zainab Abaid discusses this in her article "Dyeing Ourselves in the Color of Allah." She says,

> It is difficult to tear ourselves away from the shimmer and glitter of the colors of duniya (sic), of the hundred different lifestyles that beckon to us all at once. It is difficult to bleach off the color we have grown up in and adopt a different color entirely. But in all the beauty and glow of the world, in all its shining colors, there is not a single one so beautiful, so rich, so vibrant, and so completely mesmerizing, that its beauty cannot be described in words—it can only be experienced, and then only by donning it. That loveliest of colors is what the Quran calls *sibghatullah*—the color (or dye) of Allah.[5]

She follows this with a description of the bleaching and dying process on fabric, reminding us that we cannot dye fabric without knowing what fabric it is and how it should be dyed. We need to know what process to use to remove the old color and to apply the new one. Similarly, we must know ourselves if we are to be soaked in the way of God.

Inventing the Self

This is particularly important for a convert, for inherent in the conversion process is the idea of the invention of self. There is much for her to think about and do. Abaid says:

> Becoming a Muslim is an arduous affair. There are layers and layers involved in the process. A new Muslim has already changed her belief system. She must think about Jesus in a new way (if she was a Christian), and get to know Muhammad ﷺ. The book she will now read for guidance and light needs a new language for full access, and—while she may always have believed in God as One—she now has a new name to get used to (Allah).
>
> A new Muslim must change her habits. She will begin to pray in a certain way—and in order to do so must memorize words and phrases that will, for a time, carry little meaning. She will change what she eats, and how she eats it. She

> may have to drop friends, perhaps the boyfriend that introduced her to Islam. She will have to deal with many people telling her what is "right" and what is "wrong"—often with contradictory opinions. She may hear erroneous claims that challenge her fledgling belief, and she may get frustrated with her new "friends" and their strangeness.[6]

Complicating matters is the very real spiritual component in Islam that encourages all good Muslims to eliminate their bad qualities, to purify themselves from diseases of the heart, and to free themselves from bad habits. So there is a question facing the convert: Is this a bad habit I need to leave behind? Or is this an indicator of my core self that I need to recognize and hang on to in order to move forward in my faith?

Western (and especially American) men and women tend to start out their lives in a global cottage, not a global village. They know those "other" countries exist but, for the most part, have very little interest in understanding them or their citizens. When Islam enters one of their lives, that cottage becomes a vibrant and often confusing city. The convert is suddenly meeting people who speak to each other rapid-fire in a language that is not her own (for Americans especially this is shocking—doesn't the whole world speak English?). She is eating foods that are bright with new smells and tastes and dressing up for gatherings in clothes that carry a very different definition of dressy than she has been used to. A convert might join the fun of her new friends from Pakistan, Palestine, or Somalia and easily fall into dressing, eating, and talking like her new sisters, which is fun and exciting if it is seen for what it is—a venture into a new and exciting culture. But if she feels that her new religion is part and parcel of this new culture, she is in danger of growing tired of both. And of course, her new religion is indeed part of the new culture in some ways: the lack of alcohol and bacon and the addition of hijab are not cultural quirks. Curried lentils and styles of hijab are, however. So the convert needs to know herself so that she can work to dye her life with her faith, while at the same time taking care not to oversaturate the fabric of her life with things that are unnecessary.

In order to pause and reflect on who we are, we will first think together about issues of childhood, habits, and personality. In the next section, we put the spotlight on how our names, what we call ourselves and what others call us, influence who we are and who we become. In the final section of this module, we will talk about culture and how it informs our sense of self. There will be more activities around culture and how we build relationships in the last module, Tend Your Ties, but here we will be looking at the ways our cultural backgrounds influence our behavior, attitudes, and sense of self.

BACKGROUND

When the Past Is Painful

There is a lot of pain in the world. And sometimes converts come to Islam having experienced a month, a decade, or even a lifetime of trauma and heartache. Substance abuse is rampant, families are falling apart, children are neglected, and people are groaning in pain.

The American child is bombarded with stress. More than seven million children live with a parent who has alcohol problems; the Unites States has an increasingly high divorce rate, with about 48% of first marriages ending in divorce;[7] and child abuse is rampant, with a new report of abuse made every ten seconds.[8] Of the documented abuse cases, 74.9% are cases of neglect.[9] One out of every four children in America is in a home without a father,[10] and children in America are also poverty stricken, with one in five living below the federal poverty line.[11] The United Kingdom is not much better. In England and Wales, 42% of marriages end in divorce,[12] and 30% of children live below the poverty line.[13]

Childhood can hurt.

Children and youth enter a world of bullying and sexual predators.[14] Pressure to drink alcohol and engage in sexual activity begins early, and with little parental supervision, many young people cave. The psychological results manifest as food disorders, such as anorexia, bulimia, and obesity; self-injury activities, such as cutting, hair pulling, and burning; and rampant depression, anxiety, and suicidal thoughts and actions.[15]

The teenage years can be deadly.

Neither this statistical backdrop nor an individual's personal trauma disappears when they become a Muslim. And while Islam certainly provides a sense of spiritual peace and a model upon which to base our actions and lives, it does not provide an automatic aha! moment when all of our scars and internal traumas disappear. While finding Islam brings comfort to the confused and offers tools for health, it does not remove or prevent trauma or abuse. When we convert, we bring our baggage with us; Islam meets us at the customs desk, helping us leave behind the bad habits we don't need so that we can begin to find healing. But it takes work. Recognizing that the path to healing is available can be euphoric at first, but soon every convert realizes that she will have to continue to make good decisions, work through hurt and pain (perhaps going even deeper to find forgiveness), and create new habits that make her a better person. That said,

Islam does indeed help with healing, and there are plenty of examples in the lives of the companions of painful pasts and recovery.

When the Past Is Just the Past

Not every childhood is painful, nor are the teenage years always filled with angst. Many of us come to Islam from families who did their very best to provide us with happy childhoods, warm surroundings, and good memories. This can manifest in different ways: as a longing for a childhood memory, as a desire to "just be normal," or as a strength that carries us forth into the normal challenges of life.

In the process of bringing our full selves to God and to Islam, we will need to interact with the self we were before Islam. Our childhood, our habits, and our personalities are all part of the puzzle of understanding ourselves.

ACTIVITY: REFLECTING ON YOUR CHILDHOOD

Answer the following questions.

1. What was the best thing about your childhood? What was something you didn't like?
2. What is your most vivid memory of your childhood home?
3. Who besides your parents had the biggest impact on your childhood? Why and how?
4. What part of your background do you carry with you into your convert story?
5. What part of your background do you leave behind as part of your convert story?

TRAUMA AMONG THE COMPANIONS

Fathers

Salīm mawla Abū Ḥudhaifa was a young boy when he was taken away from his family and sold into slavery. He grew up in the home of Thubaita bint Yaʿar and her husband Abū Ḥudhaifa ibn ʿUtba. He was treated well, and when the couple became Muslim, Thubaita freed Salīm and Abū Ḥudhaifa adopted him. He then married Salīm to his niece, Fāṭima bint al-Walīd ibn ʿUtba.

Using the language of today, he grew up in a fatherless home, for although he did live in a loving foster home, he did not know who his father was, nor did he see him or visit him. He was not abused by his foster parents, but after his conversion to Islam he was harmed and abused by the Quraysh because of his religion. This abuse occurred because of his lower societal status, which was directly related to his status as a foster child (or *mawlā*).

Ibn ʿUmar narrates that the Messenger ﷺ formed brotherly ties between some of the *muhājirīn* before the hijra.[16] One of those pairs was Salīm mawla Abū Ḥudhaifa and Abū ʿUbayda ibn al-Jarrāḥ. Abū ʿUbayda was one of the earliest Muslims. He was a merchant from a noble family. After he became a Muslim, we know that his father began to abuse and torture him in an attempt to force him to leave his faith.

Two men. One grew up in a loving home but didn't know his biological father; the other knew his father but suffered at his hands. The Prophet ﷺ put these two men together, and together they both grew into significant figures of the early Muslim community, overcoming their respective hardships and shining the light of faith into society.

Mockery and Differing Abilities

Some of the *ṣaḥāba* faced attitudes of *jāhiliyya* (ignorance) rooted in physical prejudices. The Arabs had an age-old respect for strength and size, but the Prophet ﷺ taught them to judge on a different scale.

ʿAbdullāh ibn Masʿūd is described as a "thin, short, and frail man with skinny legs." We understand that his physique was not of the norm when, at one point, the Prophet ﷺ asked ʿAbdullāh to climb a tree to retrieve something, and the companions began to laugh and tease him about his legs.[17] In modern terms, we would call this bullying. Anyone who has been teased or bullied because of her size (whether too small or too big) knows what it means to not fit in to a cultural norm. Yet when we read the *sīra*, we do not remember ʿAbdullāh ؓ as a man who didn't fit in but rather as the great carrier of Quran.

It is interesting to note how the Prophet ﷺ interacted with him. Upon their first meeting, when ʿAbdullāh was just a boy, the Prophet ﷺ put his hand on his head and said, "You are a learned lad [or marked or designated]." We imagine the boy, having heard of Prophet Muḥammad ﷺ, feeling shy about his physical frailty and wondering how the Prophet ﷺ would interact with him. Imagine the boost to his self-esteem when the Prophet ﷺ spoke to him about his intellect, his future, his hopes.

ʿAbdullah was to become the Prophet's personal assistant, preparing his wuḍūʾ water, carrying his shoes, and most importantly, reciting Quran in front of him ﷺ. And when the Prophet ﷺ witnessed the teasing of the companions (about his legs) he said, "What are you laughing at? One of Abdullāh's legs will weigh more than Mount Uḥud on the Day of Judgment."[18] His consistent attitude toward ʿAbdullāh washed away any remaining insecurity regarding his size. ʿAbdullāh became one of our great examples—we are forced to see him for his whole, healthy psyche, and we as an *umma* barely remember his physical stature.

Managing Muslims

Those who entered Islam from tribes that were hostile to the Muslims—like ʿIkrima ibn Abū Jahl and Ṣafiyya bint Ḥuyai—had to struggle to find their place in Muslim society. The Prophet ﷺ specifically warned his companions not to curse ʿIkrima's father, who was an avowed enemy of Islam and the ringleader of the Qurayshi oppression and maltreatment of the Muslims and even the Prophet ﷺ himself: "It does not reach the dead and it hurts the living."[19] He helped Ṣafiyya stand up to the women who teased her. Ṣafiyya bint Ḥuyai, a Jewish woman from Medina, was a young girl when she heard her father in a conversation with her uncle. "Is it him [the expected prophet]?" her uncle asked.

"Yes, it is," answered her father

"Can you clearly determine that? Can you verify it?"

"Yes, I can verify it with accuracy."

"What now?"

"Hostility, for as long as I live."[20]

It is curious to contemplate how Ṣafiyya would have reacted, on a deeply personal level, to words such as these. Certainly, she would have been observant over the next years of the interactions between her father and this man

Muḥammad. When the Prophet ﷺ later gave her the choice to enter Islam and be honored as his wife or to remain in Judaism and follow her tribe, she chose Islam.

Ṣafiyya entered the community as the daughter of an enemy of the Prophet ﷺ and, as a result, some of the women teased her about her heritage. The Prophet ﷺ gave her the words to answer anyone who judged her and ridiculed her. He said, "Tell them, 'How are you better than I am? My husband is Muḥammad, my father is Aaron, and my uncle is Moses (peace be upon them all),'" thereby empowering her to self-defense and psychological health. He didn't tell her to "put up with it" or justify her ridiculers by offering the excuse that, "Well, your father was really bad to me," or any other response that would have suggested that her feelings of hurt and rejection were unfounded. Rather, he uplifted her.

HABITS

Islam beautifies and refines. "The best of you in *jāhiliyya* (the time previous to Islam—a time of ignorance) are the best of you in Islam,"[2.1] is an oft-quoted hadith of Prophet Muḥammad ﷺ. The good qualities that a convert carries with her to Islam help her walk along the path. The people of Banī al-Azd are an excellent example of this. A delegation of seventeen new Muslim men of Banī al-Azd (converts!) came to the Prophet ﷺ in the ninth year after the hijra. They were full of confidence in their new religion and in the habits they brought to Islam. When the Prophet ﷺ first saw them, he was impressed with how they presented themselves and asked them, "Who are you?"

"Believers."

"For everything said, there is proof; what is the proof of your belief?" the Prophet ﷺ asked with a smile.

They listed five things the Prophet's messenger had instructed them to believe in and five things he had ordered them to do as proof of their belief. But most meaningful to this discussion, they also listed five habits of goodness that they brought forth from their lives before Islam: "gratefulness in times of plenty, forbearance in times of trial, contentedness in the face of bitter fate, courage in times of battle, and the leaving of gloating over enemies."

The Prophet ﷺ was pleased. He said, "Wise and learned, their depth of understanding brings them to [the level of] prophets."[2.2]

When a convert begins her new journey of faith, the first weeks, months, and years can mean some rejection of where she came from. But here, in the *sīra*, is such a beautiful example of a people who understood that Islam beautified their beautiful habits and qualities—and they were ready to grow some more. When we bring our whole selves to Islam, we can be like Banī al-Azd and come forth with a myriad of good habits that we have already developed and be ready for deeper growth in *tawḥīd* and worship habits, or anything else we need to work on.

Thinking about Habits

Islam is a religion of habits. We are trained to drop everything five times a day, turn toward Mecca, say "Allahu Akbar," and enter into a state of spiritual connection with our Creator. A literal habit of spirituality.

We learn to stop eating constantly during Ramadan, to limit sleep during hajj, and to make a habit of generosity whenever we have a bit extra.

In Surat Hud God says, ﴾ *Verily good deeds remove bad deeds, this is a reminder for those who are mindful* ﴿ (Q. 11:114). In this verse, we are given a clear path to creating a life of good habits: increasing them in order to seek forgiveness from God for the (hopefully few) mistakes we make along the way.

Before I (Tamara) became a Muslim, I was a good student. I had excellent homework habits, and I was a reader. My eating habits, however, were terrible, and after I became a Muslim, I spent a lot of time working on improving them. Today I have some admirable habits that I can thank Islam for and some poor habits that I still haven't been able to improve. But as I continue to walk the path of faith, I continue to work on all of them, striving to imitate the example of our Beloved Messenger ﷺ.

What about Really Bad Habits?

What about addictions? Or sinful habits? This book is not the place to address the steps to overcome alcoholism, drug addiction, or pornography addiction. For that, we strongly recommend that you seek professional help and recognize that Islam will be a wonderful support for you, but it is not an automatic cure for serious problems. However, a strong worship habit will definitely help. To that end, we offer the following series of verses that may help your quest to overcome the bad habits that are facing you down. Each one reminds us of the straight path and the possibility of forgiveness. We recommend repeating them often.

> ﴾ *You alone do we worship, and You alone do we call for help. Keep us on the right path. The way of those on whom Thou hast bestowed Thy Grace, those whose (portion) is not wrath, and who go not astray.* ﴿ (Q. 1:5–7)

إِيَّاكَ نَعۡبُدُ وَإِيَّاكَ نَسۡتَعِينُ ٥ ٱهۡدِنَا ٱلصِّرَٰطَ ٱلۡمُسۡتَقِيمَ ٦ صِرَٰطَ ٱلَّذِينَ أَنۡعَمۡتَ عَلَيۡهِمۡ
غَيۡرِ ٱلۡمَغۡضُوبِ عَلَيۡهِمۡ وَلَا ٱلضَّآلِّينَ ٧

﴿ *They are on (true) guidance, from their Lord, and it is these who are successful.* ﴾ (Q. 2:5)

أُوْلَٰٓئِكَ عَلَىٰ هُدٗى مِّن رَّبِّهِمۡۖ وَأُوْلَٰٓئِكَ هُمُ ٱلۡمُفۡلِحُونَ

﴿ *Verily We have granted thee a manifest Victory: That Allah may forgive thee thy faults of the past and those to follow; fulfill His favor to thee; and guide thee on the Straight Way; And that Allah may help thee with powerful help.* ﴾ (Q. 48:1–3)

إِنَّا فَتَحۡنَا لَكَ فَتۡحٗا مُّبِينٗا ١ لِّيَغۡفِرَ لَكَ ٱللَّهُ مَا تَقَدَّمَ مِن ذَنۢبِكَ وَمَا تَأَخَّرَ وَيُتِمَّ نِعۡمَتَهُۥ
عَلَيۡكَ وَيَهۡدِيَكَ صِرَٰطٗا مُّسۡتَقِيمٗا ٢ وَيَنصُرَكَ ٱللَّهُ نَصۡرًا عَزِيزًا ٣

Habit Hub

What are some good habits you brought to Islam?

What are some bad habits you left? Hope to leave?

What new habits do you hope to develop?

Activity: Changing Habits

Gandhi is often quoted as having said, "Your beliefs become your thoughts, your thoughts become your words, your words become your actions, your actions become your habits, your habits become your values, your values become your destiny." Part of growing in Islam is growing in good habits. Once something is a habit, we can do it on autopilot and free brain space to focus on the deeper spiritual aspects of our worship or do other things in our lives.

Changing habits can be very difficult. We often default to old habits when faced with stress or difficulty. However, research is rich in tips and tricks for habit development. We suggest you read a book or two about it (see Appendix B for a list of possibilities). In this activity, we will practice two habit-changing strategies: motivation and the elimination of barriers, and to make sure that we don't forget about it, we'll send ourselves a reminder letter.

1. Look at the chart for examples of how to eliminate barriers to change habits.
2. What one single habit would you like to change?
3. Now try to narrow down that habit even more. Not "I want to stop eating so much," but instead "I want to eat smaller portions" or "I want to stop eating after 8:00 p.m."
4. Why did you choose this habit? Think for a few minutes, and then write yourself a letter explaining why you want to change the habit.
5. What is stopping you from making this change? Make a list.

Stuff in the way of change

6. What could you do instead? Make another list. Include both lists with your letter.

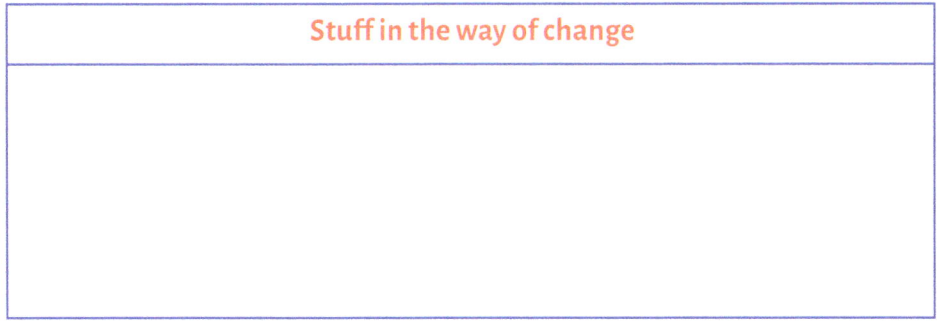

Stuff that might help me make a change

Mail the letter to yourself and when it arrives, make a poster plan! Hang your poster somewhere to remind you about your new habit-changing goals.

Habit	Barrier	Remove Barrier	Stopping A Bad Habit Or Starting A Good One?
Snacking	Chips and candy bars in desk drawer	Empty drawer	Stop a bad habit
Pray *tahajjud*	Waking up early is hard	Create a support system, go to bed earlier	Start a good habit

Personality

A painful experience that some converts endure is being made to feel that their personality is "not wanted" in Islam, or that they need to fundamentally change who they are in order to adhere to and grow in their new faith. Many an extroverted Western woman has been told that she needs to learn to love quietude and solitude in order to be a good Muslim, and some quieter introverted converts have been pushed into community service that burned them out. The archetype of a "good Muslim woman" or a "good Muslim man" is rooted in a number of modern circumstances mixed with actual religious text and habit. It can vary across cultures, and weighing oneself against this seemingly-accepted ideal can be especially challenging for converts.

Is there a better personality? Or are all personalities welcome and needed to build healthy communities? A perusal of the companions who loved and lived with the Prophet ﷺ helps us to see the vast differences in personality that were present in and benefitted the first community.

- Abū Hurayra was a quiet and goal-oriented man. He was content to follow the Prophet ﷺ from place to place. He sought learning and cared little for physical comforts. We might think of him today as an academic type.
- Khālid ibn al-Walīd was a strategist. He was smart and tough. He was a leader of men and the Sword of Islam. We would label him a military type or a commander type who leads fearlessly.
- Asmāʾ bint Yazid was an Ansari woman who was forthright, outspoken, and assertive. She often went to the Prophet ﷺ with her questions and was concerned about the rights of women. We might think of Asmaʾ as an activist and defender of women's rights.
- Māria al-Qibṭiyya, on the other hand, was quiet and shy. She disliked conflict and drama. She cared little about status and did not like to be in the limelight. She was a Ma Ingalls type, or an introverted homebody.

Each of these Muslims, along with the thousands of others, was a necessary part of the early community. Likewise, each of our personalities brings something unique to the global *umma*. In fact, our personalities give us insights into our spiritual selves. Carl Jung (d. 1961) believed that psychology is incomplete and fundamentally misconstrued if it is disconnected from the spiritual self. At one point, he said, "Human thought cannot conceive any system or final truth that could give the patient what he needs in order to live: that is, faith, hope, love and insight."[23]

There are many ways to think about the self. All of them are tools made by human beings, and all of them have benefit. The Myers-Briggs Type Indicator (MBTI) is one such tool that helps us understand our core personalities, strengths, and blind spots. Another is the Enneagram types, which were used by early sheikhs to help them understand their students so they could, in turn, help them. We should never pigeon-hole ourselves or anyone else based on a psychological test; however, these tools help us gain deeper understanding of why we do the things we do and think the things we think. The purpose of these tests is to help us identify our innate tendencies and work on using our strengths (and our weaknesses) constructively. They can help us grow, but they are not labels to define and restrict people. Rather they are for understanding ourselves and each other.

Jung's work in personality types was further developed by the mother-daughter team Myers and Briggs. They developed a tool (MBTI) to test typology that is now used in workplaces around the world to help people bring their full selves to the job. Here we suggest that you visit myersbriggs.org and quiz yourself to find your own Meyers Briggs type. You can then use that understanding to help you bring your whole self to Islam.

Dear __________,

I want to ____________________________________ because ____________

____

____

____.

Tamara's MBTI Experience

I (Tamara) remember the first time I took the MBTI (Myers Briggs Type Indicator). My husband had just taken it at work, and he came home full of the fervor of this new way of thinking. Our mutual discovery about our differences helped us understand each other better and learn to interact with more wisdom. My test told me that I was an extreme extrovert. His told him that he was an extreme introvert. It was a light bulb moment. His discouraging me from going out to see friends was directly related to his own lack of interest in such events. And my desire to attend events and be social was directly related to the way I draw energy—from being around people. We decided to free each other from the demand to be just like each other, and it was wonderful!

Najiyah's MBTI Experience

When I was a senior in high school, they instituted a new rule that in order to take honors classes, one had to take an IQ test. Mind you, I had taken and done well in Honors History, Honors American Government, Russian History, and Honors English in my junior year. I excelled in debate and speech and had the medals to prove it. But I had an Achilles' heel. I was weak in math and science. I only took math through Algebra II, and for my required science credit, I chose Anatomy and Physiology, which isn't considered a hard science. I'm also a very linear thinker. I couldn't think my way out of a barn. Literally. Too much spatial thinking.

On the IQ test there were a lot of mathy, sciencey, and spatial questions. I got a 94. I was barred from taking honors classes. My entire identity was destroyed.

So I was a bit wary of taking the MBTI test at my first Project Lina workshop.

But I was so glad I did! The description of my type (ENFP) fits me to a tee. I've learned to understand my tendencies and traits, which helps me let the positive ones shine and gives me the insight to identify and work on my weaker ones.

Knowing about MBTI also helps me accommodate and work better with others' personality traits. I can say to myself, "Ahh, she's probably a J" (which means she's organized and likes to plan ahead). This will give me a heads-up that my strong P personality (spontaneous and going with the flow) might annoy her, so I'd better do my best to channel my inner J, even though it's hard for me.

MBTI can also help parents tailor their strategies to their children's types. One of my daughters, who is an introvert (an INFP to be precise), said to me once, "Mom, I used to hate it so much when you would push us to meet new people and drag us to people's houses and try to make us be friends with their kids."

"I'm so sorry," I replied. "I didn't know about MBTI back then!"

Benefits of MBTI in Spiritual Life

Learning about type can help us along our spiritual path. When we understand ourselves, we understand which activities can best help us grow and which activities we should probably steer clear of. We can learn how to become better worshippers and more effective community activists and volunteers when we figure out our strengths and weaknesses.

Knowing ourselves can help us get along better with our children, our coworkers, our friends, and our spouses, but for the purposes of this book, we are hoping it will help you get along better with yourself and find new avenues to spiritual growth.

We encourage you to use a variety of tools to understand yourself. The MBTI itself is more complicated and offers more insight than what we will accomplish here, but books and programs by licensed MBTI specialists will help you dig deeper into the theory and its tools. See Appendix B for recommended books about type theory and other tools to help us discover who we are and how we grow.

What's Your Type?

The sixteen psychological types of the MBTI begin with eight preferences. There are four pairs of preferences, and each pair represents a continuum upon which people fall. The eight preferences are as follows.

Extraversion	Energy Source	Introversion
Sensing	Information Location	Intuition
Thinking	Decision-Making	Feeling
Judging	Lifestyle	Perceiving

These preferences come together to make sixteen personality types.[24]

Overview and Brief Summary of the Sixteen Personalities Described by the Myers-Briggs Type Indicator			
ISTJ	**ISFJ**	**INFJ**	**INTJ**
"Doing what should be done"	"A high sense of duty"	"An inspiration to others"	"Everything can be improved"
Organizer, compulsive, private, trustworthy, rules, practical	Amiable, works behind the scenes, ready to sacrifice, accountable	Reflective, quietly caring, creative, intuitive, good with words	Theory based, skeptical, strategist, need for competency, "my way"
Most Responsible	Most Loyal	Most Contemplative	Most Independent
ISTP	**ISFP**	**INFP**	**INTP**
"Ready to try anything once"	"Sees much but shares little"	"Performing noble service to aid society"	"A love of problem solving"
Very observant, cool and aloof, hands-on practicality, unpretentious, ready for what happens	Warm and sensitive, unassuming, short range planner, good team member, in touch with self and nature	Strict personal values, seeks inner order/peace, creative, nondirective, reserved	Challenges others to think, absent-minded professor, competency needs, socially cautious
Most Pragmatic	Most Artistic	Most Idealistic	Most Conceptual

ESTP	ESFP	ENFP	ENTP
"The ultimate realist"	"You only go around once in life"	"Giving life an extra squeeze"	"One exciting challenge after another"
Unconventional approach, fun, gregarious, lives for here and now, good at problem-solving	Sociable, spontaneous, loves surprises, cuts red tape, juggles multiple projects, quip master	People oriented, creative, seeks harmony, the life of the party, more starts then finishes	Argues both sides of a point to learn, brinksmanship, tests the limits, enthusiastic, new ideas
Most Spontaneous	Most Generous	Most Optimistic	Most Inventive
ESTJ	**ESFJ**	**ENFJ**	**ENTJ**
"Life's administrators"	"Hosts and hostesses of the world"	"Smooth-talking persuader"	"Life's natural leaders"
Order and structure, sociable, opinionated, results-driven, producer, traditional	Gracious, good interpersonal skills, thoughtful, appropriate, eager to please	Charismatic, compassionate, possibilities for people, ignores the unpleasant, idealistic	Visionary, gregarious, argumentative, systems planners, take charge, low tolerance for incompetency
Most Hard-Charging	Most Harmonizing	Most Persuasive	Most Commanding

The following chart may help you understand your own path and the paths of your loved ones.[25]

Type	How to be Helpful to This Type	Common Stumbling Blocks for This Type	Paths of Growth for This Type
ISTJ	Offer specifics and real-life examples	Rule minded—might miss the big picture	*Fiqh* is an interesting and engrossing subject to learn
	Give clear details about new topics	May doubt growth because too aware of need for more self-improvement	All organized religious activities

Type	How to be Helpful to This Type	Common Stumbling Blocks for This Type	Paths of Growth for This Type
ISTP	Give tangible advice in the moment	Worship may feel awkward or intimidating	*Duʿāʾ* and less formal practices
	Help in times of need Provide examples of faith in action	Reducing faith to a logical formula	Strong relationships with a trusted source to discuss issues as they come up
ESTP	Withhold judgments about how much Islam is being practiced	Focusing so much on this *dunyā* (what feels "real"); it can be hard to focus on spiritual life	Having fun with religious people
	Help to see the lighter side of a spiritual/religious life	Belittling sin, as in "Does God really care?"	Engaging in spiritual retreats with other people
ESTJ	Demonstrate practical application of spiritual ritual	Avoiding new experiences	Structured academic study
	Work together toward a goal	Demanding so much proof that practice takes a back seat	Leading community projects
ISFJ	Offer help because ISFJ folks find it difficult to ask for it	Filling time with "all that needs to be done," especially in helping others, so self is neglected	Organized ritual in small groups
	Share your spiritual side	Experiencing difficulty seeing the overall plan	Study of specific practices that can be easily applied to personal life

Type	How to be Helpful to This Type	Common Stumbling Blocks for This Type	Paths of Growth for This Type
ISFP	Offer warmth and emotional support	Keeping opinions to self	Memorizing Quran while understanding the meanings
	Allow time for quiet work	Experiencing fury when feeling their core values have been violated	
	Give space to do her own thing	Avoiding conflict and perhaps building up bitterness as a result	Learning about practical matters with a spiritual emphasis (spiritual parenting for example)
ESFP	Spend time with them Help by giving, as ESFPs are self-sacrificing	Expecting spiritual practices to be organized by themselves	*Group dhikr*
	Be available to talk it out	Forgetting to pray/ neglecting time for spiritual matters	Caring for the needy in the community—elderly, alone, etc.
ESFJ	Show love in concrete, helpful ways	Being driven by "should" and aiming for the elusive "perfect"	Honest self-evaluation with a plan of action
	Talk about personal journeys	Sweeping conflict under the rug	Academic study
INFJ	Cheer them on	Overfocusing on their own vision of what should be, missing suggestions of others	A worship group that holds each other accountable for agreed upon goals
	Meet with them in a small, disciplined group that has a plan of spiritual action	Finding it difficult to ask others for help	Studying sacred texts

Type	How to be Helpful to This Type	Common Stumbling Blocks for This Type	Paths of Growth for This Type
INFP	Understand that this type's spirituality is deep and very personal	Believing others do not care enough	Learning paths of *dhikr*
	Recognize their sincerity before addressing shortcomings, as they live out their own values imperfectly but with conviction and sincerity	Taking negative feedback personally	Learning about personalities in Islam
ENFP	Go easy on rules and judgments	Jumping from one thing to another	Reading and talking with people who ask questions
	Act as a "family"	Moving too quickly for contemplation	Attending learning retreats
ENFJ	Provide a caring environment	Assuming their way is the most altruistic and therefore best	Long periods of worship, especially in a group
	Help this type deal with conflict	Lacks patience	Academic learning that allows discussion
INTJ	Intellectually discuss religiosity	Expecting others to see issues as they do	Spending time in liturgies
	Offer advice, not description of ritual or religion	Not feeling competent in prayers and other rituals	Research with a guide
INTP	Recognize feelings and emotions even though they prefer reason and analysis	Skepticism	Learning about spirituality intellectually before attempting to live it practically
	Don't talk in excess, but get to the crux of the matter	Overlooking the heart	Setting up a model for a concrete spiritual life that is rational

Type	How to be Helpful to This Type	Common Stumbling Blocks for This Type	Paths of Growth for This Type
ENTP	Engage in a relationship deep enough to share	Lack of a spiritual routine	Spiritual retreats
	Share stories of people who have overcome stumbling blocks	Gathering information continuously with little practice	Group *dhikr* practices
ENTJ	Understand that this type seldom looks to others for help in spirituality	Applying rigorous standards to self and others	Rigorous study to become a scholar
	Offer opportunities to slow down and "waste time" on social interaction	Not taking time to build important relationships	Getting involved in big projects that keep ENTJs connected to spiritual people or a vision of self and society that can be created by work.

ACTIVITY: YOUR MBTI TYPE AND YOUR SPIRITUALITY

Reflect. Think about the chart above. How well do the suggestions fit your needs?

Expand your reflection. Think about your background and your personality.

Think about symbolic representations of self. Draw pictures and symbols to represent things that have changed and things that have stayed the same during your conversion process. For example, I (Tamara) might draw a microphone in both pictures because I have always been a speaker and/or performer (choir in church and drama and debate clubs in high school), but on my postconversion microphone, I may draw in books to represent the new scholarly use of my speaking talent.

Tips for Self-Reflection and Self-Development

Inner work and introspection are part and parcel of a spiritual life. As Muslims, we recognize that our inner life is seen by God, and our outer life is seen by both God and the world. Both must be in sync. The definition of *ʿaqīda*, or creed, is "those ideas and matters that a person believes in with certainty, and without doubt or suspicion. It is that which inhabits the heart and conscience and touches the emotions, affects one's behavior and character, and settles deeply in the psyche such that it cannot easily be shaken."[26] Beliefs determine our behaviors. Hence, our work to beautify and refine our innermost thoughts and practices in demonstrating goodness and joy is part of what it means to be a Muslim.

Name It and Claim It

If we want to grow, we must be willing to get real about our problems. We must stop blaming the unfairness of individuals, other Muslim cultures, or anyone else for our issues. The process of getting real about our problems is of course complicated by very real and sincere questions and struggles. Islam brings with it a new sensibility, and we rightly wonder if our previous sense of right and wrong is valid.

We see the early companions questioning themselves in this way. Hind became a Muslim soon after *fatḥ* Mecca (the opening of Mecca), and on that day she questioned some of the previous practices that had seemed normal to her. Her husband, Abū Sufyan, was stingy, and Hind would help herself to his money stores in order to manage living with him. Her conscience pricked her about this once she entered Islam, so she asked the Prophet ﷺ, "O Messenger of Allah! Verily Abū Sufyan is a stingy man and does not give me what is sufficient for me and my children, so I take from him without his knowledge." And he ﷺ responded, "Take what is enough for you and your children, within reason."[27] Hind was able to examine her life through her new lens of Islam, ask a question, and then continue to manage her life with wisdom.

When we realize that we are the only ones accountable for our decisions and our lives, we become better Muslims. Sometimes that means solving our personal and relationship issues, which takes time, wisdom, *taqwā* (awareness of the presence of God), and patience.

Other times our problems are simpler; we don't know Arabic, for example, and therefore find prayer (salat) difficult. In this case, we see a problem, and, without romanticizing it or exaggerating it, we decide to acquire those skills.

Many converts would do well to remember that the same good sense that brought them to Islam will help them move forward in faith as well. Too many converts check their internal voice at the door, listening instead to closed-minded ideologies that call themselves Islam, but these converts end up spiraling themselves back out the door. When we stay clear with ourselves—recognize when difficulties are a result of our own weaknesses and/or very human interactions—we have a better chance of navigating life with joy and faith.

Stop the Blame Game

There are approximately 1.8 billion Muslims in the world. To expect every one of them to be well-behaved and to fulfill an idealistic image of what a follower of Muhammad ﷺ should be is ridiculous at best. This is not to say that it is not terribly disappointing to run into Muslims who pray and cheat or Muslims who declare loudly their Islam and then treat their families without an iota of respect. But our responsibility to be good and do good lies squarely on our shoulders. It will not be acceptable on the Day of Judgment, nor is it acceptable in this life, to make the behavior of another an excuse for our own deficits or poor behavior. When we learn to say, "I am not praying my prayers because I am not making the necessary effort," instead of "I am not praying because I don't like the way people who pray behave," we set out on a road of spiritual health.

We will meet Muslims who will hurt us. Some will shock us with their poor behavior. Some will think in ways that make our eyes pop out and our hair turn gray. But we will also meet Muslims who are good and kind, wise and well-mannered. We will meet Muslims who are generous and fun and some who make us laugh and love. No matter who we meet, we create our own experience as Muslims. We must acknowledge and accept responsibility for our lives. Islam is a religion of accountability. We recognize and believe in the accountability of the Day of Judgment, and hence, we must practice personal accountability in this *dunyā*.

What's the Payoff?

How are you benefitting by missing prayer time and again? Certainly, on the surface it seems to be a ridiculous question, but perhaps it is easier to miss the morning prayer than to get up every morning because you stay up very late at night. Perhaps you do not want others to know you are Muslim, so you are gaining anonymity by not praying at work.

At the time of the Prophet ﷺ, seeing the Prophet ﷺ smile was a highly motivating reason to do many things. And he eliminated cultural norms that were once payoffs for bad behavior. Once there was a man who saw the Prophet ﷺ hug and kiss his grandson al-Hasan ibn ʿAli, and he boasted that he had never hugged or kissed any of his ten children. Certainly, he expected to be rewarded for this statement—thinking he'd be admired for his "strength" or however he defined his lack of emotion. And even today we understand that men struggle to show emotion and especially to speak about it. Yet the Prophet ﷺ said, "Whoever does not show mercy will not be shown mercy,"[28] thereby cutting off the payoff and forcing him and all listeners to rethink what works.

In our own lives we must also examine what works and why. In this way, we can make positive changes that help spur us along on our chosen path. This is especially pertinent if, in converting to Islam, we were seeking an identity instead of a faith. While identity is certainly part of being Muslim—it is not enough to hold us up. And if identity is our only foundation, we will find ourselves angry at Muslims most of the time. As Abdal Hakim Murad succinctly puts it,

> A hundred years ago the founder of the Anglo-Muslim movement, Imam Abdullah Quilliam in Liverpool, was writing that those British people who convert for Allah and His Messenger, will, by the grace of God, be rightly guided. Those who convert for any other reason are in serious spiritual trouble. . . . Islam will not work for us unless we have entered it in faith, out of a sincere questing for God's good pleasure. If things are not going right for us, if we find no delight in our prayers, if Ramadan simply makes us hungry, if we cannot seem to find the right mosque or the right company to take us forward, then we would do well to start by examining our intentions.[29]

Life Rewards Action

Make careful decisions, then act. Belief is intricately intertwined with action. The Quran describes the people of heaven as ﴾ *those who believe and do good deeds* ﴿ in a number of verses:

> ﴾ *Those who believe and do good deeds are the best of creation* ﴿ (Q. 98:7);
>
> ﴾ *And keep up prayer in the two parts of the day and in the first hours of the night; surely good deeds take away evil deeds. This is a reminder to the mindful* ﴿ (Q. 11:114);
>
> ﴾ *The Lord of Mercy will bestow affection upon those who believe and perform righteous deeds* ﴿ (Q. 19:96);
>
> ﴾ *To whomever, male or female, does good deeds and is a believer, We shall give a good life and reward them according to the best of their actions* ﴿ (Q. 16:97).

While we know that Allah looks to our intentions, we also know that intending is not enough. Hence, we stand up to pray, close our mouths to fast, travel to hajj, and hand over money for zakat. We are a faith of action. Our lives must reflect this if we are to reach inner peace and happiness.

Warning!

If a husband is weaponizing polygyny to punish or bully his wife, or to make her jealous, that is not a cultural filter. That is spiritual and emotional abuse.

Find Your Filters

Each one of us comes to Islam with her own preconceived ideas about what is fair and what is right. Islam is a religion that encompasses vast geographical and historical borders. Not every Muslim culture will feel like home for a convert, but that does not make the cultures weird or wrong. When we acknowledge our biases, we can move beyond them.

In the case of polygyny, for example, many Western women downright reject the institution for their own lives, and it is their right to choose not to live in a polygynous marriage. But some have trouble acknowledging that it could be a healthy institution for others. They cannot believe that there are some women who prefer polygyny because of what it provides them of children and freedom. The same culture that supports multiple lovers does not support multiple spouses. Acknowledging our own cultural filters helps us live happier lives. We can choose not to be a second wife without ridiculing the institution itself. Once we can recognize that our filters are real, we can be more respectful of other filters and choose which ones we want to keep and which ones we want to modify.

Life Is Managed, Not Cured

Life is a long road. There will be continuous trials and tests that ask us to hone and tone our very selves and our reliance on God. ﴿*Do people think that they will be left alone upon saying, "We believe," and that they will not be tested?*﴾ (Q. 29:2). As we go through life's questions and tests, we keep in mind that this too shall pass, or, even better, ﴿*Surely after hardship comes ease*﴾ (Q. 94:6–7) and in that way manage each turn of events with the uprightness of a person of faith. Here are some tips for managing life.

a. **Always pray.** Never decide that prayer is unimportant. If you find it difficult, don't give up. Muslim prayer (salat) is our most important tool to work through the trials of life.
b. **Keep promises and commitments.** Either don't make promises or make sure you keep the ones you make. It will make personal relationships easier and hence, our spiritual growth smoother. And it will make you a person of integrity in front of Allah.
c. **Continue to learn.** Islam is a vast and nuanced faith; learning means you will avoid stagnation. Go to local lectures or *ḥalaqa*s (study circles), ask a respected friend or scholar for recommended reading lists and charge into them, or enroll in online or in-person classes where you can learn Arabic and Islamic sciences. Enroll at ribaat.rabata.org, and engage in traditional learning using modern teaching methods. There is always more to learn, and learning strengthens faith and helps us stand firm on our chosen path.
d. **Keep a personal garbage can.** Dump erroneous claims and poor behavior into it, and don't be afraid to use it often. This metaphorical garbage can is useful for both the outrageous behavior of others and our own slipups. Admitting we were wrong about something or behaved badly is not a sign of weakness; it is a step up to a higher station.
e. **Talk to God.** Make *duʿāʾ*. Long, earnest *duʿāʾ*s, alone and in company, are an integral part of Islam in many Muslim-majority countries, but somehow this tradition got diluted in the transition from East to West. I (Najiyah) once led a prayer where I closed with a long English *duʿāʾ*, and a woman thanked me afterward, saying that she

was born Muslim but didn't realize we could supplicate like that—openly and directly pleading to and thanking Allah for specific things in our lives. Not only is it acceptable to call out to God in *duʿāʾ*, but talking to Allah is one of the most effective ways to strengthen our relationship with God. And that is what Islam is all about.

We Teach People How to Treat Us[30]

Own, rather than complain about, how people treat you. Learn to treat people well and insist on being treated well. This is a powerful concept and a difficult one to swallow. It is easy to complain and whine about how people treat us, but if we recognize our accountability, we will have more successful and rewarding relationships.

My (Tamara's) sister was once having dinner with some people who started to ridicule me and the way I dress. She stated clearly, "If you talk about my sister like that, I am leaving the table." They continued to do so. Now, before we see what happened next, let's answer the question about why they continued to do so. It was because prior to that dinner conversation, she had "taught them" that it was OK to ridicule others in front of her. Even though she didn't like it, she had fumed internally rather than speaking up, for fear of upsetting them. When she decided to teach them how to treat her (in this case how to speak about her family), she changed the rules. They tested her and continued to speak in the old way. At this, she stood up and left the table. She did not push back her chair roughly, nor did she slam the door, nor did she flip them the bird. She simply followed through on her intention to no longer allow people to speak badly about me. In so doing, she taught them what was acceptable and what was not. They never spoke ill of me again, and they all remained friends. Once we understand that our own actions influence how people treat us, we can begin to improve our lives.

ACTIVITY: DO YOU HAVE A HEALTHY SELF?

Ask yourself the following questions.

Healthy Self?	Yes/No
1. Do you spend hours watching one YouTube video after another?	
2. Do you throw a wrinkled abaya over pajamas and leave the house?	
3. Are you feeling bitter over what you are "missing out" on?	
4. Are you suddenly without friends?	
5. Have you gained a lot of weight since becoming a Muslim?	
6. Do you believe that getting married will solve all your problems?	
7. If you are married, does your spouse fall short of your expectations daily?	
8. Have you cut off family ties because your family members are "*kuffār*?"	
9. Have you stopped eating the food you like because none of your new friends eat it?	
10. Are you a closet Muslim, living two identities?	

Here are some strategies for any problems you may have identified.

Problem	Possible Solutions
1. Watching too many random online videos	YouTube videos can be interesting, fun, and even educational. They are not, however, a replacement for real learning. Sign up for a series of courses that have an organized curriculum (like Ribaat), or start local classes. If you do not have access to either, choose the videos you watch based on content, and try to build up your knowledge with strategy and planning. One idea is to work with an elder mentor to choose which videos to watch, take some notes, and discuss them with friends on the path.
2. Feeling unkempt, sloppy, or messy	Just as you took care of your appearance before Islam and before you started to wear hijab, it is important that you do the same now. Choose clothing that fits. Clothing that is your size is not the same as tight-fitting clothing. Clothing that is four sizes too big is going to make you feel sloppy and frumpy.
3. Being afraid of "missing out"	Reality check here. Start living your life. If you miss parties, invite some lonely sisters over for an alcohol-free party. If you miss barhopping, find some nice coffee shops, bakeries, or tea shops to spend time in. If you miss friends, be proactive about making new ones. Go to a *ḥalaqa*, have a hijab swap party, or invite people you don't know well over for dinner.
4. Having a lack of personal ties	Make time to build relationships with other sisters, even if it means driving an hour and a half to have a coffee. Look to online relationships to help fill the gap as well. Sometimes our like-minded beloveds live far away, but we can still be connected.
5. Gaining weight	Stop making excuses and find solutions. Don't say, "I can't exercise since I wear hijab." Instead, find ways and places to move and be healthy.

Problem	Possible Solutions
6. Thinking marriage is a quick fix for personal difficulties	Do not get married in order to take the proverbial problem-solving pill. Marriage is a lot of work, and cross-cultural marriages are even more so. Work on your own happiness and strength of faith. Bringing a joyful, knowledgeable self who is settled in her faith into a marriage puts you light-years ahead of the game compared to bringing an uncertain, spiritually immature self.
7. Criticizing your spouse	Work on your own happiness. Stop expecting your spouse to provide it for you. It may help to remember your own flaws, accentuate his positives, look at baby pictures of him (so fun!), and remember that he is human. Also, keep in mind that love is a verb, so acting loving often brings deep and fulfilling feelings of love.
8. Cutting off family ties	It is very important to keep family ties, both for your health and for the hope of your family's guidance. It is also an Islamic requirement to keep family relationships. Do your best (more about this in module three).
9. Pining for a type of food	Have a piece of pie and a steak. Try turkey bacon or beef bacon. Stop eating foreign food for a couple of weeks, until you rebalance your taste buds and your lifestyle.
10. Having a split identity	Bring your two identities back together. Maybe change your profile name to include both names for a while, while people get used to calling you the name you've chosen.

What's in the Self?

So many things. This section has reviewed issues of childhood and background, habits and character, as well as personality issues. It has given us tips and tricks to improve ourselves and hopefully, to bring our whole selves to Islam, becoming in the process fully contented, like those in the verse:

﴾ *O contented self, return to your Lord well-pleased and pleasing* ﴿ (Q. 89:27–28).

Now we will turn to another aspect of the self—our names.

PART TWO: WHAT'S IN A NAME?

Malcolm X was one of the greatest American Muslims who ever lived. His devotion to truth was inimitable, and his influence on Muslims around the world was tangible. After joining the Nation of Islam, Malcolm, like many of his contemporaries, took X as a surname, rejecting the surname that had been handed down to him by a slave owner. The Nation of Islam would provide last names for followers who requested them, or some families would choose new last names for themselves. Indeed, whole families would have their names legally changed. All of their documents would carry this new name, as would their children. The rejection of a name that indicated oppression, and the adoption of a new name that indicated their choice of religion was an empowering part of the movement. It helped young men and women redefine themselves and pull themselves out of a history that haunted their psyche. Malcolm X changed his name again when, in 1964 following his hajj, he became El-Hajj Malik El-Shabazz in honor of his continued growth into Sunni Islam.

Just as the Nation of Islam helped its followers to shake off the shackles of oppression, a name change can help a new Muslim walk away from an old life that haunts her. Just as some of the companions of the Prophet ﷺ changed from ʿAbd Shams (worshipper of the sun) to ʿAbd al-Rahman (worshipper of the Merciful), some new Muslims today find solace in a new name. But a name change can also have a negative effect—splitting up families, separating the new convert from her true self, or just inducing stress.

The Name Game

There are some converts who, in changing their given name, broke their parents' hearts, struggled with a split identity, and were confused by a belief that taking a new name was necessary for their Islam to be complete. In many cases, immigrant imams, aunties, and other community leaders with good intentions told converts that they had to change their names, but it was often with troubling results. For many young converts, the new "Muslim" name was used only in the Muslim community, and her original given name was still used at work, at home, and with old friends. As a result, a dichotomy began to grow. Two people emerged from one, manifesting itself in a confused identity. Even today, some converts will have two Facebook pages and essentially live two lives. One woman said to us, "After fifteen years of living with two names, I'm beginning to forget who I am to different people. I get phone calls and I can't remember if I should say that I am Khadija or Carol. I'm exhausted and I don't know what to do about it now. I feel it's too late to do anything."

"Your New Name Is Maryam!"

Following a Project Lina workshop, one young woman went to her local mosque to declare her faith and, just as she finished, an older woman leaned in and said, "What's your name dear?" to which she replied, "Tracy." The woman smiled, pointed her finger at her, and said, "Now you are Maryam." Tracy thanked us profusely the next day, saying that because she had heard us talk about Muslim names and name changes, she was able to smile and say "No, I'm keeping Tracy, thank you," without wondering if her inclination was sinful.

Call Me Whatever You Want

Another young woman we met in Minnesota introduced herself to other Muslims as Khadija. When we asked her about it, she said, "I don't really care; it's easier for them." In other words, since her name was too difficult for them to pronounce, she let her Muslim acquaintances call her whatever they wanted to.

"What is your given name?" we asked.

"Hannah."

"Hannah? We know Arab women who were given that name at birth!"

She shrugged and said, "I don't know."

My Name Just Is Not Me

In California a woman confided to us that she had never connected with her "Islamic" name of the past fourteen years. She had really lost herself and was now struggling to get her identity back. We made a point to use her given name when talking to her, at least for that weekend.

Is My Name a Sin?

An Asian woman, also in California, told us with a measure of pride and a measure of shame that she had a prefix to her name that went back fifteen generations. For the past four hundred years, all the women in her family had carried the same prefix. She said, "I've been told it is terribly haram, and I don't know what to do. I don't know what to tell my family or how to have it taken off my paperwork. And is it really necessary?" She asked the last part with trepidation.

"What does it mean?" we asked her, assuming that it had some pagan meaning related to Buddhism.

"The kind and gentle one."

"How do you pronounce it in your language?"

Her answer was a syllable that neither of us could reproduce.

"How do you spell it in English?"

So the problem was that when this beautiful and historic name was written out in English it looked like this: Dieu. Someone who had taken a little French in college saw this and decided that this young woman wanted herself addressed as "God." Sigh. She had carried around unnecessary guilt and sadness.

My Sheikh Gave Me My Name

Some converts take on new names for personal reasons. A good friend of ours was given the name Fatima by her sheikh, and for years she vacillated between Fatima and her birth name. Recently, however, she has begun to hold she has begun to hold on to the name Fatima tightly, so that when we mistakenly call her by her given name, the name we have known her by for over thirty years, she gently corrects us.

Name Stories

Names are important. They are the labels that tell the world who we are. For every name we have, there is a corresponding story. Our birth names tell us something about our history, nicknames might say something about relationships, and chosen names can hold great nostalgic significance.

Tamara's Name Story

When my mother was pregnant with me, she wanted to name me Tracy, but lo and behold, her college friend had her baby girl first and stole the name, so I was left nameless. My maternal grandmother walked into the hospital and offered the name Tamara. "You can call her Tammy." Maybe it sounded close enough to Tracy—or maybe it was just meant to be—but it stuck. I became Tammy for the next seventeen years. (I am still Tammy to many of my closest family members, but please note that if you call me that, I will not be amused.) As family lore goes, this story is part of my history; my father tells this story at the same time that he tells stories that point to my stubbornness and my desire to leave home (which I did at two years old, doll in tow). When I became a Muslim, I had already ordered the world to call me Tamara, and my new college friends had no idea I was once called Tammy. Perhaps because of the Arabic word for "date" (tamar), my name was accepted, and I was rarely tormented with remarks about changing it.

Najiyah's Name Story

When I became Muslim, I was excited to take on every single part of my new identity. I put on my scarf, bought dresses at the thrift store to go over all my jeans, and made a sign for my entryway that said, "This is a Muslim home. Please remove your shoes." I was so proud! So proud that I had found the Truth, and I wanted everyone to see me, be intrigued, and, of course, just by seeing my transformation, convert immediately! Isn't that the way it happens?

I was also completely enamored of all things Arabic and all things Muslim which, at the time, were all mixed up in my head together. I revered anything I saw written in Arabic because I didn't know what was Quran and what wasn't. Ditto Arabic cultural practices and actual Islamic tenets.

This attempt to absorb, don, and inhabit my new identity extended to my name. I had never liked my name (which I see now was more of a self-esteem issue than a name issue. I was actually more uncomfortable with the person Diana *was* than with the name Diana.) But I loved the name Iman. I loved its meaning (faith) and its sound, and I thought that if I adopted it, I would be completing my metamorphosis into a Muslim.

My then-husband disagreed. "There isn't anything wrong with the name Diana," he insisted. "And nothing in Islam that says you need to change your name." So for seven years, Diana I remained.

Then one day in the middle of my seventh Ramadan, we went to pick up the visiting prayer leader and take him to dinner at a friend's house. On the way, out of the clear blue sky and with the imam as a witness, my husband said, "I have a gift for you, if you'd like to accept it. My grandmother's name was Najiyah. Would you like to take that as your name?" I was ecstatic! Both its sound and its meaning (one who has been saved) were more beautiful than I could ever have chosen on my own.

Najiyah is an old-fashioned name, like Bertha or Gertrude, and it isn't commonly used these days. So I had the added benefit of a unique name that most Arabs have fond memories of from the old days. I loved it and embraced it without hesitation, although I never changed it legally, mostly out of (rather belated) consideration for my parents' feelings.

So I have been Najiyah for twenty-four years, and to this day I cherish the name. I moved back to Kansas to be near my parents recently, and my birth name came back to life as they and my old acquaintances started calling me Diana. I do use both names now, but I don't feel a sense of split identity. I want my neighbors to know the Muslim they see and talk to is one of them—a homegrown daughter of the prairie. And of course, the last three decades of deep personal work have given me a foundation where using two names is not confusing for me internally; rather, it has become empowering.

Religion, Culture, and Name Changing

A Saintly Name

Many Christians place an emphasis on a child's name at the baptismal ceremony. For Catholics, Canon 855, "Parents, sponsors, and the pastor are to take care that a name foreign to Christian sensibility is not given,"[31] guides the choice of a child's name. In the early twentieth century, that often meant that a saint's name would be tacked on to the child's birth name.

Hebrew It Is!

Jews require the use of Hebrew names for certain rituals, and as a result some Western Jews will have two names—a secular name and a Hebrew name. These names are both given at birth. For Orthodox Jews, however, the child is given a Hebrew name only. This is related to the ethnic nature of the Jewish faith. All Jews (other than converts) are ethnically Jewish, whether or not they are believers in the Judaic creed, and the shared language of all Jews is Hebrew.

Trendsetters!

Names in Western cultures follow trends. The cultural importance of celebrities means that children will often be named after famous politicians, authors, film stars, or musicians during a certain decade. American families do not often pass down names, at least not as much as was done historically and in Europe, but parents do spend an enormous amount of time worrying and fussing over meaning, sound (with the surname), and what the initials spell. Early Puritans tended to give their children names with blatantly obvious meanings like Temperance or Prudence. A perusal of the most popular names at the top of the last five decades tells us that, in general, Americans name their children names with either positive or benign meanings.

Popular American Baby Names by Decade

Decade	Name	Language Origin	Meaning
1960	Mary	Hebrew (Miriam)	Unknown, but one theory is "wished-for child," another is "beloved by God"
1960	Susan	English (Susanna)	Variant meanings, refers to an Old Testament heroine
1960	Linda	German	"Soft, tender"
1970	Jennifer	Welsh (Guinevere)	"Fair, white, and smooth"
1970	Lisa	English (Elizabeth)	"My God is abundance"
1970	Kimberly	English	From a place called Kimberley
1980	Jennifer	Welsh (Guinevere)	"Fair, white, and smooth"
1980	Amanda	Latin	"Worthy of love"
1980	Melissa	Greek	"Bee"

Popular American Baby Names by Decade			
Decade	Name	Language Origin	Meaning
1990	Jessica	Hebrew (Jisca, pronounced Yiskah), first used in this form by Shakespeare	"To behold"
	Ashley	English (surname)	"Ash tree clearing"
	Brittany	French	From the region of Bretagne, named after British settlers who fled to the region
2000	Emily	Latin (Amilius)	"Rivalry"
	Hannah	Hebrew	"Favor/grace"
	Madison	English (surname)	"Son of Maud"
2010	Isabella	Latin (Elizabet)	"My God is abundance"
	Sophia	Greek	"Wisdom"
	Emma	German	"Whole or universal"
2020	Emma	German	"Whole or universal"
	Olivia	Latin	"Olive tree"
	Ava	Latin (meaning "bird"), Hebrew (Eve)	Possibly "life or living one"

Who Names the Child?

Parents in Western cultures tend to place great importance on personally naming their children. In the past, and in other cultures, it has been and remains less important for the parents to name the child. Either the child carried a family name or she was named by grandparents or a tribal member. In modern Western societies, however, we often find that children have elaborate name stories, in which they hear about all the other names that were considered and how the parents finally settled on the given name. In light of this cultural component, when a person enters Islam, it can be very hurtful to parents if the child gives up her name in favor of a new "Muslim" name. The parents can feel resentful and bitter over this complete loss of their child.

Considering Parents' Feelings

It is important to remember the emphasis Islam places on parents and their role in our lives before we decide to change our name. When contemplating a name change, consider their feelings first.

Joe Bradford, an American scholar of Islam, tells us in his article "What's in a Name: Why You Don't Have To and Shouldn't Change Your Name in Islam,"[32] about an experience he had in Medina while studying:

> While I was there, I was studying under a prominent scholar in Medina, and he would constantly call me "Joe." Once in class he did this, and someone said, "His name is Hud." To which he replied, "Yes, but he is Joe to his parents."
>
> Another time something similar happened. After class he pulled me to the side and said "Joe..."
>
> "Hud," I cut him off and corrected him.
>
> He smiled and said, "Your parents named you Joe, and I would hate for you to change something good that they gave you." He continued, saying, "Think of Allah's statement in Surat Yusuf (12:68) ﴿ *And when they entered according to their father's advice, it did not avail them in the least against the Will of Allah; but it met a need in Jacob's heart that he needed fulfilled.* ﴾ See how he requested something that wasn't essential, wasn't necessary, and the only purpose was to fulfill a personal need he had? Allah orders us to respect our parents in all cases; we can only disobey them if they order us to commit *shirk*. Even then we must respect them and treat them kindly. Even though they may accept you using another name, keep your original name out of respect for them, out of respect for their choices. You'll be rewarded for that."[33]

He goes on to talk about realizing that his parents' feelings mattered. After his father's death, he decided to drop the Arab name he had acquired and honor his father with the use of his given name. When converts who have changed their name decide to reclaim their heritage, it is often difficult to reteach our Muslim brothers and sisters our original name. It takes courage to insist that instead of Amina, you are now (once again) April. But if done for the sake of your parents or rooting your identity in Islam, it is well worth it.

We will talk more about parents and how to ensure their *riḍa* (pleasure) in module three, but for now, suffice it to say that before you change your name, ask yourself the question, "Is it worth my parents' hurt feelings and anger?"

Names, Literature, and Society: Anne Shirley

Literature mirrors life, and the character of Anne Shirley in the Anne of Green Gables series is an excellent example of a turn-of-the-century Western female in search of her identity. That identity is intertwined with her name. Anne (with an *e*) is attempting to move out of her sorrowful life and chooses a new and romantic name, Cordelia, to help her. Her guardian, sensible Marilla, will not concede, and thankfully so, because Anne Shirley will grow into a mature young woman with a clear identity throughout the books.

> "Well, don't cry any more. We're not going to turn you out-of-doors to-night. You'll have to stay here until we investigate this affair. What's your name?"
>
> The child hesitated for a moment.
>
> "Will you please call me Cordelia?" she said eagerly.
>
> "Call you Cordelia? Is that your name?"
>
> "No-o-o, it's not exactly my name, but I would love to be called Cordelia. It's such a perfectly elegant name."
>
> "I don't know what on earth you mean. If Cordelia isn't your name, what is?"
>
> "Anne Shirley," reluctantly faltered forth the owner of that name, "but, oh, please do call me Cordelia. It can't matter much to you what you call me if I'm only going to be here a little while, can it? And Anne is such an unromantic name."
>
> "Unromantic fiddlesticks!" said the unsympathetic Marilla. "Anne is a real good plain sensible name. You've no need to be ashamed of it."
>
> "Oh, I'm not ashamed of it," explained Anne, "only I like Cordelia better. I've always imagined that my name was Cordelia—at least, I always

have of late years. When I was young I used to imagine it was Geraldine, but I like Cordelia better now. But if you call me Anne please call me Anne spelled with an E."

"What difference does it make how it's spelled?" asked Marilla with another rusty smile as she picked up the teapot.

"Oh, it makes such a difference. It looks so much nicer. When you hear a name pronounced can't you always see it in your mind, just as if it was printed out? I can; and A-n-n looks dreadful, but A-n-n-e looks so much more distinguished. If you'll only call me Anne spelled with an E I shall try to reconcile myself to not being called Cordelia."

"Very well, then, Anne spelled with an E, can you tell us how this mistake came to be made? We sent word to Mrs. Spencer to bring us a boy. Were there no boys at the asylum?"

The Importance of Being Earnest

In the nineteenth-century play *The Importance of Being Earnest*, the main characters take on a fake name (Earnest) in order to avoid social responsibility. They bumble around making mistakes and attempting to fix the mistakes they make—all because of the fake name. It is in the first act that the name problem is discovered, and it is the cause of much farce and difficulty. The

Algernon:	Besides, your name isn't Jack at all; it is Earnest.
Jack:	It isn't Earnest; it's Jack.
Algernon:	You have always told me it was Earnest. I have introduced you to everyone as Earnest. You answer to the name of Earnest. You look as if your name was Earnest. You are the most earnest-looking person I ever saw in my life. It is perfectly absurd, your saying that your name isn't Earnest. It's on your cards. Here is one of them. [*Taking it from case.*] "Mr. Earnest Worthing, B. 4, The Albany." I'll keep this as a proof that your name is Earnest if ever you attempt to deny it to me, or to Gwendolen, or to anyone else. [*Puts the card in his pocket.*]
Jack:	Well, my name is Earnest in town and Jack in the country...

symbolic emphasis of the play, however, is in the demonstration of hypocrisy as represented by having two personas in one person, where each is displayed in different company.

In real life, as in literature, our names are inextricably wrapped up in our identities. For converts to Islam who have made a decision to believe in a new faith, their identity is in a process of redefinition, and the decision whether to change a name or not should be taken in that context.

Names and Cultural "Correctness"

Westerners, and especially Americans, are very big on cultural understanding, and the politically correct movements of the late twentieth and early twenty-first centuries have placed great emphasis on using the correct name for individuals and groups of people. Hence, in the Western hemisphere, it is considered an important point of etiquette to attempt to pronounce someone's name correctly. Teachers often struggle with this the most when looking at a roster of names that originate in all countries of the world. On a teacher forum, for example, one teacher laments that she had a student on her summer list with the name of Yaralize. She says, "All summer I sort of practiced saying it just the way it looks, 'Yaralize.' Then her mother came into my classroom and said, 'This is my daughter Jahdi,' and I told her that I didn't have any students by that name. She pointed to 'Yaralize' on my list and told me, 'It's pronounced "Jahdalise" and her nickname is "Jahdi."'" The teacher complains on the forum because of the effort she went to in order to pronounce the name and her frustration that the child's actual name was pronounced so differently than it was spelled.

Names, both first and last, originate from a variety of places in immigration-heavy countries. Hence, the sensitive Westerner has grown accustomed to making at least a reasonable attempt at the pronunciation of letters and syllables that are unfamiliar to them.

For peoples in places that have not experienced two hundred years of multiethnic immigration, however, there is less social pressure to pronounce a foreign name correctly. Indeed, in countries where colonialism held sway, Western names tend to carry a negative connotation, one that indicates an enemy or an unfriendly entity in one's midst. In countries that are majority Muslim, this cultural tendency gets mixed with a deeply principled loyalty to the faith of Islam. Thus, often when converts meet up with Muslims, they are told, "You need to change your name," or "Your name is now (fill in the blank)" or "You need an Islamic name." In more modern times, and with more and more Western converts (as well as a large second generation of Muslims who have grown up in Western countries) this problem seems to have become less of an issue, though it still remains in Muslim communities that are dominated by immigrant Muslims.

Prophet Muhammad's Name Story

The Prophet's name ﷺ was a chosen name. It taught people who he would become. Ibn Sa'd reports Amīna, the mother of the Prophet, as saying, "I did not realize that I was carrying him, and I did not feel heaviness as women usually do, yet I thought it strange that I no longer menstruated. I heard a voice ask me while I was between wakefulness and sleep, 'Do you realize that you are with child?' and it was as though I answered, 'I do not know.' And the voice said, 'You are carrying the master of this nation and its Prophet.'" That was on a Monday. She said, "This confirmed the pregnancy to me. Then again, close to the time of delivery, I heard the same voice tell me, 'Say, as soon as you give birth, "I seek refuge in Allah from the evil of all enviers," and then name him "Muḥammad."'"[34]

His ﷺ name story continues, "It is narrated that when Amina delivered the Prophet ﷺ, 'Abd al-Muṭṭalib took him, kissed him, and then entrusted him to Abū Ṭālib saying, 'I entrust him to you; this son of mine will be renowned.' He then ordered sheep and camels to be slaughtered, and he fed the people of Mecca for three days. Then he slaughtered a camel in all the glens of Mecca, so that no human, beast, or bird was prevented from eating."[35]

On the seventh day he circumcised him ﷺ, as was the habit among the Arabs,[36] slaughtered a ram, and invited people to dinner. He named him Muḥammad (meaning "the praised one"), which was an unfamiliar name to the Arabs, so when the people of Quraish heard it, they wondered at it, and found it strange. They asked 'Abd al-Muṭṭalib, "Why did you not use his family's names?" He answered, "I wanted him to be praised in heaven by Allah and on earth by His creation."[37]

Peace and blessings be upon him.

Arabic Names at the Time of Revelation and the Prophet's Response

Arabs had a tendency to name their children with words that were quite specific to who they were. Names such as Khālid (eternity), Walīd (newborn boy), and 'Umar (the enduring) were common, and the Prophet ﷺ did not change these names. (Though, today Muslims from all over the world name their children these names, not for their intrinsic meaning but for the namesakes they represent.)

The Arabs also named their children in honor of their pagan rites. So the name ʿAbd Shams (worshipper of the sun) and ʿAbd Manāf (worshipper of the idol Manaf) were prevalent amongst them. The Prophet ﷺ did change these names; one of the most famous early companions of the Prophet, ʿAbd al-Raḥmān ibn ʿAwf, was originally ʿAbd ʿAmr. Any companion with the name ʿAbd al-Raḥmān was most likely a carrier of a pagan name before his Islam, because the name for God al-Raḥmān (the Gracious) was not known to the Arabs prior to Islam.

The Prophet ﷺ also discouraged names that carried a negative meaning. He was visited by a man named Qaṭiʿ ibn Ẓālim ibn Sāriq, who came to him to become a Muslim. He was a tall and dignified man, and when he came to see the Prophet ﷺ, he was wearing a long yellow robe. The Prophet ﷺ asked him his name, and when he said, "I am Qaṭiʿ (the one who cuts off ties of kinship), son of Ẓālim (the oppressor), son of Sāriq (the thief)." The Prophet ﷺ said, "You are Abū Ṣufrah (father of yellow); leave off the use of the other names."[38]

It was and remains a common practice among the Arabs to nickname each other "father of so-and-so" and "mother of so-and-so." Usually she or he would be nicknamed after their eldest son and would also retain her or his given name, father's, and grandfather's names. For someone like Qaṭiʿ, who was a dignified leader claiming lineage to the king of the high seas, this lineage would be even more important. Yet the Prophet ﷺ renamed him and told him to leave off his lineage when telling people his name. The man looked at the Prophet ﷺ. He had already arrived in order to enter Islam, but now he gazed at him with the eyes of certainty and said, "Truly, truly, you are the Messenger of God. I have eighteen sons and only one daughter, and her name is Ṣufrah." So the Prophet ﷺ had actually nicknamed him after his only daughter. The man found this miraculous and embraced Islam (and his new name) with fervor and deep belief.[39]

Abū Hurayra is a famous companion of the Prophet because of his numerous narrations of hadith. His given name was ʿAbd Shams ibn Ṣakhr and the Messenger ﷺ changed his name to ʿAbd al-Raḥmān. Then, when he found him carrying a cat in his sleeve, he nicknamed him Abū Hurayra (father of the little cat), and that was the name that stuck.

How Did the Companions Manage Their Name Changes?

One clear characteristic of those who did change their name at the time of the Prophet ﷺ was that the name was adopted completely. We do not read of companions living double lives, using one name in Medina and another in Mecca.

The Case of Abd al-Rahman ibn ʿAwf

ʿAbd al-Raḥmān ibn ʿAwf's given name was ʿAbd ʿAmr. The Prophet ﷺ changed his name to ʿAbd al-Raḥmān. ʿAbd al-Rahman had a friend in Mecca who was an idolater and an active oppressor of the Muslims. When this man heard of his friend's new name, he scoffed and said, "Oh ʿAbd ʿAmr! Have you rejected the name which your father gave you?"

Have you ever had a "friend" or relative who knew just what to say to throw you off your game? The one word that would trigger a deep and emotional reaction? We both do, and it is truly difficult to hold on to our deeper values when poked and prodded in this way. But ʿAbd al-Raḥmān held strong. We know the Arabs held family ties as the highest of values. Breaking them was shameful. Even so, ʿAbd al-Rahman responded with a simple "yes." Strong and firm, and without unnecessary explanation that could draw them into an argument. But this friend would not acquiesce. He would call out "ʿAbd ʿAmr," and ʿAbd al-Raḥmān would not respond. Finally, he said to him, "Since I do not know 'al-Raḥmān,' choose a name that will be between you and me that I may call you by it; you do not answer me when I call upon you by your given name, and I will not call upon you using a name of which I know not." So for a time they settled on ʿAbd al-Ilāh (servant of the God) as a compromise of sorts.[40]

ʿAbd al-Raḥmān ibn ʿAwf's story speaks to the importance of being our full selves with all people, even those who will chastise us for our beliefs and our values. He both insisted on his new name and then compromised within his values. Here is a lesson against rigidity that is at the same time a lesson in a principled stance. As we think about our names and our other life choices, we can remember this example and be both firm and loving when interacting with the people who have known and loved us since before our Islam.

The Internet

The internet offers us avatars, fake accounts, and enough anonymity to open up the possibility of creating entirely new identities on social media. These extra identities cause some people to act in ways that are not in keeping with their true morals and values, under the guise of an anonymous person. In this state of anonymity, people have found themselves involved in numerous haram and illegal, as well as unethical and just plain wrong, activities while online.

If we look at real life, it is normal for many of us to take on a somewhat different persona at work and at home; indeed, we often must. But here we are not talking about the benefits or potentially damaging risks of being assertive at work and passive at home. Here, the issue at hand is religious identity. So if no one at work knows you are a Muslim or if you have two Facebook accounts—one for the Muslims and one for everyone else—there is a chance that you are facing a dangerous identity crisis.

It is important to be an authentic person. This does not mean that we have to be comfortable, for comfort is not the same as authenticity. We may feel strange in the beginning of our conversion telling everyone about our deepest beliefs. And while that is perfectly normal, developing a double identity can be dangerous to your psychological and spiritual health. At some point, the various parts have to merge on one path to God and come together to support your new religious identity.

How Many Identities?

Here is what a few converts have told us about how they grapple with the many identities that result from having more than one name.

- "I feel split into two, the old me and the new."
- "My past only shadowed my present in thoughts and memories. As time passed, I remembered the story of my name that my mom gave me. Eventually I took her name back."
- "Even after fourteen years, I sometimes forget who knows me as what!"
- "I like my Muslim name, but I missed my old name and changed it back at work. Then it stuck."
- "Over time I did not like having two names and gradually my Muslim name fell into disuse."
- "I feel frustrated that some people who knew me as my Muslim name when I initially converted still insist on calling me that despite numerous corrections."
- "I love both names, but when I hear my given name, it brings about a whole different feeling."

What, Then, Is in a Name?

In this section we looked at the connection of names to identity, discussed some possible drawbacks to changing your name upon conversion, and some possible benefits. We considered how the Prophet ﷺ interacted with the names of people around him and discovered that, for the most part, he had no comment. He ﷺ only offered a new name when names carried blatantly idolatrous or unethical meanings. This both reminds us of the importance of our names, perhaps pushing us to find a "Muslim name," and underlines the significance of our birth name, which may give us needed permission to hold on to it.

In short, there is no right or wrong answer to the question of "Should I change my name?" Indeed, it is the wrong question. Instead, we can ask "What is in my name?" and if the answer is "worship of an idol" or "ugliness (of any kind)," then we might consider changing it. If, however, the answer is "me," then whatever your name is, it becomes a Muslim name by virtue of the very fact that you are a Muslim.

ACTIVITY: NAME THAT SELF!

What is your name? Take some time to think about all of your names—nicknames, fun names, and first, middle, and last names. Then fill in the blanks below:

My name: ____

My "Muslim" name (if applicable): ____________________________

My nicknames:

____

____

____

My favorite nickname, how I got it, and who calls me by it:

____

What is the story of your given name?

____

____

____

What is the story of your acquired name?

____

____

____

ACTIVITY: WHO CALLS ME BY WHICH NAME?

List who among your family, friends, and acquaintances calls you by which name:

Who calls me...	Given name	Acquired name
Family (parents and siblings)		
My close friends today		
Acquaintances		
Other		

PART THREE: WHAT'S IN A CULTURE?

Jane opens her eyes. The clock says 5:30 a.m., still some time before the sun rises. She pulls herself out from under her quilt and stumbles to the bathroom. Freshly *wuḍū'*ed, she prays the morning prayer and then heads to the kitchen to start her day. Coffee on, she turns on the morning news and goes to make her bed.

Jane folds her prayer clothes and calls her mother. Thanksgiving is in two weeks, so they are negotiating dinner. It's important to Jane that the family comes to her house, and it's important to her mother that she gets to make the pies. An agreement has been made—her mother will make the pies and Jane will whip the cream.

Later that morning Jane, in a denim skirt, long-sleeved T-shirt, and matching jersey hijab, stands in line at the bakery. There are three people ahead of her, and while she waits, she ogles the cookies she always promises herself she won't buy. There are snowflakes, Santa heads, and a cute little Christmas tree with sparkles. She spies her personal past favorite—maple bacon doughnuts. It's finally her turn, and she smiles at the cashier. They exchange niceties, and Jane leaves—diet, begone!—with her bread and a dozen sugar cookies, leaving behind the maple bacon doughnuts.

Culture

Culture is found in our routines, the foods we eat, and the beverages we drink. We see culture in the clothes we wear and the celebrations we participate in. It is found in our behaviors, our manners, and in the trappings of life. Culture is what helps us cope with our world.

When someone becomes a Muslim, she wakes up at a different time of day, eats different foods, changes her routine, and begins to rethink her celebrations and habits. As she continues in this new lifestyle, her very behavior and demeanor may change, and she may one day look in the mirror and not recognize herself anymore. At this point, if she hasn't realized how much her personal culture has changed, and if she has difficulty differentiating between religion and culture, her very faith may be challenged.

Muslim Culture

Muslim cultures around the world are colorful and beautiful examples of the diversity of Muslim peoples. Malaysian culture, for example, is vastly different from Syrian culture—yet both are deeply religious societies. Malaysians eat spicy food and a lot of fish, and their desserts are just barely sweet. Syrians eat sour food and a lot of meat, and their desserts are sticky sweet. But culture is more than just food, of course, and when I (Tamara) lived with Malaysians, they were gentle and quiet, very unlike the loud and talkative Arabs of the Mediterranean. My experience with Kuwaiti culture was very different from my experience with Syrian or Lebanese culture, though all are Arab countries. Even within the Gulf region, you will find that Kuwaiti culture and Emirati culture are distinct from one another. The women I have met from Hyderabad, India have had different cultures from the Pakistani women I have met. And Kashmiri women have demonstrated different ways of living from all other women from the Indian subcontinent. Culture is a beautiful and defining part of who we are.

Sometime in the midnineties, I (Tamara) recognized the loss of culture that was happening to converts all around me. I was still living in Syria, and I invited a group of American friends for a potluck dinner. One of my friends was from the beautiful state of Georgia, and I had a hankering for Southern sweet potatoes, so I called her up and asked her to make them. She hesitated, making me think she didn't know where to buy them, or that she wouldn't have time to comb the city looking for them (sweet potatoes were not readily available in Damascus at the time), so I offered to pick them up and deliver them to her. She hesitated again, and I became confused. After a few moments, she admitted that she wasn't sure she would be able to make them. She had been married to a Syrian for thirteen years, and during that time she had never made any of the dishes of her childhood. Her husband and in-laws objected to Western or "non-Muslim" food, and so she had almost lost touch with her own personal food memories. "My children have never tasted my food," she lamented.

As American converts, Najiyah and I have done a lot of thinking about how our culture has contributed to our convert experience. We have found that food, social expectations, and what we perceive as good manners have all played a part in our ability to bring our whole selves to Islam.

Finding Culture in Food

Pizza, hamburgers, steak, apple pie, and fried chicken are pretty universal American foods. In the North, we find hot dishes; in the South, grits and greens; in California, sprouts; and on the East coast, crab and crawfish. Most Americans like sandwiches and soup and enjoy eating breakfast all day long. Traditional comfort foods are usually fried and/or buttery. Americans are willing to have a meal that doesn't include rice, and they will eat soft macaroni mixed with cheese. Chips include dip, hot chocolate is made with milk, and salad comes with creamy dressings instead of lemon and olive oil. We eat popcorn with butter, and we call thinly sliced potatoes that are fried and salted, "chips."

Bosnians eat fried bread for breakfast, dipped in soft cream cheese. Syrians prefer spice mixes and thick yogurt, covered in olive oil and eaten with thin pita bread. Dinner time for my Italian grandmother was a series of courses, a thin soup followed by pasta, followed by meat and salad, followed by dessert, whereas dinner for my German grandmother meant individual portions on plates with sides of pickles and sour things laid out on the table.

Food is how we share with others. The type of food, how it is prepared, how it is presented at the table, and how we eat it together are all deeply ingrained in our nostalgic memory of caring and love. When I (Tamara) first became Muslim, I was invited to eat dinner at a convert friend's home. She placed a platter of rice on the floor and asked us to sit around it and eat with our hands. I was appalled. Nothing about this felt comfortable or caring. I was worried about germs and how to scoop up the rice dish without most of it winding up decorating my dress. Nearly thirty years later I was invited to a traditional Bosnian dinner where thirteen people sat around a large tray and shared the soup—each of us dipping our own spoon into the communal bowl—and I felt comfortable and cared for. What was different about these two experiences? At the first dinner, I was told that that mode of eating was the "right" way to eat, and my own culture of forks and individual plates was looked down upon as wrong. On the second occasion, I was a guest at a traditional Bosnian dinner, respecting the culture of a historic people. I thoroughly enjoyed it. I felt at ease and was honored by the work that had gone into the meal. No one even implied that their way of eating was "correct" or that the way I ate at home was "incorrect." They were just sharing their tradition with love.

Food nourishes us in many ways. Converts who enter into a new culture either via marriage or community can both enjoy the new food experience *and* be sure to bring their own food culture forward into their new life experiences.

Culture in Common Knowledge and Expectations

Americans are often surprised to visit England and find that many bathroom sinks still have separate spouts for hot and cold water. The first time my mother visited Syria, her most harrowing experience was needing to use the bathroom at the Jordanian airport and finding "a hole in the ground!" She found it both gross and perplexing. On the other hand, a Syrian woman I once knew found it shocking and quite disgusting to sit on a toilet—where so many had sat before—finding it gross and perplexing from her own perspective.

Americans expect that people around them will stand in line. In fact, one of the lessons of elementary school, taught every single year, is the importance of the straight and orderly line. In other parts of the world, those who wait in line are considered foolish. Why would you wait? Go forth and get![41]

During colonialist rule, Western governments and missionary schools introduced their own beliefs about femininity to Muslim lands. Their concept of the delicate and fainting woman clashed strongly with the example of bravery in battle of Safiyya bint Abdul Muttalib ﵂ but it began to permeate local cultures nonetheless. Eventually the "ideal woman" who cooks, cleans, docilely serves her husband, and gently raises her children became part and parcel of *khutbas* and *halaqas*—all without questioning where that ideal came from in the first place.

The sexualization of women, and especially Muslim women, also became part of the feminine ethos. The harem became an orientalist trope while, in reality, it remained the *haram*—the place where women gathered to do laundry and cook without the need for hijab in a space where men were not allowed.

Images of traditional families come to us in television shows. We are taught that mom and dad and two and a half children make up an ideal family. Post–World War II, the US invented the suburb and social workers began to endorse "nuclear family separateness and looked suspiciously on active extended-family networks." For most women, this move to nuclear families separated from other supportive family members meant more housework and fewer support systems. Sitcoms in the 1950s showed so-called "ethnic" men as unable to "control" their wives, whereas the middle-class white housewife was well-behaved. An image of ideal femininity attached to gentle and sweet housewifery was born and then exported across the world via movies and television for peoples of every culture to absorb. Suddenly, in Muslim societies, there was women's work (housework) and men's work (office work)—though our very Prophet ﷺ had never endorsed this distinction.

Muslims care very much about family, and we were particularly susceptible to the image of perfect happiness, submission, and feminine "light." It was, however, only an image. The breaking up of the extended family and the locking in of one definition of femininity has had tragic consequences. Emotional needs cannot be met by so few people, same-sex networks have dissolved, and success outside of family has been defined as individual, strategic, and smart, while success inside the family is described as sacrificing, selfless, and involving an intentional disregard for rationality. The result has been unhappiness. In the sixties, many women tried to rectify their emptiness by throwing themselves into the workplace and demanding equal access and equal treatment. "The acquisitive, competitive values women adopted when they forsook domesticity led them to become 'clones' of men." Feminine qualities then, without examination, became associated with being weak and a failure. A nostalgia grew for "the traditional family" but most people had forgotten what that actually was (the original extended version).

If the image of the domesticated woman is a false ideal, what is the Muslim version of womanhood? We need to be careful not to adopt tropes that we did not define and that are not exemplified in our history. Instead we must look to the Quran and Sunnah to discover the characteristics of womanhood and femininity.

(Excerpt edited for clarity from Tamara Gray, "Courage and Commitment: The Femininity of Muslim Women," *Yaqeen*, July 18, 2019, https://yaqeeninstitute.org/tamara-gray/courage-commitment-the-femininity-of-muslim-women.)

Cultural questions around which traits are praiseworthy and which traits are bothersome can also be painful for the convert who suddenly finds that her well-honed manners no longer receive the same approval that they once did. Below we have included an excerpt from an article written by Tamara that addresses issues of femininity and how women have been affected globally by expectations of a particular type of perfection.

These different expectations are often most glaring in relationships. Cross-cultural marriages struggle partially because of differing expectations of married life, of communication, of family roles, of parenting—an unending assortment of differences.

Americans expect their young children to obey them and their teenagers to "sow wild oats," while many Arab and Desi parents don't mind their young children "running wild" and eating piles of junk as long as their teenagers hold up the family name and are carefully loyal and obedient.

Common expectations tie people together and make us feel comfortable. When converts find themselves amongst many people with varying and diverse expectations—and especially if they are now a minority in that experience—it can be discombobulating. Recognizing that we can enjoy and learn from other cultures without ignoring our own becomes very important.

I (Tamara) went to Friday prayer one week, and because I was a little late, lunch was already being laid out in anticipation of the postprayer crowd. There was a rich smell of tomato, curry, onion, and spice. Nostalgic smells for many—but not for the American convert. If a convert has come to Islam from a Christian background, the smell of food at church was probably limited to egg salad, spaghetti dinners (no garlic, just tomato sauce), and a constant smell of brewing (possibly burning) coffee. (I [Najiyah] grew up Baptist and always enjoyed their favorite joke: How many Baptists does it take to change a lightbulb? One hundred. One to change the bulb and ninety-nine to have a potluck supper.)

The same week I (Tamara) ate lunch at the Friday prayer, I spoke at a church. The timing made the contrast between church culture and mosque culture extremely evident. At the church, there were three greeters whose job it was to make everyone feel welcome, help them find where to go, introduce them to others, and show them where they might find the (burning) coffee. When lunch was served at the mosque, it was a bit of a free-for-all. Children and adults were rushing through and filling up plates of food. Lots of children were weaving in and out between the tables and the lines of people. I wasn't sure where to start or where to sit. Neither of these cultures is right or wrong, but the expectations are very different. The folks at the mosque were indifferent to the high-energy children and organized chaos of the food serving, but I was uncomfortable and left without eating. Because of these different cultural expectations, converts sometimes quit going to the mosque because the feeling is just not what they expect in a place of worship. Instead of bitter frustration, converts can learn to accept the chaos and enjoy the exciting food, while at the same time planning events that fit their expectations of a sacred place.

I (Najiyah) have often suffered from church envy as a result of this cultural clash. One of the things I realized long ago is that what we experienced as Christians is 100% a product of our own culture. It has nothing to do with Christianity or its theology or Jesus, upon him be peace. What Western Christians have done is to completely wash Jesus's own culture out of their beliefs and practice (and even portrait) of him. He was a Middle Easterner. He was a Jew his entire life. And the disciples remained practicing Jews after he had left this earth. His culture and language and faith were nothing like what we find today at Western churches.

One way to verify this is to travel the world and see how other Christians practice. Trust me, you wouldn't even recognize it. Christians in the Middle East don't have the doxology song, the youth groups, the Sunday schools, or the potluck suppers that we had. Because they have Middle Eastern culture. Those things are culturally unique to America (or the West). And we miss them because they are what we grew up with. If we had grown up with something else, we would miss *that*. That's how nostalgia works.

So what is the answer for all our missing? It is to import those things into our lives as Muslims. We and our children are those who will forge and form the practice of Islam in the West. We are the pioneers. That's lonely, but it's a great opportunity. Bring your love of song to your sisters' groups. Bring the level of organization and outreach that you remember to your mosque.

There is, after all, some inevitable culture shock and adjustment that will necessarily be part of becoming a Muslim and interacting with the community wherever one may be. It is important, however, that the new convert (and the seasoned convert) hold on lovingly to the parts of her culture that do not contradict Islam and that fill her with nostalgic feelings. She should also begin to invent and develop new habits and memories as they lay the groundwork for her new faith culture (and what may eventually become her children's nostalgic memories).

Seeing Culture in Holidays

Culture is often most obvious at holiday time, and there are three categories of holidays that could pose challenges.

1. Holidays that are celebrated by the dominant culture and by her family, where the question is whether or not she will join in these celebrations.
2. Islamic holidays (the two ʿEids), where the question is how she will create joy and happiness in these holidays, without any childhood nostalgia or a memory map of how to manage the holiday.
3. Muslim celebrations celebrated in her community and outside of her community.

Islamic Holidays

The definition of an Islamic holiday is a holiday that is found in sacred texts. In other words, for a holiday to be Islamic we must find evidence of the celebration of the holiday either in the Quran or in the words and/or practice of the Prophet of Islam ﷺ. The two ʿEids, for example, are Islamic.

ʿEid al-Fitr, or the Holiday of Breaking the Fast

ʿEid al-Fitr follows Ramadan (the month of fasting). Ramadan is ordained in the Quran:

> ﴿ *The month of Ramadan is that in which the Quran was revealed, a guidance to humanity and clear proof and the criterion. So whoever of you is present in the month, he shall fast therein, and whoever is sick or on a journey, a number of other days. Allah*

> *desires ease for you, and desires not hardship for you and that you should complete the number and that you should exalt the greatness of Allah for having guided you and that you may give thanks.* ﴾ (Q. 2:185)

Following the month-long work of fasting—a deed that only we and God know whether we actually succeeded in or not—we are called upon to celebrate together. The Prophet ﷺ forbade fasting on the first day of Shawwal (the first day of ʿEid), ensuring that even Type A personalities wouldn't start making up their fasts or fasting sunna fasts without a celebration. Similarly, the ʿEid that follows the hajj is meant for communal gatherings and eating.

ʿ*Eid al-Adha*, or the Celebration of the Sacrifice

ʿ*Eid al-Adha* is a holiday of celebrating our Muslim brothers and sisters who have completed the hajj (and are still performing some of the rites of hajj on the first day of ʿEid) and of course celebrating our prophet Ibrahim's ﷺ complete trust in and submission to God. This holiday is known as the holiday of sacrifice because we are called upon to purchase a small animal (or shares of a larger one) and distribute its meat to the poor. God says in the Quran, ﴿ *So pray to your Lord and make your sacrifice to God alone* ﴾ (Q. 108:2).

Muslim cultures have many traditions around these holidays: visits, gifts, and new clothes, among others, and as Muslim converts it is important to consider what traditions we would like to build for ourselves and our families.

ʿEid for Tamara

As a new Muslim I was so excited about my first ʿEid. A holiday! My mother had raised me on a diet of lavish holiday celebrations: the churches I had attended were always decorated and welcoming with a special holiday spirit, and I was, of course, used to the entire community (including local grocery stores and even gas stations) decked out in holiday finery and supplies. I (quite naively) expected no less from my newfound Muslim community.

Needless to say, I was disappointed. When I got married, my hopes soared again as I imagined all of my husband's childhood traditions playing out in my house. Unfortunately, my introverted husband was only interested in sleeping. For years, I was bitter and frustrated and really downright sad about ʿEid. I was, that is, until I finally remembered that I was making choices in my unhappiness. The next ʿEid, I imported a number of my earlier Christmas traditions (special foods, morning presents that "appear" for the children, twinkle lights and other decorations) and began to find my own inner holiday happiness while building nostalgia and tradition for my children. (See module three for tips on tending ties during holidays and creating a sense of nostalgia for your children.)

ʿEid for Najiyah

Like Tamara, I expected my first ʿEid to be as magical and stirring as Christmas had always been. I imagined presents and sparkle. I dreamed of coziness and family. What I got was stress, and that was about it.

Looking back, I can see that there were two main factors that set me up for so much disappointment. The first was that, as you read above, I had wildly unrealistic expectations. Presents and sparkle? My husband insisted on giving money instead of presents, and he disapproved of decorating. Coziness and family? ʿEid was in June. It was hot. And my family was miles away.

The second factor was that I allowed my hurt feelings to overcome my festive mood. I was so bitterly disappointed and frustrated and angry that I let any chance of fun be snuffed out.

Eventually we worked out an enjoyable ʿEid routine. After the prayer we would go to Cracker Barrel for brunch, and this is still an ʿEid tradition today, even though the kids are grown, and we are all far flung. Wherever we are, we go to CB and share the pictures on our family WhatsApp group. And now the grandkids love it as well.

As the years went by and I began to make money, I would buy the kids gifts when I could afford it. I also made a tradition of giving them new prayer clothes in Shaban. In this way I was able to enjoy my style of celebrating.

So stay flexible, but invent your own ways to make ʿEid fun. Just because it isn't a precise replica of the holidays you remember doesn't mean it can't have beauty and meaning. My kids taught me that. They love ʿEid in the way that I loved Christmas, and the traditions we made up warm their hearts with sparkle and coziness to this day.

Other Islamic Holidays

We do not have other required Islamic holidays, but nonetheless there are numerous days of recognition that are beneficial to the developing Muslim.

'Ashura'

A number of hadith refer to the day of 'Ashura' (a holiday once celebrated by the Jews of Medina) and recommend fasting on this day. Shi'a Muslims are averse to this holiday because the grandson of the Prophet ﷺ was killed on this day; they believe that as a result, it should not be a day of celebration. However, in a *ṣaḥiḥ* hadith, the Prophet ﷺ is quoted to have said, "Verily, 'Ashura' is a day among the days of Allah. Whoever wishes to fast may do so, and whoever wishes to break fast [not fast] may do so." So we recognize that it is indeed a sacred day and that there is reward for recognizing that with fasting.

In many Muslim countries, special foods have grown out of the tradition of fasting 'Ashura'—many of them are pudding-style dishes made from beans. If you are so inclined, you might find your own special 'Ashura' food, as so many others have done before you.

Mawlid

The Prophet's ﷺ birth was not celebrated by the first generation of Muslims. However, only three centuries later it became a state holiday under Muslim governance and today is celebrated in almost every place and space that Muslims live, so it is worth some attention here.

The Prophet ﷺ was born on the 12th of Rabi al-Awwal. He arrived in Medina on the 12th of Rabi al-Awwal and later passed away on that same day as well—needless to say, it is an important date in Muslim history. We have evidence that he referred to the day of his birth as "blessed"[42] and that he would allow poets to recite poetry that praised him on his birthday.[43]

The actual celebration of this day is a point of disagreement for some. However, it can be a beautiful and wonderful way to ignite love for the Prophet ﷺ in our hearts and the hearts of our families. Celebrating Mawlid has support from great early scholars such as Ibn al-Jawzi, who said,

> The people from the two sacred sanctuaries, as well as Egypt, Yemen, the Levant, and the other Arab lands from East to West, continue to celebrate the birth of the Prophet ﷺ and express happiness when the new moon heralding Rabi' al-Awwal appears. They go to great lengths in singing religious odes and reciting narrations of the Prophet's ﷺ blessed birth, and in all of this, they shall obtain a bountiful reward and mighty triumph.[44]

Scholars support celebrating with recitation of Quran, poems in praise of the Prophet ﷺ, hospitality, feeding people, and other good deeds and encouragement to be joyful and happy. In module three you will find some rich resources for creating new family and community traditions that build our relationship with Prophet Muhammad without compromising our commitment to the tenets and traditions of Islam.

Muslim Holidays

The definition of a Muslim holiday is a holiday that, though not found in any sacred text, does not contradict the teachings of Islam and is celebrated by Muslims. All national days and independence days, as well as Mother's Day, Father's Day, and other days of appreciation would fall under this category. See module three for tips on using these days to tend your relationships with love, thoughtfulness, and care on occasions that are important to your beloved family and friends.

ACTIVITY: COMPARE CULTURES

Coffee should be served . . .	My family's culture:
	A Muslim culture that I know:
When someone is sick I should . . .	My family's culture:
	A Muslim culture that I know:
At holiday time . . .	My family's culture:
	A Muslim culture that I know:

A clean house can be described as . . .	My family's culture:
	A Muslim culture that I know:
Elder family members . . .	My family's culture:
	A Muslim culture that I know:

Culture

Alan Watts writes that "We seldom realize, for example, that our most private thoughts and emotions are not actually our own. For we think in terms of languages and images which we did not invent, but which were given to us by our society."[45] Part of the work of converting to Islam is learning to hold on to our personal cultures while embracing the mosaic of Muslim cultures around the world, all without losing touch with core Islamic principles. Much of our internal culture is found in the food we eat, the holidays we celebrate (and how we celebrate them), and in common expectations. In bringing our whole selves to Islam, it is important to reflect on the food we eat and share, the ways we celebrate, and what we expect from holy places and people. We can build our own culture that includes the culture we grew up with and adds the beautiful touches of Islam.

The Whole Self

Bringing the whole self to Islam does not mean changing the whole self, but rather knowing the self. We encourage you to heal any remaining fragmentations of self, to work to understand yourself, and to work through any childhood pain. All of this will help strengthen you spiritually, and when we are strong, we can link arms together and hold each other up.

MODULE TWO

DECLARE INDEPENDENCE

2

INDEPENDENT THINKING

Al-Tufail al-Dawsi stuffed his ears with cotton in order to avoid hearing anything from Muhammad ibn ʿAbdullah ﷺ. The Quraish had warned him not to fall under the "spell" of Muhammad and thereby lose his authority amongst his people. They said to him, "On no account listen to anything he has to say. He has the speech of a wizard, causing division between father and son, between brother and brother, and between husband and wife." Regardless of the cotton, he heard some of what Muhammad ﷺ was saying and said to himself, "What are you doing al-Tufail? You are a perceptive poet. You can distinguish between the good and the bad in poetry. What prevents you from listening to what this man is saying? If what comes from him is good, accept it, and if it is bad, reject it."[46]

At this point al-Tufail crossed over the bridge toward independent thinking. He was indeed a talented poet and knew himself capable of discerning the quality of Muhammad's ﷺ words, so he decided not to follow the Quraish's directions but to determine for himself the validity of the words and message that Muhammad ﷺ spoke.

He followed the Messenger of God ﷺ and asked about his mission. They talked, the Prophet recited some Quran to him, and al-Tufail stretched out his hand and converted to Islam.

Becoming al-Tufail

This chapter is dedicated to our own independent thinking. In the *sīra* (study of the life of Prophet Muhammad ﷺ), we are often introduced to companions at the point of their conversion with the following phrase: "He [or she] became a Muslim and made good his [or her] Islam (*ḥassana Islāmahu*)." This refers to his or her commitment and practice.

Over the years, as we have met and spoken with converts, we have been surprised by both a running theme of uncertainty as well as a certain underlying dependence on Muslims to behave in a certain way in order to "prove" the validity of this new faith.

The same strong, independent, and confident woman who, previous to her new faith, knew very well what she believed, might now respond to the question "What do you believe about X?" with panic or anxiety and a lack of certainty.

Such vulnerability leaves her open to misinformation and skewed understandings that can challenge the deep-set foundations of her conversion. In this module, we will cover some basic vocabulary, the foundational creed, and recommended tools for continued learning. In this way, we hope to stem the inevitable frustrations of interacting with humanity. Human beings are always imperfect, but Islam is complete.

Books and Bias

Sometime in 1985 I (Tamara) received an entire box of books about Islam, which I set eagerly to reading. This was prior to Google, and my local Minnesota bookstores were limited in their choices. Not far into the pages of these books, I found myself frustrated and upset. I could not stomach the tone regarding women. I soon decided to quit reading. I continued to be hungry for knowledge about Islam, so I needed to go back to reading, but I needed a plan to protect myself from bitterness and misinformation. I began to read with more discernment—looking for bias and anything that did not seem right. I was not a poet like al-Tufail, but I was a good student and, having been an active Christian, I understood that Muslims were people and that the best-intentioned writer still had implicit bias. I changed my strategy and started reading book after book, attempting to find the common points of actual knowledge while setting aside the tone or attitude or commentary that I found disturbing. I would read books and deposit anything that didn't jive with my knowledge about God and His Prophet ﷺ in a file in my head to either ask about later or to shred with the rest of the stuff I didn't need. This helped me read many books without losing my core faith and understandings. I would use the same strategy when listening to lectures and speeches. Of course, we didn't have a plethora of online resources then, which was both a help and a hardship.

This Module

The three components of Declare Independence are: know the terms, know the belief, and know the tools. Each one of these is important in its own way and is a piece of the foundation necessary to develop a deep and independent faith.

Know the Terms

Language is how we learn, how we teach, and how we create culture. Arabic is the language of the Quran, and there are a number of religious terms that just cannot be translated. In this section, we create an interactive glossary of sorts in order to create a common language and develop a deeper sense of some common Islamic terminology.

Know the Belief

A solid footing in basic creed (*'aqīda*) is critical and will hold us in a loving hug during hardship. This section is a straightforward description and explanation of the six tenets of Islamic *'aqīda*: *tawḥīd* (the Oneness of God), angels and the unseen world, sacred texts, prophets and messengers, the Day of Judgment, and divine destiny.

Know the Tools

What are the tools we need to grow? In order to stand solidly on our own two feet, we need some tricks, tips, and tools. This section will spell these out and help you get started using them.

PART ONE: KNOW THE TERMS

One of the keys of language learning is to reach a place where the new language has intrinsic meaning. We are both English teachers and curriculum developers, and one of our most important messages to parents and teachers over the years has been to step back and allow your student to learn the words in such a way that they begin to own the words. How does one "own" a word? Certainly not in translation alone. In fact, the problems of translation are many and could severely distort the connotative or even semantic meaning of a word or word phrase. Thus, it is important for language students to learn the foreign word as it is used in the structures and contexts of its original usage.

Muslimese

There is a whole body of words that are considered daily Muslim speak—and these words need to be understood for more than just their translations. Muslim terminology demands attention to connotation, semantics, and emotive syntax. Complicating this new language are the many words thrown around by Muslim speakers and scholars (and we are guilty of this) without any translation, as though everyone already had a strong background in the language of Muslimese. When audiences hear new words and lean over to their neighbor asking, "What does that word mean?" they may get a translation that was not intended by the original speaker. Muslimese needs to become part of our internal language coding. Words like *taqwā* and *tawba*, and words like *ṣalawāt* and sheikh all need to become part of this new language and its attendant emotions in our brains and hearts.

One young woman we know was born a Catholic. Raised on a diet of fearing God and threats of punishment, she was delighted when she found Islam and its balanced view of reward and punishment. Then she got married. Her husband—a well-meaning Arab man—informed her that the translation of the phrase "*ittaqillah*" (have *taqwā* of God) was "fear God," and he proceeded to salt and pepper his conversation with that phrase. So when she wondered about where to go shopping, he said, "*ittaqillah*," and when she thought she might go visit her parents, "*ittaqillah*." And when she had lunch with friends, "*ittaqillah*." And certainly when they argued, "*ittaqillah*." Of course he was using the phrase as a colloquialism meaning "be careful" or "whatever you want is fine." But she didn't realize that, and it didn't take long for the resentment she had experienced in Catholicism to resurface. One day she exploded: "I did not leave a religion of 'fear of God' to enter another one with the same theme," and she stormed away. Her shocked husband had never thought about how this one phrase and his surface translation of it was affecting his wife.

Labels

Labels plague our vocabularies as well. Some words are thrown back and forth in accusations of disbelief and blasphemy. It can be very confusing to hear from a Salafi anything about a Sufi, or from a Sufi anything about a Salafi. What do these two words actually mean? What are the historical meanings? How are they used today?

Then there are the titles. All these different names for our leaders. What is an imam? How is he different from a priest? What is a sheikh? What about women? Can a woman be called "Imam so-and-so?"

And for that matter, what in the world does *anse* mean?

Define, Define, Define

Thus, if we are to stand on our own two feet in this gorgeous religion of ours, we are going to have to know its language well. We must own these words and carry their meaning with us, so that we can avoid misunderstandings. Furthermore, we must insist that others do so as well. When people begin to talk about any murky issue—usually underlined by its controversial nature—our very first comment or question should be, "Could you please define what you mean by . . . ?" This insisting on a definition was the habit of early scholars and is a healthy practice to carry forward.

I (Tamara) once participated in a panel discussion about social justice. They sent me a working definition, but when I arrived at the venue, they changed the rules and asked us to define it according to how "we think of it." One of the panelists was late and thus struggled to catch up because she was ready to talk about the definition that had been provided. Definitions mold how we think about things.

As a guest speaker at another event, I (Tamara) was speaking about culture in relation to converts, and one of the young listeners stood up and asked me what I meant by culture. More specifically he asked if I was referring to the cultural imperative put forth by Dr. Umar Faruq. I appreciated this question greatly and responded as such. I was actually referring to the nostalgic pieces of culture—the smells of home, family foods, and holiday traditions. I was not referring to a movement or even a vision of Muslim culture. His question clarified my message.

And When We Do Not Define

In a local mosque, Faith listened to the imam give a scathing talk against Sufi practices and Sufis in general. She was very hurt because she had recently begun her own spiritual journey. After the class, she confronted the imam with her experience amongst spiritual people, and he said, "Well, of course I didn't mean any of *those* Sufis, only the ones who do not hold on to sharia." Although comforted, she was also frustrated because she felt that while she had been able to clarify the actual meaning of the imam's lecture, others may have gone away with fear in their hearts towards the practices that had just recently begun to bring her peace after a long stint of emptiness.

The misunderstandings that occur because two people are talking about completely different things but are using the same word are too numerous to count.

Readers of early books often misunderstand the meaning of texts because they read the Arabic word in its modern meaning. An interesting example of this is the word *ṣūra* (as in "photograph," not as in "a chapter of the Quran"), which according to early dictionaries meant "an effigy, statue, or something like an icon,"[47] and according to Arabs today means "a photograph."[48] So it's important to ask ourselves the definition to help us understand the words we are encountering.

Words, Words, Words

From a mosque talk to a YouTube lecture, everywhere we listen to people speak, we hear them using new words. Some words are common across geographical distances, and others are common only in books. The number of words that must be learned by the early convert can be overwhelming, and there is no way we could provide an exhaustive list. But to begin the journey toward independence, the following is a glossary of sorts. Words are grouped together and then explained separately with old and new definitions and anecdotal accounts. We hope that this brief beginning of a Muslim vocabulary will start you out on your road to independence!

Terms: People

Islam is a religion without a formalized clergy, and as such, we do not have priests, pastors, ministers, or rabbis running our mosques or institutions. Islam has instead grown a population of *ʿulamāʾ*, or scholars, who have worked to preserve our religion, teach the faith, and set a good example of what it means to be a Muslim. These scholars, leaders, and teachers have different names that indicate their level of knowledge, their geographic origins, and sometimes their ancestral origins. Some of the titles have very specific connotations, while others leave a wide berth.

Imam

Definitions:

1. The person who leads prayer in a mosque
2. A title of various Muslim leaders, especially of successors to the Prophet (in Shi'a Islam)
3. One who is followed in words or deeds
4. The one who stands in front[49]

The title of imam is the most heavily used in Western cultures and is often used to indicate an equivalency with heads of churches. Imam Warith Deen Muhammad was the first to popularize the term in American religious life. As the son of Elijah Muhammad, he took leadership of the Nation of Islam after his father's death and, as imam (leader), led them through a dramatic but smooth transition into mainstream Sunni Islam.

The title of imam is usually given to men in modern contexts, and usually in their context as mosque leaders. The qualifications for this job differ based on the mosque they lead. Generally, they will know enough Quran to lead the daily prayers and perhaps the Ramadan *tarāwīḥ* prayers as well. In some places, they have traditional learning and in others they do not. While a woman can lead the prayer for other women, and in some rare opinions, for men and women, she is generally not called Imam or Imama as a title. One exception to this was Imam Halima Krausen, who led her German mosque for twenty years and carried the title of Imam during that time.[50]

The Arabic word "imam" can be either masculine or feminine. Some add the *tāʾ marbūṭa* (ة) to the word, so that it becomes imama, and others use imam to refer to men or women because they see it as a noun and not an adjective. Ibn al-Sakit said that the Arabs say, "Our leader is a woman (using imam in the masculine gender) . . . because the majority are of men and the minority are women."[51]

We also use the term imam as a title for the founders of the four major Sunni schools of thought: Imam al-Shāfiʿī, Imam Abū Ḥanīfa, Imam Mālik, and Imam Aḥmad. Though these men were some of our greatest scholars, we use the term imam (and not sheikh or any other term that might denote great knowledge).

An imam is sometimes a paid position and sometimes a volunteer position. When it is paid, it is usually underpaid. Many imams work more than sixty-hour weeks. Religious service is hard and usually underappreciated. Be gentle and forgiving of your imam's imperfections (even as you are empowered to speak your mind and ask for your needs at your place of worship).

An imam is not equivalent to a pastor or priest. He may not have had any training in Islamic theology or law. Or it could be that the local imam is a trained Islamic scholar, but that does not mean he is equipped to deal with counselling, pastoral care, or complicated issues of Islamic law, let alone congregants from different cultural or ethnic backgrounds from his own. So keep this in mind when seeking guidance and help.

An imam also has most likely not had experience or training in running a nonprofit, school, or religious organization. He may have little experience in issues of fundraising, dealing with volunteers, and creating safe spaces for members. The community can provide opportunities for training, but he should not be expected to be an expert in these areas.

With these points in mind, you can inquire as to your local imam's training before seeking help that is outside of his scope of practice.

Sheikh and Sheikha

Definitions:

1. An Arab leader, in particular the chief or head of an Arab tribe, family, or village
2. A leader in a Muslim community or organization[52]
3. An elderly man

But the meaning in the dictionary is far from the implied meaning within devout circles. While it is true that the word still refers to political and tribal leaders in Gulf countries, and may be attached to a local community leader, it implies an array of knowledge and spiritual acumen not mentioned in the English dictionary definition. For this, we must turn to the celebrated historical Arabic language dictionary *Lisan al-ʿArab*, which gives us a much more accurate and nuanced definition of the word "sheikh" (and therefore "sheikha," the feminine form of the Arabic word).[53]

- A sheikh(a) is one who makes the road/way/path of truth clear and guides through the dangerous and scary places, guiding the seeker and pointing out what will help them and what will harm them.

- It is also said that a sheikh(a) is one who settles the rules of sharia and the ways of the faith into the hearts of their students.

- A sheikh(a) is one who loves God and the servants of God enough to bring them to God. Therefore, God's servants will follow them and love God as well, and they are the most beloved of the servants of God to God.

- They are holy in their very person.

- They are a pillar of religion, chosen.

- A sheikh is one who removes the love of *dunyā* and other things from the heart of the seeker through the strength of their insight, such that nothing is left in the seeker's chest of rancor, jealousy, cheating, evil, or attachment to *dunyā*.

- Muhammad al-Husaini said, "It is not of the sheikh to walk on water or fly in the sky, rather he is the one who is known by the souls in their graves, and found by the souls of prophets, and carries divine attributes and actions. And one will repent and move beyond holdings of this world because of his life. And these meanings are rare today [the 7th century AH]. So whoever finds a leader with such qualities, let him take him as his *khalifa* (his leader)."[54]

For those on a spiritual path, the term sheikh refers to their teacher, the one who helps them and guides them along the road.

A sheikh is one who is on the straight path,

> follows the rules of shari'a, and is knowledgeable about the book of God and the sunnah of the Prophet ﷺ. Not every *'alim* or knowledgeable one is of the category of sheikh. Rather the honorific of sheikh implies one who is not attached to this dunia, has no need for popularity or fame, and should have taken the road from a sheikh who came before him in a chain or line of authority and piety that leads back to the Messenger of God ﷺ. He eats little, sleeps little, and mixes little with people of the marketplace. He has much fasting, prayer, charity, and other deeds of the like. In one sentence, he carries the character of the Prophet ﷺ.[55]

The title of sheikh is sometimes designated incorrectly and other times missing in the title of a person worthy of it. It is a word with a vast range of meaning, so as we navigate the leadership world, we will always want to be respectfully discerning when introduced to someone carrying this title.

Ustadha and *Ustādh*

In modern use, the word *ustādh* means teacher—one who is learned and can teach. In religious terms it usually means that he or she is under a sheikh or is a beginning teacher. In the Arab world, the term is used in schools instead of the Western Mr. and Ms. It is also used in mosques to designate a young teacher of the faith, as the title of sheikh is generally reserved for those who have more life experience and knowledge.

Mufti

The term mufti is a legal term that refers to a person who has received enough training in a certain school of thought that he or she may give legal rulings. Not every scholar is a mufti.

Ḥāfiẓa and *Ḥāfiẓ*

A *ḥāfiẓ(a)* is one who has completed the memorization of the Quran. See *The Crowning Venture* by Dr. Saadia Mian for stories of women who have memorized the Quran in modern times. This is a title that even young children can carry. Certainly, the imams who pray *tarāwīḥ* for a large congregation are *ḥāfiẓ* and could be addressed as such out of respect. For example, Ḥāfiẓ Imam Ahmad.

Al-Ḥājja and al-Ḥājj

The famous al-Ḥājja Maria Ulfah, who is mentioned in the 2017 *500 Most Influential Muslims* carries the title *ḥājja*. This means that she has been on hajj. Historically, Muslim communities have granted the honorific *al-ḥājja* to anyone who has been on hajj, with an eye of deference to the completion of their religion, the fulfillment of an important and difficult requirement, and the spiritual growth that is implied. In Indonesia today, many still hold to these earlier ways of honoring one another, so even though al-Ḥājja Maria is famous for her Quran recitation, her honorific is not "*al-qāriʾa*" (the reciter) or "*al-ḥāfiẓa*" (the memorizer), but rather "*al-Ḥājja*." El-Hajj Malik El-Shabazz (Malcolm X), upon his return from Hajj, took on the honorific when he changed his name and declared himself part of the larger Muslim *umma*.

Anse

Finally, an answer to the question, "What does *anse* mean?" Many people think this is my (Tamara's) first name, but it is in fact a very colloquial term for "teacher," used in Syria to indicate respect for female teachers, whether schoolteachers or religious instructors. Similar to *ustādha* (classical Arabic), *anse* is a replacement for the Western Mr. or Ms. and is used to denote respect.

Amongst my friends, we learned to call one another *anse* so-and-so out of a practice of old-school *adab* and respect for one another. My students in Syria called me *anse*, and I myself called my elders and teachers *anse*.

When I arrived back in the United States in 2012, my students asked me what they should put on the posters for my speaking tour. I instructed them to use *anse*. My students replied, "But no one knows what that is. How about sheikha or *ustādha*?" I had much sorrow and longing for Syria, so I insisted on *anse* because it reminded me of home. Nostalgia is a powerful emotion. I also expected to soon return to my beloved Sham, so I saw no reason to take on a new title. At the time, I had also recently learned that the *ḥabāʾib* of Yemen use the honorific *ḥabīb* to reflect their scholarly leadership and relationship to the Prophet ﷺ, so I thought if they could use a term that most people don't recognize, so could I!

At this point, I'm not so particular about what people call me, and I recognize that I've caused some confusion using *anse*, but I am still nostalgically connected to the word, and I still love it and prefer it to others.

ACTIVITY: WHO LIVES IN YOUR SPIRITUAL LIFE?

Who are some leaders who have been influential in your growth? Fill in the chart with local and nonlocal leaders in your spiritual life.

Honorific	Definition	Local	Nonlocal
Imam		Imam Zaid Shakir	
Sheikh/Sheikha			
Ustādh/Ustādha	Instructor		
Ḥāfiẓ/Ḥāfiẓa	Completed the memorization of Quran		
Al-Ḥājj/Al-Ḥājja		Al-Hajja Maria Ulfah	
Anse			

Legal Terms

Islam is a religion of rules. This can be both comforting and daunting for the convert. On the one hand, a sense of order pervades, along with the feeling that there is a right and wrong way to do things. On the other hand, the rules can be overwhelming, and the new Arabic terms meant to sort and simplify become hindrances to the non-Arabic-speaking convert. Complicating matters is the very real semantic issue of formal and informal language. The same words that are used to formally define categories of rulings are also used to speak of the mundane in casual conversation. You might hear a father exclaim to his daughter, "Haram!" when telling her not to have a third cup of coffee. He means she shouldn't do it because of the caffeine, but the convert having dinner with them might think there is a ruling about coffee—two cups only.

The following is a preliminary list of Muslim legal vocabulary. These words were chosen because of their popular usage, but certainly there are many more possible words to add here. We suggest that every reader make the study of the Arabic language a lifetime habit and hobby.

Sharia

The word sharia is tossed around in the public arena quite a bit. Islamophobes and hatemongers have introduced antisharia bills in forty-three states, and fourteen have enacted antisharia laws.[56]

But the question of what exactly sharia law is remains unanswered. Is it an oppressive and static group of laws? Certainly not. Sharia law is a dynamic system wherein rulings are based on Quran, sunna, *qiyās* (analogy), and *ijtihād* (diligent study and analysis). It takes into account custom (*ʿurf*) and therefore manifests itself differently in various geographical and historical contexts. It is impossible to pull out a book and say, "Here is sharia law." What the Islamophobes are afraid of does not exist. And scary men on YouTube calling for a "sharia law" that implies violence and oppression are so far from a recognizable Islamic system of law as to be the antithesis of it.

The general definition of sharia law is the body of law, as well as the system of coming to legal decisions, that began at the time of Prophet Muhammad ﷺ and has continued through the ages. It encompasses systems of worship, family, politics, economics, war, the environment, trade, and just about every other situation a person might find themselves in. These systems have rulings that are absolute, in that they are not subject to interpretation or cultural manifestations, as well as rulings that are more dynamic, in that they are fluid and subject to interpretation and cultural manifestations.

Fatwa

The Arabic word for "ruling" is fatwa, and throughout history, juristic scholars have issued fatwas about both personal and public matters. Some of these fatwas were meant for one person, and others were meant as general rulings for everyone to follow.

The creation of a fatwa is not a simple process and must take into consideration various facets of law and custom. Imam al-Shafiʿi was a famous early scholar and founder of one of the four major schools of thought. He lived in Baghdad for a period of time, during which he wrote his first treatise of Islamic law. He then moved to Egypt. Upon his arrival, he was inundated with people who had been eagerly awaiting him with legal questions and requests for fatwas. He refused to answer any of their questions, saying that he did not know the customs of their society and therefore could not be expected to give reasonable rulings. After living amongst the people for nearly a year, he began to issue fatwas.

In today's Google-a-fatwa society, this seems overly cautious. The internet is inundated with sites that have questions and answers, or individual fatwas. To be clear, if someone is asking a question about an absolute ruling, for example, "How many times a day should I pray?" then there is no context or custom involved in the answer. If, however, someone were to ask a more personal question, "My family is against my faith, should I pray in the house anyway?" the fatwa would be more nuanced. How does the mufti (the one to make the fatwa) know the seriousness of her situation? Are there other places to pray? Is her life threatened? Can she make hijra (travel, move)? I (Tamara) was once asked this question by a young woman, and before I had time to ask questions, she herself decided to pray outside in the snow. It was a wise and wonderful decision. Her family saw that she had respected their boundaries (no praying in *this* house), and over time their hearts softened, and they allowed her to pray indoors without resentment. But what if someone outside of the American (Minnesotan) context had decided that she should leave the house immediately? Would she have been left homeless in the freezing cold? Would she have decided to forget prayer and eventually Islam as well? Would her relationship with her parents have been irreparably damaged? The world of fatwas depends on context; it is sensitive and needs wisdom and understanding.

Halal and Haram

Certainly, Islamic law includes those things that are permitted (halal) and prohibited (haram) regardless of context. There is some semantic confusion, however. Many Arabic-speaking cultures use the word "haram" to refer to anything they think is inappropriate, wrong for today, sad or deserving of pity, or even just expensive. I (Tamara) have myself used the word to lament the price of good coffee (which I then sheepishly paid anyway). In Islamic law, however, there are actually very few things which qualify as haram. It is haram to drink intoxicants and haram to eat pork products. The word haram is related to the world of sin and retribution. So if one does something haram, she is punishable by God. The flip side of this, though, is that if one avoids haram, she is rewarded by God. So every day a Muslim does not drink alcohol, or eat bacon, or have an illicit sexual relationship is a day she gains reward from God.

While the word halal means permitted, it is not necessarily related to sin and good deeds. Things that are halal are things that are not haram. They are so numerous that they could in no way be listed. What is not clearly haram is halal. However, the fact that something is halal does not mean that it incurs a reward. For example, it is halal to sit in a chair, but that doesn't make it a rewarded act. Unless, of course, you sit in the chair with the intention to please your mother, who bought you the chair and wants a picture of you in it. But here the reward is related to the intention, not the halal nature of the chair.

Prophet Muhammad ﷺ, in a hadith *qudsi*,[57] spoke about the types of things that bring great reward,

> Allah (mighty and sublime be He) said: "My servant draws not near to Me with anything more beloved to Me than the religious duties I have enjoined upon him (that which is *farḍ*), and My servant continues to draw near to Me with supererogatory (*nafl*) works so that I shall love him. When I love him, I am the hearing with which he hears, the seeing with which he sees, the hand with which he acts, and the foot with which he walks. Were he to ask of Me, I would surely give to him, and were he to ask Me for refuge, I would surely grant him it."[58]

Farḍ

When something is an absolute obligation, or *farḍ*, then it is something that must be done. *Farḍ* is a word that implies positive action. These are things that a believer must engage in. Prayer five times a day within allotted times is *farḍ*. Fasting Ramadan is *farḍ*. Pilgrimage, or hajj, is *farḍ*. When a person fulfills an obligation, she is rewarded, and when she does not do it, she stands ready to receive God's retribution, while still hoping for His mercy. As we see in the aforementioned hadith—fulfilling *farḍ* acts draws us near to God in beauty and joy. If we miss a *farḍ* deed of any type, it affects us spiritually and should inspire us to repent and continue to try and fulfill our *farḍ*s.

Most of our daily life does not fall under that which is *farḍ*, nor that which is haram, but rather those things that lie somewhere in between. These are the rewarded (sunna/*mustaḥab*) acts, the disdained (*makrūh*) acts, and those that are simply permissble (*mubāḥ*).

Sunna and Mustaḥab

It is sunna to smile, there are extra prayers that are sunna, it is *mustaḥab* to eat with your right hand, and *mustaḥab* to fast Mondays and Thursdays. (Sunna and *mustaḥab* are interchangeable, although in *fiqh*, there can be a nuanced difference in meaning). There are long lists of those beautiful acts that imitate the Prophet ﷺ in detail and in principle, and each of them is rewarded. If we do not imitate him in those particular ways, then we are without retribution, though missing out on reward.

These acts of love, or sunna and *mustaḥab* acts, are positive in their energy. Our engaging in them is in response to a deep desire to imitate and to draw near to the Messenger ﷺ. Engaging in them, we gain reward, God's pleasure, and an understanding of who the Prophet ﷺ was. Some of these beautiful deeds have become engrained in Muslim cultures to such a degree that we might hear "haram" when someone eats with her left hand, for example. But it is not haram to eat with your left hand. It is, rather, *makrūh*, or disdained.

Makrūh

The Prophet ﷺ was clean and promoted good health. The Arabs at the time ate with their hands and cleaned themselves after relieving themselves with stones, leaves, and their hands. The Prophet ﷺ gave each hand a job: the right hand to eat with and the left hand to clean with. It was a genius solution to avoiding germs and staying healthy. In Muslim culture, the *makrūh* nature of eating with the left hand has grown into a strong culture of eating with the right hand, even for left-handed folk. And sometimes, out of ignorance (and thinking it is haram to eat with the left hand), Muslims can be hard on lefties.

We once met a woman who had a paralyzed hand as a result of a hospital error. Her hand looked normal but did not function. Through tears she told us of the women who scorned her and scolded her, who told her she was eating with Shaitan and that she was doing something haram. It got so bad that she had stopped eating with Muslims. She asked us for a retort. She said "I know they are wrong, but I want a retort that will quiet them." We told her of the companions who lost limbs in war. Those who lost legs and arms. Those who lost hands and fingers. Those who retained their limbs but, like her, could no longer use them. Those unknown soldiers who continued to live with their injuries—to eat and use the bathroom—without any judgment or difficulty from the *umma*. *Subḥanallāh*. We wanted to say to all the women who had hurt her feelings, "Are you above the *ṣaḥāba*? Are you a mufti? Are you changing Islamic law?" We wanted to take her to dinner and ask every single woman to eat with her left hand, not in the breaking of a sunna, but rather in the upholding of the sunna of caring for and supporting each other. The ruling of eating with the left hand is that it is *makrūh* for those who can eat with their right hand. A *makrūh*, or disdained, action is one that you are rewarded for not doing, but are not held accountable for if you do it. In the case of a woman who does not have use of her right hand, it is not *makrūh* to eat with her left hand because it is the only hand she can eat with.

However, avoiding things that are *makrūh* is part of loving God. And, our fantasy of teaching our *umma* how to live in the shelter of one another notwithstanding, it is a beautiful thing to see these little details and attempt to fulfill what is sunna or *mustaḥab* and avoid what is *makrūh*.

Definitions, Consequences, and Examples

Ruling	Translation	Doing	Not Doing	Prayer Example	Other Example
Farḍ	Obligation	Reward	Punishment	Fajr prayer	Zakat[59]
Haram	Prohibition	Punishment	Reward	Praying to an idol	Eating ham
Sunna/ *Mustaḥab*	Imitation of the Prophet ﷺ/ Preferred	Reward	Nil	*Tahajjud* prayers	Charity
Makrūh	Disdained	Nil	Reward	Praying when the sun is at its zenith	Divorce

All things begin at the point of halal, or permitted. There must be textual proof to make something illegal, or haram. This is not to cast judgment upon the modern use of the term amongst Arabs, as the connotation is different. As a convert, however, it is important to recognize that just because someone says, "Haraaaaaam" does not necessarily mean that it is haram.

The companions of the Prophet ﷺ used to leave nine-tenths of the halal for fear of falling into the haram. So we do have a tradition of conservatism and restraint. There is a difference, however, between how one lives one's life and how one legislates. A jurist may be very conservative at home, choosing to buy only fair-trade coffee and chocolate and hormone-free, *dhabīḥa*-slaughtered, grass-fed beef. However, she should be gentle with people and make things easy and smooth for them. In this way, she can encourage others towards restraint and care in food and worship in an effort to raise a generation of strong believers who are full of light, love, and joy and are ready to uplift the *umma*, rather than a generation full of artificial constriction and resentment.

Mubāh

Mubāḥ acts are all those parts of life that (without an intention to make them rewarded) are just part of life. The kind of chair you sit in and the color you paint your walls are both *mubāh*. Eating fruit is *mubāh*, unless you intend to eat it to strengthen your body to serve God, in which case it becomes a rewarded act by virtue of the intention attached to it. *Mubāḥ* acts are inherently halal and have no significance outside of the intention attached to them.

ACTIVITY: EXAMPLES

Think of examples of *farḍ*, sunna, haram, *makrūh*, and *mubāh* actions. Write them in the boxes.

Farḍ	
Do it	reward
Don't do it	retribution

Examples of *farḍ*:

Sunna	
Do it	reward
Don't do it	

Examples of sunna:

Haram	
Do it	retribution
Don't do it	reward

Examples of haram:

Makrūh	
Do it	
Don't do it	reward

Examples of *makrūh*:

Mubāḥ	
Do it	
Don't do it	

Examples of *mubāḥ*:

ACTIVITY: GOOD DEEDS

Discussion question. Have you ever thought of categorizing your deeds? What are some ways to think about the words sunna and *makrūh*? Have you ever been told something is haram, only to discover later that it was just too expensive?

ACTIVITY: POSSIBLE RULINGS

Think about each aspect of the following gathering and all the possible rulings that might apply to the different circumstances.

Aspects of a Gathering	Possible rulings (*mubāḥ, makrūh, haram, farḍ, sunna*)
Pizza	
Beer	
Popcorn	
Chips	
Music	
S'mores	
Hot dogs	
Maghrib time	
The gathering	

Terminology: Food

Rulings around food are some of the first that new Muslims must contend with. Anyone who has been used to thick and juicy BLTs will find turkey bacon a poor substitute. Some new converts come to Islam and are still addicted to haram substances. Whether drugs or alcohol, pork products, or any other substance that it is haram to eat, drink, or smoke, the convert must first remember that she is on a journey. A slipup, a succumbing to base desires, or a night full of regrets does not nullify your faith.

Converts quickly develop a read-the-label habit, looking for lard, gelatin, and other questionable ingredients. And while struggling against the ever-present pig in Western food products, she is then presented with the larger question of "Is it *dhabīḥa?*"

Dhabīḥa

Dhabīḥa (sometimes pronounced "*zabiha*") means that the animal was slaughtered according to Islamic rulings and principles. It should have been humane and done in the name of God, and the animal should have been without fear. The animal should have been treated well while alive and fed from good foods that the animal eats naturally (as opposed to food that it does not eat naturally, which can cause disease).

Some news reports over the past few years have questioned the legitimacy of the *dhabīḥa* labels of some companies that claim to be Islamic; there have been accusations of meat mills and cows in regular slaughterhouses with CD players repeating "Allahu akbar, bismillah" on a loop, while the animals are stunned and abused. Numerous scholars have reminded us that the Quran says "halal and *ṭayyib*" regarding food, *ṭayyib* meaning "good." We are continuously warned that we should only eat that which is well cared for, carefully fed, and carefully slaughtered. This idea of *ṭayyib* has circled back, as Muslims question the Islamic ethics of *dhabīḥa* companies and wonder if it wouldn't be better to get meat that is slaughtered humanely (organic) even if not slaughtered by Muslims.

And what of the meat of the People of the Book? The Quran clearly states that the meat of the People of the Book is halal for us, so the question is not "Can we eat the meat of Christians and Jews?" but rather "Who are the Christians and the Jews?" Jewish folk have made this easy. Their political clout and careful eating habits have ensured that a number of different symbols on food—from K to Pareve to U—indicate if products are kosher.

The Christian question is more difficult. Are the farmers supplying meat to the grocery store the People of the Book? This has been a matter of scholarly disagreement for decades.

The Assembly of Muslim Jurists of America published a "Resolutions and Recommendations" paper that resulted from their ninth annual conference, during which they addressed the issue of eating meat from the People of the Book.[60] (See the sidebar for the full text.) In sum, they say that based on the following verse, ﴾ *This day [all] good foods have been made lawful, and the food of those who were given the Scripture is lawful for you and your food is lawful for them* ﴿ (Q. 5:5), the meat of the Jews and Christians is halal for Muslims.

More Detail

The Quran permits the meat of the People of the Book (Jews and Christians) without placing any clear-cut restrictions or conditions upon it, except that it cannot be one of the forbidden types of meat. And because neither the Quran nor the sunna make it clear that the Christians or Jews are to slaughter their food as Muslims do, scholars have differed about this issue. Some held the view that they are to slaughter according to the same conditions that Muslims do,

The Animals Slaughtered by the People of the Book of American Society

(The following text has been edited for clarity and can be found in its original form at the AMJA website).

In order for any slaughtering to be acceptable and sound, it must be done by a Muslim or one of the People of the Book (a Jew or Christian). Their slaughtering is considered to be sound and acceptable as long as there is no proof to the contrary.

- The description of "People of the Book" is appropriate for those who ascribe, in a general sense, to Judaism or Christianity, as Allah has addressed them with that description. Most of the inhabitants of the United States meet this description, ascribing themselves to Christianity in general. Such will be considered the case with respect to those who slaughter meat, unless it is specifically mentioned that the slaughterer was not of that nature.
- One is not allowed to eat meat slaughtered by anyone who does not believe in the divinely revealed religions (Islam, Judaism, or Christianity). These are people such as idol worshippers, atheists, or members of any other religion.
- According to the strongest opinion among the scholars, it is not a condition that the People of the Book mention the name of God upon slaughtering their animals. Allah has permitted their slaughtered animals while it is known that most of them do not mention the name of God.
- The slaughtered animal of anyone who can be described as a Muslim is permissible, regardless of the extent of his sinfulness or heresy. However, if he reaches a point where he openly displays something that nullifies Islam, the animal he slaughters would not then be permissible.

while others held that it is sufficient that the meat come from the People of the Book, as long as it is not established that the meat is from one of the forbidden categories. So it then becomes a Muslim's duty to mention Allah's name over the meat (to say bismillah), especially since it has been reported that once some of the companions came to Allah's Messenger ﷺ complaining that a people offered them meat, but they didn't know if Allah's name had been mentioned over it, and the Prophet's reply was, "Then you mention His name."[61] All of this is to say that for a convert who is visiting family and dealing with so many other issues, the question of *dhabīḥa* meat can be less complicated.

Every convert will have to make her own decision. If it happens that one takes the view that it is permissible to eat the meat of the People of the Book, even if they don't slaughter as Muslims do, and as long as the animal is not of that which is impermissible (for example, an animal that was dead previous to the slaughtering process), then there is no basis for condemnation because the scholars of Islam have differed much about this matter, and she is following the clear fatwa of the Assembly of Muslim Jurists of America. No one should object to her decision because it is not permissible to object to a person doing a thing if there is no unanimous consensus (*ijmāʿ*) that the act is impermissible.

If another person decides that she will eat only *dhabīḥa* meat, we should not condemn her for overzealous behavior. Rather, we should support her decision to be scrupulous in her eating.

The beauty of this flexibility is that each convert can manage her particular experience in a way that is best for her, her family, and her ability to practice Islam.

The Default Status of All Things Is Halal

There are many other questions of permissibility that converts will grapple with. It is important here to remember that the default of all things is that they are halal, until proven that they are from a haram category or come from haram sources.

Terminology: Islamic Sciences

Becoming a Muslim is so easy. Two sentences that play in the corners of your mouth and reach down into your heart. The intimate crowd of witnesses shed tears and (hopefully) serve you cake and shower you with gifts.

All bets are off, however, when it is time to learn. Islam is a religion of scholarship. Hence, there are tomes, opinions, schools of thought, rulings, and debates.

Caveat!

When I (Tamara) was in eighth grade, I learned about the US government and its laws and suddenly thought that I could and should be the president of the USA. After all, I knew all there was to know and was certain that I could do a better job!

This is a typical eighth-grade belief; knowing a little makes you believe you are an expert. Of course, it is experts who truly know how little they know.

Be careful in your learning journey not to get stuck in an eighth-grade mindset. Remember to be thankful for a little knowledge and humble in the knowledge that there is always more to know.

When I (Tamara) became a Muslim in 1985, it was pre-Google and pre-Amazon, so my learning began with every book I could find in my local bookstore. Next came the care package of books I received from my mentor in California. I had been a Muslim for four weeks, and I already had more books about my religion than I had had as a Christian! The more I read, the more questions I had. Sometimes I thought to myself "No way, it can't be," especially if the book seemed particularly culturally oriented or misogynistic. Other times I struggled to swallow the knowledge I found in a book because I could not get past the typos and spelling errors.

My struggle was one of a paucity of decent books, coupled with a community that discouraged seeking teachers. The end of the twentieth century was antiteacher, and all around me Muslims claimed they could know everything about their religion from books. They mocked anyone who sought a teacher. I sought one anyway. The sea was chock full of garbage, and I was afraid I would sink right into it or just leave the boat.

Today's converts do not suffer from scarcity but rather from a dizzying cacophony of available information. Teachers are aplenty, but not all are principled. Although new Muslims are still in a dangerous sea, in general, seeking a teacher and an organized curriculum is the best way to learn this beautiful religion.

This section will describe the most important Islamic sciences and offer some tips to learning the basics.

Disciplines

Of course, none of the disciplines we study today existed at the time of our beloved Prophet Muhammad ﷺ because he was a living and breathing example of Islam (the religion), *īmān* (faith), and *iḥsān* (excellence). But it is a sign of the blessing of God and His promise to protect and preserve our religion that these disciplines grew.

God said in Surat al-Hijr, ﴾ *Indeed, it is We who sent down the Remembrance and indeed, We will be its guardian* ﴿ (Q. 15:9), and He has been the guardian of the Quran and the sunna of Prophet Muhammad ﷺ through these disciplines. Here we learn what has been passed down from generation to generation, discussed and applied, believed and lived. It is in these sciences that we find that the breath of Prophet Muhammad ﷺ lives on, as we take it in and send it back out into the universe.

The following table shows the main branches of Islamic knowledge.

Discipline	Description
ʿAqīda	Creed, theology, philosophy of faith
Fiqh	Jurisprudence, law, rules of prayer, etc.
Hadith	Words and deeds of Prophet Muhammad ﷺ
Tafsīr	Exegesis and explanation of the Quran
Sīra	Life and lived history of Prophet Muhammad ﷺ
Taṣawwuf/Tazkiya	Self-betterment and spiritual upbringing
Thaqāfa	Culture and civilization
Usūl	Origins and foundations of disciplines
Geography	Muslim lands, resources, and how Islam entered these lands
History	History of Islam and Muslim peoples
Tajwīd	Rules of pronunciation (of the Quran)
Arabic	Grammar, linguistics, semantics, and rhetoric

ʿAqīda

Muslims began to develop a science of belief and faith in response to the encroachment of Greek philosophy around the third century after hijra. It was originally called *ʿilm al-kalām*, or "the science of words," and its purpose was to use the methodology of the Muʿtazila (Muslim theologians who relied on Greek philosophy to explain matters of faith) to refute them. Springing from this work, a few early scholars wrote out creeds that could be easily learned. They were an early type of CliffsNotes®, though they eventually came into lives of their own. Three famous theologians of this period were al-Ashʿarī, al-Māturīdī, and al-Ṭaḥāwī. Their work became the foundation, or orthodoxy, of Sunni Islam.

ʿAqīda books teach about the six pillars of faith as listed in the famous Hadith of Gabriel: God, the angels, the revealed books, the messengers, the Final Day, and divine destiny.

Fiqh

As Islam spread, and those who had known the Prophet ﷺ began to die off, it became increasingly important to codify Islamic law—to record for posterity the correct positions of prayer and rulings around charitable giving, along with all the other rules and directions of living a pious life.

There were many scholars working on this enormous project, but the four whose Sunni schools (*madhhab*s) survived are: Imam Abū Ḥanīfa, Imam Mālik, Imam al-Shāfiʿī, and Imam Aḥmad (ibn Ḥanbal). Each school of thought is known for its unique methodology, and as Muslims we look upon each as correct, even when they differ. Today we find the schools of thought anchored in global locations, so families from India and Turkey will probably follow the Ḥanafī *madhhab*, Somali and Malaysian families usually adhere to the Shāfiʿī school, Moroccan and Algerian Muslims tend to follow the Mālikī school, and Saudis tend to follow the Ḥanbalī school.

In recent history, some would say as a response to modernism, Muslims have been encouraged to "just be Muslim" and not "fall into sects by following a *madhhab*." This is a gross misunderstanding of the purpose of *madhhab*s as well as the epistemology of Islam.

*Madhhab*s make things easy. The differences between schools are attributed to their different methodologies and how they interact with texts. Scholars collated hadith and Quran, discussed and debated to reach agreements, and recorded moments of disagreement. These great historical scholars handed down this knowledge to their students, who continued to massage it into the lives of those around them.

The slight differences in prayer styles that we see at the mosque are usually rooted in these global differences of schools of thought, even if the practitioner does not realize the origins of where she puts her hands. So you may find one woman moving her forefinger for the testimony of faith at the end of the prayer and another holding it still; you may see some women pray with their hands at their sides and others hold their hands up upon their chests. These are all slight differences between *madhhab*s.

It is problematic to approach hadith as though each hadith is a ruling on its own. Islamic law is a joining together of the Quran and the sunna, not the application of one hadith. Hence, the choice to interpret a hadith on one's own in order to make decisions about how to pray or when one can pray a traveler's prayer is problematic.

We fall safely within the bounds of correctness when we follow any of the *madhhab*s, but we run the risk of making mistakes when we choose one hadith and attempt to build a life of practice around it.

The study of *fiqh* is divided into two primary subject areas: the *fiqh* of worship and the *fiqh* of deeds. The *fiqh* of worship includes matters of purity, prayer, fasting, pilgrimage, and mandatory charity. The *fiqh* of deeds includes social, political, and economic matters of life.

For most people, the study of the *fiqh* of worship is sufficient to ensure a healthy life of piety. The *fiqh* of deeds is usually the stuff of scholars, to whom we go with questions about laws of marriage, inheritance, money, and leadership.

Studying Fiqh

Certainly, the best knowledge of the *fiqh* of worship would be to know the methodologies and rulings, as well as the opinions of individual scholars from all four major *madhhab*s. Al-Azhar, a famous Egyptian university that has been teaching Islamic studies for centuries, teaches five *madhhab*s (they include the Jaʿfari school as well). But for practical purposes, it is best to choose one *madhhab* and learn it well.

You can choose which *madhhab* to study and learn based on the community you live in and your access to teachers. If you have chosen a spiritual guide, then whatever his or her *madhhab* is should be yours, since you will most likely be engaging in worship together and it makes sense to be following the same *madhhab*.

In our modern global, digital culture, with classes online and in person, there are many opportunities to learn basic *fiqh*, such that there is really no excuse not to embark on a *fiqh* journey.

While everyone's learning experience will be unique, a typical path looks like this:

1. Learn basic worship rules from a friend or local teacher (or even YouTube if necessary). For this first stage, be patient with yourself and put some time into the learning process. You may want to write the

prayer down in Arabic (with English letters) and read directly from the notebook during prayer. In order to learn the prayer phrases and Surat al-Fatiha, you will need to spend some time listening and reciting. Do not worry about getting it wrong; fill your heart with joy during the learning process. Remember that all the schools are correct, so little differences between the people teaching you, YouTube, and the folks at the mosque do not indicate that anyone is doing it wrong, just that this blessed religion has flexibility and accessibility.

2. Find out what *madhhab* is followed by your chosen community. If you attend a mosque, ask the imam. If you are married to a Muslim, ask your spouse and/or his or her family. If you do not have a local community yet, look up the school of your favorite virtual instructor or your online community. Find out what classes are available.

3. Choose a short informational book about the *madhhab* and maybe its founder. See suggestions in Appendix B.

4. Once you have some basic knowledge, practice what you've learned. As questions arise, pose them to your teacher, a local learned person, or a learned friend. Begin to expand your understanding of *fiqh*.

5. Now you are ready for a full-blown class about the *fiqh* of worship. Sign up locally or online. Ribaat has a class called Fun and Friendly Fiqh just waiting for you! Go to ribaat.rabata.org and sign up.

6. The next step is formalized study. You can sign up for more advanced classes in *fiqh* and other sciences at ribaat.rabata.org.

ʿUlūm al-Ḥadīth

This is the study of the classification, chain of narration, and text of hadiths. The most beautiful aspect of this topic is learning about the hard work our ancestors did to verify and uphold truth and accuracy in our narrations.

Remember junior high school history class? We took the details of world history for granted. But if most of the stories we learned were put to the tests of veracity that hadith have been put to, they would fail miserably. Most would not even qualify as weak, and only a few would qualify as *ḥasan* (good). We are doubtful that any would qualify as even close to *ṣaḥiḥ* (authentic).

Here is a beginning chart of what you might learn in *uṣūl al-ḥadīth*, which is one part of *ʿulūm al-ḥadīth*. (This chart is full of terms you will probably not be familiar with, and this is not the forum for teaching them. The point of including them is only to underline the complexity of the subject matter).

The categories in the farthest column on the right are the only categories usually known by today's layperson, but as you can see, the science of hadith is a vast and detailed topic.

Another category of hadith studies is hadith memorization. Here, our early scholars memorized vast numbers of hadiths and became experts in one or more of the books of hadith (for example, Bukhārī, Muslim, etc.).

For a convert or a new Muslim, we suggest getting to know the words and phrases of our beloved Messenger ﷺ through a collection of forty hadith. The first to collect hadith into a set of forty was Imam al-Nawawī, and since then there have been a number of various collections compiled around themes. (See Appendix B for recommendations.)

Tafsīr

Tafsīr is the exegesis of the Quran. It includes *asbāb al-nuzūl,* or the contextual reasons for the revelation of particular verses; grammatical points; an explanation of vocabulary; related hadiths or stories from the life of the Prophet ﷺ; and commentary (although not all *tafsīr* books include personal commentary). *Tafsīr* can be as simple as a translation of the Quran. The translator has interpreted the meaning and rendered it into English; hence, it is a *tafsīr* of the Quran more than it is the Quran itself. We also have heritage tomes of *tafsīr* like those of Ibn Kathīr, Ibn ʿAbbās, and others.

Sīra

Sīra began as the documentation of the battles during the time of the Prophet ﷺ and grew into a complex compendium of the entire lived history of the Prophet ﷺ. His life, his relationships, his manners, his experiences, what he did and did not do – all these all add up to his *sīra*. His life is a blessed example of a lived Quran and how best to live on this earth.

Taṣawwuf/Tazkiya

Taṣawwuf and *tazkiya* are the study of how to purify the self. They include the qualities of a believer, qualities of a disbeliever, and methods of identifying and treating diseases of the heart. *Taṣawwuf* and *tazkiya* teach spiritual ethics and

Classification of Hadith according to...

A specific authority	Qudsī Marfu‘ Mawqūf Maqṭū‘
Number of reporters	Mutawātir Āḥād Mashhūr ‘Azīz Gharīb
Links of isnād	Musnad Mursal Muttaṣil Munqaṭi‘ Mu‘ḍal Mu‘allaq
Nature of the text & isnād	Ziyadat al-thiqa Munkar Mudraj
Reliability of reporters	Ṣaḥīḥ Ḥasan Ḍa‘īf Mawḍū‘

how to gain piety while living in the world in the manner of those who were and are beloved to God.

Uṣūl

Uṣūl is the origin or the foundation of sciences. *Uṣūl al-fiqh*, for example, teaches us the history of the subject matter and how rulings are reached. We can also study *uṣūl al-ḥadīth* (see above), *uṣūl al-Qurʾān*, and others.

Geography and History

These are important parts of Islamic knowledge. Through it we gain an understanding of the earth, its peoples, Muslim civilizations, natural resources, and international relations.

Tajwīd

Tajwīd is a Quranic science that teaches us how to pronounce the letters of the Quran, including elongations and rhythmic recitations. It is a science open to all, and we highly recommend learning as much of it as you can before you attempt to memorize too much of the Quran, because inevitably if you memorize before learning *tajwīd*, you will need to unlearn and relearn much of what you memorized if you were pronouncing it incorrectly.

The Tapestry of Islamic Sciences

The Islamic sciences have a rich history, and each one adds to the tapestry of our faith, bolstering and enriching us individually and as a community. Part of declaring independence as a convert is understanding the very vastness of our faith, so that when closed-minded or uneducated (and often well-meaning) Muslims say things that just don't sound right, we can recognize that there is an ocean of knowledge that they may very well be missing. There is no need to correct them or become upset; simply accept that this Muslim may be connected to a pond instead of the ocean.

Even if we do not know all of the drops of the ocean, knowing they are there can stave off doubt and frustration when we are faced with confusing information or ignorant people.

ACTIVITY: THE SCHOLARS AND THEIR SPECIALTIES

Look at the timeline. Who was a *faqīh* (a scholar of *fiqh*)? Who was a hadith specialist? Who was a *sīra* scholar? Who was known for more than one subject area?

Look up a biography of one or more of these scholars. What strikes you as unique? Important?

Work with a friend—look up the scholars and match them to their specialty area.

Name	Specialty
Abū Ḥasan al-Ash'arī	history
al-Tirmidhī	hadith
Ibn Kathīr	*'aqīda*
al-Ṭabarī	*tafsīr*

Terminology: Labels, or Things We Call Each Other

"Don't go to that mosque! They are Salafi!"
"Don't go to that *ḥalaqa*! They are Sufi!"
"Be wary of that restaurant! It's run by Ahmadis."
"Don't listen to that speaker! He is Shi'a."

Labels come crashing into the lap of the convert with rules about who to listen to and who to avoid. We are told to stay clear of one speaker, adhere to another, reject one mosque, and accept another.

Some of this advice may go against our intuition, but, nonetheless, many people will think it is their business—and often they are coming from a place of sincerity—to tell you where to learn your religion.

However, you are not three years old. In fact, you are one of the rare people capable of making the life-changing decision to convert, to take on a new faith. You are powerful! Just as you were able to heed your healthy heart and choose Islam, you should be able to think it through and choose which mosque to attend, which speaker to listen to, and whether to take a mentor or not.

It is true that Islam, at the time of the Prophet ﷺ, was without labels and divisions. It is also true that there is a sadness and a weakness in division. But human beings also tend to create groups. Each of us has lived in Syria, and we were happy and comfortable in our lives, yet we still attended the monthly American Women of Damascus meetings so that we could hear women speaking English (correctly) and talking about American stuff like sports, politics, and crafting. Across America, Canada, Britain, and Australia, Muslims in larger cities build ethnic mosques. They find comfort in sharing food, language, and

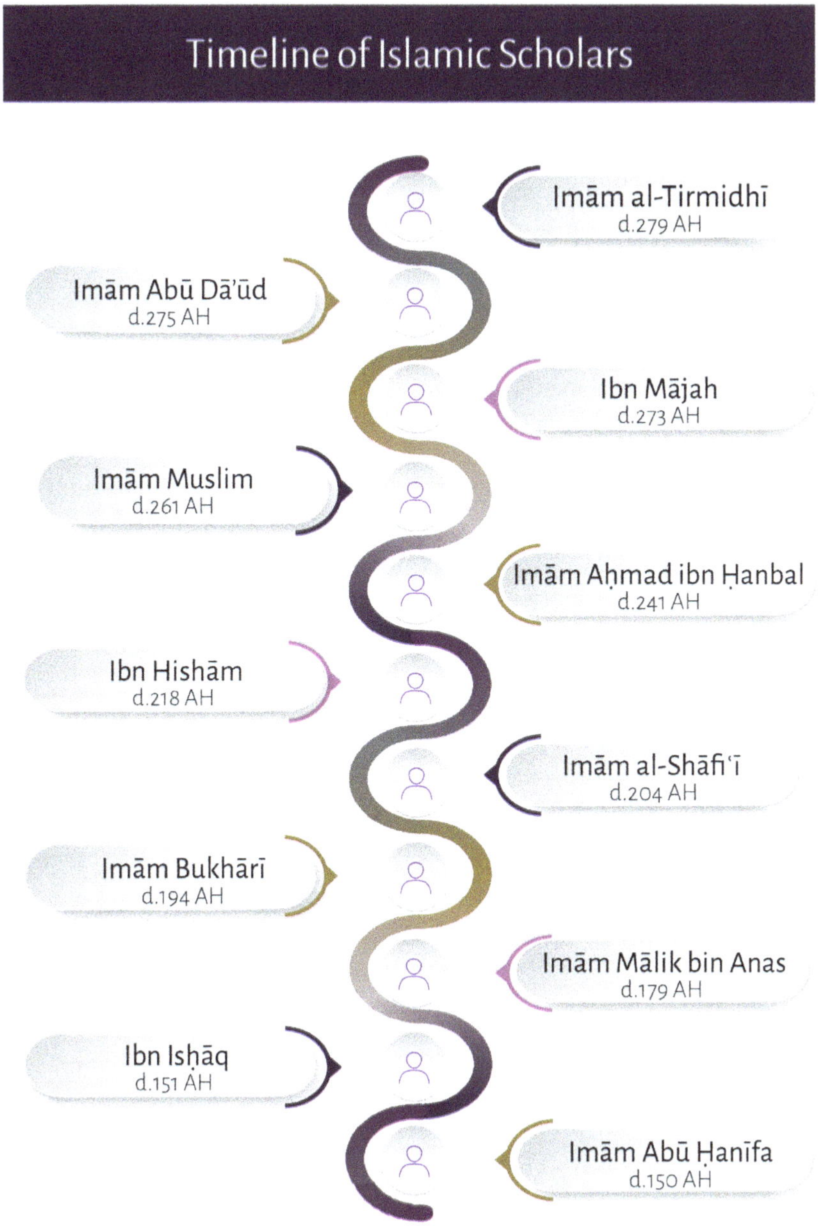

expectations. People gravitate to the familiar and create social groups and communities of practice in those spaces.

This is a problem only when racism, exclusion, xenophobia, and cultural clashes step in to prevent the formation of a healthy spiritual community.

Converts need to deal with these divisions and make our own choices about how to practice our faith. While we can certainly take advice and sincere warnings from our friends and family, it is also important that we do not allow anyone to bully us into a life that is not authentic to us or that lacks spiritual grounding.

Islam is a religion. It should be a spiritual fountain quenching the thirst of our parched selves. When it becomes anything else, it may be time to find a new community.

The major theological groups in the world today are the following: Sunni, Salafi, Progressive, and Shi'a. Some would categorize Sufis as another theological group, while others would categorize them as people who acknowledge and practice the spiritual aspects of Sunni (or Shi'a) Islam.

Sunni Muslims

The majority of Muslims identify as Sunni Muslims. This epistemology grew by leaps and bounds from the first century to the third century and called itself "the people of the sunna and the collective" (*ahl al-sunna wa-l-jamāʿa*), basing their methodology on the Quran, the Sunna, and the lived example of the companions instead of philosophy or literalism.

Shi'a Muslims

A minority of Muslims identify as Shi'a. This epistemology began as a political movement that believed that Ali, the Prophet's cousin, should have taken leadership after him. It later developed into an epistemology based on the Quran, the life of Muhammad ﷺ, and the sayings and rulings of twelve designated imams. They exclude the examples of some companions and include others.

Sufi Muslims

Historically, Sufi Muslims were considered part and parcel of Sunni Islam. In fact, you couldn't be a good Muslim without the ethics and spiritual practices of one Sufi *ṭarīqa* (path) or another. The connection to sharia was clear, and piety could not be separated from the law. Today some organizations claim to be Sufi but not Muslim. This is a new and strange development, for though there were those laypeople in the past who took Sufi practices into the realm of superstition and exaggeration, the founders of the major Sufi paths were scholars of law and theology.

You may hear this Sufis are a group of heretical innovators who do things like dance in mosques, listen to musical instruments, pray to saints, and join little cults called *ṭarīqas*, none of which has anything to do with "pure" Islam. They are innovators—people of *bid'a*.

but Sufis say this Sufism is the practice of *taṣawwuf*, which teaches the heart how to detach from all things in this world and turn completely to God. It began at the time of the Prophet ﷺ and developed into a science around the second century.

Salafi Muslims

The Salafi movement is a postcolonial reform movement that calls for a return to the Quran and the ways of the first generation of Muslims: *al-salaf al-ṣāliḥ* (the righteous early Muslims). It ascribes itself ideologically to the thinking of Ibn Taymiyyah and in general takes a very literal epistemological view.

You may hear this Salafis are a group of literalist modernists who reject Sunni scholarly tradition, teach anthropomorphism, and adhere to a narrow-minded view of Islamic law. Those who don't agree with them are labeled as nonbelievers. They are the root of modern extremism.

but Salafis say this Salafism is pure Islam as it was understood by Prophet Muhammad ﷺ and his immediate followers with little interpolation. We reject all forms of innovation.

Progressive Muslims

In the late twentieth century, a new reform movement began based on the values of the general progressive movement in the United States. Like Salafism, this movement rejects much of Sunni scholarship, but unlike Salafism, it calls for a new hermeneutic of the Quran that is more compatible with modern times.

You may hear this

Progressive Muslims don't adhere to sharia. They want to make an American Islam. They are anti-hijab, pro–free sexuality, and have an "anything goes" attitude. They see Islam as an identity more than a practice.

but Progressives say this

Muslims for progressive values promote new interpretations of heritage texts. We want to make Islam relevant to modern society.

Question for Discussion. What might be the middle way between all of these statements? Do you think labels are helpful or harmful?

Bidʿa

Another word that is common among some Muslims is the word *bidʿa*. This word labels and criticizes actions rather than people. But the word is used incorrectly in most cases.

Darla was concerned about the oppression and pain of the Palestinian people, so she organized a fast-athon and planned a gathering for iftar where the participants would raise some money and make *duʿāʾ*. She organized the whole thing herself and made a homemade pie for the potluck. Rushing to the event, she opened the door, and no one was there. "They're late," she thought to herself. But at an hour after iftar time, it became apparent that no one was coming. It wasn't a lack of interest in the plight of Palestine that had kept people away, but a community member who had labeled her event "*bidʿa*," so no one came.

The hadith used most often to close down creative thinking is, "Beware of matters newly begun, for every matter newly begun is an innovation (*bidʿa*), every innovation is misguidance, and every misguidance is in Hell."[62] But is it possible that this means that every new thing is haram? Are we like the Amish? Should we reject electricity? Spoons? Airplanes? Sheikh Muhammad Jurdani explains that "the hadith refers to matters of innovation that contradict sacred law."[63]

ʿIzz al-Dīn ibn ʿAbd al-Salām[64] categorized *bidʿa* into five categories of sacred law: that which is obligatory (a *bidʿa* that is necessary for the health of the Muslim *umma*); a *bidʿa* that is haram and therefore punishable; a *bidʿa* that is recommended or rewarded; a *bidʿa* that is offensive; and a *bidʿa* that is permissible—neither rewarded nor punished.

Categories of *Bidʿa*					
	Farḍ, or Obligatory	*Ḥarām*, or Forbidden	*Mustaḥab*, or Recommended	*Makrūh*, or Offensive	*Mubāḥ*, or Permissible
Definition	Must be done for fear that something of Islam will be lost	Must not be done	Should be done to benefit the community	Should not be done in order to protect the community from trial and tribulation	Permissible without implication of reward or punishment
Example	Writing the Quran in book form	Changing the Isha (night prayer) from four *rakʿas* to three to save time	Writing a book that teaches the memorization of the *sanad* using symbols	Not allowing women to pray in the main prayer space	Using a washing machine or dryer

And of course, this makes sense—anything that is new in life must be examined through the lens of the sunna of the Prophet ﷺ. During the course of the Prophet's life, the companions did many new things, from tying knots in rope in order to count their *tasbīḥ* or phrases of praise (Abū Hurayra), to praying after every *wuḍū* (Bilāl), to asking for a *muʾadhdhin* to be assigned to a home (Um Waraqa). Each of these creative spiritual efforts was applauded and supported by our beloved Messenger ﷺ, showing us that coming to Allah with our whole selves is the most important aspect of the sunna.

The Power of Words

Language builds meaning in our minds and hearts. Converting to Islam means a sudden onslaught of new terms and new ways of thinking. To declare independence is to own the language—to use it with confidence and to speak using the subtleties of each word. This takes time, but it begins with definitions and perfunctory use until the words become second nature and can be used wherever and whenever necessary. Words are power. You now have the power of all of the terms in this section. May the force of words be with you.

PART TWO: KNOW THE BELIEF

The scholars of ʿ*aqīda*, or our system of belief, tell us that our beliefs are mirrored in our actions. We act upon what we deeply believe. Hence, a faulty belief system will impact us negatively, and a healthy belief system will help us grow.

If you believe that a friend truly loves you and cares about your well-being, you will react with patience when she asks you again and again about your sleep and eating habits. You will smile knowingly when she makes you healthy bread chock full of raisins and nuts, and you will thank her when she orders you vitamin D from a vegetarian shop. The same actions, however, could drive you bonkers if you do not believe in the loving intentions of the person doing them. A mother-in-law who you believe is only interested in her son and doesn't really care about you will irritate you when she asks about your well-being. When she asks about your sleep and eating habits, you may blow a gasket, and if she makes you bread filled with nuts and raisins, you may respond politely but roll your eyes internally. A gift of vitamin D may be interpreted as an underhanded way of saying you are lazy. The same scenario may produce very different responses—all based on beliefs.

Belief, then, affects how we live our religion. The famous Hadith of Gabriel ﷺ, where he had a conversation with the Prophet ﷺ in front of the companions clearly lists the components of the religion (Islam), faith (*īmān*), and excellence (*iḥsān*).

> While we were one day sitting with the Messenger of Allah ﷺ, there appeared before us a man dressed in extremely white clothes and with very black hair. No traces of journeying were visible on him, and none of us knew him. He sat down close by the Prophet ﷺ, rested his knee against his thighs, and said, "O Muhammad! Inform me about Islam."
>
> The Messenger of Allah ﷺ said, "Islam is that you should testify that there is no deity except Allah and that Muhammad is His Messenger, that you should perform salah, pay zakat, fast during Ramadan, and perform Hajj to the House, if you are able to do so." Pillars of Islam
>
> The man said, "You have spoken truly."
>
> We were astonished at his questioning him (the Messenger) and telling him that he was right, but he went on to say, "Inform me about *iman*. He (the Pillars of *Īmān*

Messenger of Allah) answered, "It is that you believe in Allah and His angels and His books and His messengers and in the Last Day, and in Divine destiny, both in its good and in its evil aspects."

He said, "You have spoken truly."

Pillar of *Iḥsān*

Then he (the man) said, "Inform me about *ihsan*." He (the Messenger of Allah) answered, "It is that you should serve Allah as though you could see Him, for though you cannot see Him, yet (know that) He sees you."[65]

The six pillars of belief are belief in God, His angels, His books, His messengers, the Last Day, and divine destiny. Each can be described simply or in long, complicated tomes. For the purpose of declaring our independence, this section will summarize basic beliefs emphasizing the most important facts for a beginning student.

God

The phrase of belief, *lā ilāha illa Allāh,* is so powerful that it (along with *Muḥammadun rasūlullāh)* is the key to conversion. All of us at one time or another have declared our commitment to these two sentences.

Lā ilāha illa Allāh is a negative construction. It begins with the negative particle *lā*. This type of construction is rarely used in the English language. D. H. Lawrence, the English poet and essayist, said, "Naught is possessed, neither gold, nor land, nor love, nor life, nor peace, nor even sorrow nor death, nor yet salvation. Say of nothing: it is mine. Say only: it is with me."[66] Using a negative construction, he succeeds in emphasizing the absolute absence of possession. In the same way, the Arabic phrase *lā ilāha illa Allāh* emphasizes the absolute absence of divinity other than God.

We begin our journey with this sentence, but in order to deepen our faith there is more to understand.

Allahu Akbar

God is greatest. This is the phrase that we say in prayer and what we hear when we are called to prayer. This phrase reminds us of three important principles.

1. Know that God is present so that you can fulfill your commitments to Him.

2. Know God's characteristics and names so that you can stop turning to other than God.

3. Be absolutely certain of this knowledge in the depths of your heart to protect it from dangerous notions.

Know that God Is Present

How do we know anything? Either we have discovered it ourselves or someone we trust has told us it is true. We know the sun exists because we see it and feel it. We know it is a star, burning hot, and far away because trained and trusted scientists have reported these facts to be true.

We personally believe in the presence of God because we have known and felt that presence in our lives. We know that God's presence is complete and unending because sacred books and chosen people (prophets and the people of God) have reported this Truth.

In one of the most intimate examples of the continuous omnipresence of God, the Quran mentions the comforting words of the Prophet ﷺ to Abū Bakr when they were hiding from their pursuers during the hijra. He said, ﴾ *Sorrow not, for surely God is with us* ﴿ (Q. 9:40). These comforting words were not a suggestion but a statement of fact. God was present with them in the cave, as He is present with us in every moment of our lives.

It is in the moments of forgetfulness, when we feel alone, that we struggle to fulfill our commitment to God and to Islam. Remembering that God is ever-present and always with us brings us comfort and strength. It allows us to be strong in the face of human weakness and peaceful in the face of human anxiety.

Know God's Characteristics and Names

Who is God? This esoteric question is at the root of theology and many personal quests for spiritual fulfillment. We want to *know* God.

Islamic tradition tells us that God has ninety-nine names, and that these names, or qualities, or characteristics, if learned, will take us to Paradise. Learning the names of God changes our relationship with God. We can go from knowing God through our own limited experience to knowing God through the very words given to us by God. The Quran reminds us,

﴿ *He is Allah, the Creator, the Inventor, the Fashioner; to Him belong the best names. Whatever is in the Heavens and Earth is exalting Him. And He is the Exalted in Might, the Wise.* ﴾ (Q. 59:24)

﴿ *And to Allah belong the best names, so invoke Him by them.* ﴾ (Q. 7:180)

﴿ *Allah—there is no deity except Him. To Him belong the best names.* ﴾ (Q. 20:8)

The Prophet ﷺ encouraged us to know these names when he said, "Indeed, Allah has ninety-nine names (one hundred less one) and whoever knows them shall enter Paradise."[67]

Scholars have written about the blessing of learning God's ninety-nine names, suggested cures based on the repetition of these names, and passed down patterns of saying the names to help with memorization.

Taken together, the ninety-nine names tell us that God is beginningless. God did not become; God always was. God is after the after, eternal. God always will be. God is unique, without partner, without resemblance; He is the cause of all. God is self-existent, without any needs. God is ever-living, eternal, and independent. God is all-knowing; He has knowledge of the blades of grass, the thoughts of each mind, and the grains of sand stuck to the soles of every toddler's wet feet. God hears all and sees all, with complete hearing and seeing that is outside the limits of time and space. All will is God's. All power is God's. All existence and actions depend on God. He is Allah. The One God. Light of the heavens and the earth, and there is nothing similar to God.

Once, when one of our mentors was teaching in Switzerland, she went to spend the day at a park. There, surrounded by sunshine, flowers, and greenery, she met a very lonely woman. Our mentor greeted her with the pleasantries of a stranger—a good morning and a smile—but the woman was talkative, so she sat with her in the park and they chatted about their countries. Toward the end of the conversation, the woman said, "I live alone," and our mentor said to her, "Oh, but you have never been alone." The woman raised an eyebrow. "God has been with you every moment of every one of those days. When you thought you were alone, you were only unaware of His presence. I will pray for you to become aware of Him." At this, the woman broke down in tears, and the conversation continued late into the night.

God is al-Wali, the Friend; al-Wakil, the Trustee; al-Shahid, the Witness; and al-Muqit, the Nourisher. These names remind us of the ever-present, ever-close Reality.

Learning God's names changes our interaction with the world. Our dependence on God grows, while we remain reminded of our responsibility to make good and healthy choices and to live our life under the gaze of God's pleasure.

When we know God is al-Razzaq, the Provider, we go to work and do our best to earn money, but we rely on Him and recognize His generosity in all of our blessings.

Knowing that God is al-Khabir, the who's knowledge encompasses all things , we know that we cannot hide from God. We can hide addictions, hurtful actions, and sin from people, but God always knows. God's knowledge is complete. A deep understanding of this quality should discourage us from sin and addiction and encourage us to excel in all parts of our lives.

Each of God's names gives us a new understanding, a new window into the house of our faith.

Hence, we learn the names of God to protect ourselves from turning to anyone else for help. Even as we turn to a plumber for our plugged-up sink and a network engineer to fix our computer system, we know that we are first turning to God, the One. And these people and methodologies are but worldly tools that have been gifted to us by the Great Generous One, al-Karim.

Be Absolutely Certain of This Knowledge

The work of Shaitan is to steer us away from Truth and divine guidance. For converts, this can manifest itself in inner thoughts like "Did I make the right choice?" "Why are so many Muslims so difficult?" "Maybe I should just give up," "I feel so alone," or even "What do they think of me?" These are all dangerous notions that can misdirect a believing heart and destroy the work of years.

My (Tamara's) good friend found disbelief lurking around the corner of not-enough and a stingy husband. Her children were all at difficult and overwhelming stages of life, and her family still mocked her decision to become a Muslim. At this difficult point in her life, she entertained these dangerous notions and lost her way.

We need to dig deep into our heart of faith and deposit certainty and knowledge of God to draw on during dark moments and difficult days.

Neuroplasticity and Neurophenomenology

In his book *The Brain That Changes Itself*, Dr. Norman Doidge tells of an experiment that proves the plasticity of the brain, or its ability to learn. The experiment is simple. A university research group gathered volunteers to learn the violin. Having scanned everyone's brain using imaging technology, they proceeded to teach them how to play the violin. They then divided the volunteers into two groups. One group was given violins and told to practice five hours a day; the second group was not given violins, but instead were told to *imagine* practicing violin for five hours every day. At the end of the experimental period their brains were reimaged, and the conclusions were shocking. Both groups' brains had changed and developed the same amount. Thinking about practicing violin had the same effect on the brain as actually practicing violin.[68]

This experiment has numerous implications for spiritual life and the connection between the brain and our psyche and self. Clearly the repetition of phrases of praise—such as *subḥanallāh* and *lā ilāha illa Allāh*—will ensure that they stay with us and fortify us against whatever comes our way.

ACTIVITY: PRACTICE DEEPENING YOUR CERTAINTY IN GOD

The Prophet ﷺ said that the best *dhikr* is *lā ilāha illa Allāh*, and when asked what the best deed was, he said, "that you die with your tongue still moist with the remembrance of God."[69] Repeat *lā ilāha illa Allāh* one thousand times a day for ten days and record it here.

Day	Number
1	1,000
2	500
3	
4	
5	
6	
7	
8	
9	
10	

ACTIVITY: LEARN THE NINETY-NINE NAMES OF GOD

أَسْمَاءُ اللَّهِ الحُسْنَى Asmā᾽ Allāh al-Ḥusnā				
نَسْأَلُكَ يَا مَنْ هُوَ اللهُ الَّذِي لَا إِلَهَ إِلَّا هُوَ *Nas᾽aluka yā man huwa Allāh al-ladhī lā ilāha illā Huwa*				
السَّلامُ	القُدُّوسُ	المَلِكُ	الرَّحِيمُ	الرَّحْمَنُ
Al-Salām	Al-Quddūs	Al-Malik	Al-Raḥīm	Al-Raḥmān
المُتَكَبِّرُ	الجَبَّارُ	العَزِيزُ	المُهَيْمِنُ	المُؤْمِنُ
Al-Mutakabbir	Al-Jabbār	Al-ʿAzīz	Al-Muhaymin	Al-Mu᾽min
القَهَّارُ	الغَفَّارُ	المُصَوِّرُ	البَارِئُ	الخَالِقُ
Al-Qahhār	Al-Ghaffār	Al-Muṣawwir	Al-Bāri᾽	Al-Khāliq
القَابِضُ	العَلِيْمُ	الفَتَّاحُ	الرَّزَّاقُ	الوَهَّابُ
Al-Qābiḍ	Al-ʿAlīm	Al-Fattāḥ	Al-Razzāq	Al-Wahhāb
المُذِلُّ	المُعِزُّ	الرَّافِعُ	الخَافِضُ	البَاسِطُ
Al-Mudhill	Al-Muʿizz	Al-Rāfiʿ	Al-Khāfiḍ	Al-Bāsiṭ
اللَّطِيْفُ	العَدْلُ	الحَكَمُ	البَصِيْرُ	السَّمِيْعُ
Al-Laṭīf	Al-ʿAdl	Al-Ḥakam	Al-Baṣīr	Al-Samīʿ
الشَّكُور	الغَفُورُ	العَظِيْمُ	الحَلِيْمُ	الخَبِيْرُ
Al-Shakūr	Al-Ghafūr	Al-ʿAẓīm	Al-Ḥalīm	Al-Khabīr
الحَسِيْبُ	المُقِيْتُ	الحَفِيْظُ	الكَبِيْرُ	العَلِيُّ
Al-Ḥasīb	Al-Muqīt	Al-Ḥafīẓ	Al-Kabīr	Al-ʿAlī
الوَاسِعُ	المُجِيْبُ	الرَّقِيْبُ	الكَرِيْمُ	الجَلِيْلُ

Al-Wāsiʿ	Al-Mujīb	Al-Raqīb	Al-Karīm	Al-Jalīl
الشَّهِيْدُ	البَاعِثُ	المَجِيْدُ	الوَدُودُ	الحَكِيْمُ
Al-Shahīd	Al-Bāʿith	Al-Majīd	Al-Wadūd	Al-Ḥakīm
الوَلِيُّ	المَتِيْنُ	القَوِيُّ	الوَكِيْلُ	الحَقُّ
Al-Walī	Al-Matīn	Al-Qawī	Al-Wakīl	Al-Ḥaqq
المُحْيِي	المُعِيْدُ	المُبْدِئُ	المُحْصِي	الحَمِيْدُ
Al-Muḥyi	Al-Muʿīd	Al-Mubdiʾ	Al-Muḥṣī	Al-Ḥamīd
المَاجِدُ	الوَاجِدُ	القَيُّومُ	الحَيُّ	المُمِيْتُ
Al-Mājid	Al-Wājid	Al-Qayyūm	Al-Ḥayy	Al-Mumīt
المُقَدِّمُ	المُقْتَدِرُ	القَادِرُ	الصَّمَدُ	الوَاحِدُ
Al-Muqaddim	Al-Muqtadir	Al-Qādir	Al-Ṣamad	Al-Wāḥid
البَاطِنُ	الظَّاهِرُ	الآخِرُ	الأَوَّلُ	المُؤَخِّرُ
Al-Bāṭin	Al-Ẓāhir	Al-Ākhir	Al-Awwal	Al-Muʾakhir
المُنْتَقِمُ	التَّوَّابُ	البَرُّ	المُتَعَال	الوَالِي
Al-Muntaqim	Al-Tawwāb	Al-Barr	Al-Mutaʿāl	Al-Wālī
المُقْسِط	ذُو الجَلَالِ والإِكْرَامْ	مَالِكُ المُلْكِ	الرَّؤوف	العَفُوُّ
Al-Muqsiṭ	Dhul Jalāli wa-l-Ikrām	Mālik ul-Mulki	Al-Raʾūfu	Al-ʿAfuww
الضَّارُّ	المَانِعُ	المُغْنِي	الغَنِيُّ	الجَامِعُ
Al-Ḍārr	Al-Māniʿ	Al-Mughni	Al-Ghanī	Al-Jāmiʿ

البَاقِي	البَدِيْعُ	الهَادِي	النُّورُ	النَّافِعُ
Al-Bāqī	Al-Badī'	Al-Hādi	Al-Nūr	Al-Nāfi'
	الصَّبُورُ	الرَّشِيْدُ	الوَارِثُ	
	Al-Ṣabūr	Al-Rashīd	Al-Wārith	

الّذِي لَيْسَ كَمِثْلِهِ شَيْءٌ وَهُوَ السَّمِيْعُ البَصِيْر.

Al-Ladhī laysa ka-mithlihi shay'un wa-huwa al-Samī' al-Baṣīr

اللّهُمَّ صَلِّ أَفْضَلَ صَلاةٍ عَلَى أَسْعَدِ مَخْلُوْقَاتِكَ سَيِّدِنَا مُحَمَّدٍ وعَلَى آلِهِ وصَحْبِهِ وسَلِّمْ

Allāhumma ṣalli afḍala ṣalātin 'alā as'adi makhlūqātika sayyidinā Muḥammadin wa-'ala Ālihi wa ṣaḥbihi wa sallim

عَدَدَ مَعْلُومَاتِكَ ومِدَادَ كَلِمَاتِكَ كُلَّمَا ذَكَرَكَ الذَّاكِرُونَ وغَفَلَ عَنْ ذِكْرِكَ الغَافِلُونَ.

'Adada ma'lūmātika wa midāda kalimātika kullamā dhakarak al-dhākirūna wa ghafala 'an dhikrik al-ghāfilū

Angels

Belief in God's angels is a pillar of faith. Angels represent the unseen world—the world that lives around our seen world. Emotions such as love and intuition and attitudes of hope and inspiration all exist in this unseen world. In fact, they are a connecting point between the seen and unseen worlds. We cannot see love, but we feel it as a palpable object. We cannot put hope in a box, but we seek it in times of fear. Likewise, angels (and jinn) are real. They cannot be seen by human beings, but we are affected by their presence in our world.

Angels in Arabic are called *malā'ika,* the root of which is *aa-la-ka* (الك). The literal meaning of the Arabic word is "the one who informs, the one who bears messages, the one who carries words, the one who does what is bidden." The English word "angel" comes from late Latin *angelus* and Greek *angelos* and also means "a messenger, envoy, or one that announces."

Modern images of angels—informed by renaissance painters and Hollywood movies—as beautiful women or men wishing to marry beautiful earthly women are far from scriptural veracity. Angels were created from light to do God's bidding. They were created before Adam and Eve, and unlike humans, they do not eat, drink, or get married. In fact, angels are genderless. They can take on human shape, as in narrations that mention the Angel Jibril (Gabriel) in human form and angels at the Battle of Badr likewise. But they do not take on human qualities and characteristics. In addition, humans do not become angels upon death. Angels are their own unique creation. Their decisions are based only upon the orders of Allah; they are unblemished by mistakes and have no inclination toward evil. Their abode is in the heavens, and they visit earth according to God's command.

Angels do have wings. God says in the Quran, ﴾ *All praise is to God, Creator of the heavens and the earth, who made the angels messengers with wings—two, three, or four. He increases in creation what He wills. Indeed, Allah is over all things competent* ﴿ (Q. 35:1).

The Angels and Us

Angels play a role in matters of the universe. They are in complete service to God and bring down His mercy and punishment as He wills. They pray for us, asking forgiveness and mercy to descend upon the believers. They have jobs that exist outside our senses, and they both blow the soul into the fetus and gather the soul at the time of death. Angels are an important part of our existence.

Believing in the angels requires us to recognize their existence around us and to build a life that is inviting to them and does not repel them. We recognize that they record our deeds, pray for us, and make our spaces more peaceful.

In Surat al-Qadr, when God speaks about the Night of Power, He says, ﴾ *The angels and the spirit (Angel Jibril) descend therein by permission of their Lord for every matter. Peace until the emergence of dawn* ﴿ (Q. 97:4–5). The presence of angels brings peace, and their absence creates a dull and dank environment, one of bickering and frustration.

The Prophet ﷺ told us in a number of different hadiths that angels love purity, modesty, and good scents.[70] We can create angel magnet homes that are havens of peace for us and our family members by creating environments of purity, modesty, and beautiful scents.

Homes that are in a state of purity (*ṭahāra*) are free from those things that stand between us and prayer: blood, urine, feces, and vomit. While this is normally easy, it is a challenge while potty training a toddler or dealing with an infant boy. During these challenging times, extra work to remove the urine and feces from the places it lands will help to ensure the presence of angels.

Each family member can meet the requirements of modesty by making sure that the *ʿawra* (parts of the body that should remain covered under most circumstances) is not on regular display. So while some amount of nakedness is inevitable between dressing, bathing, using the bathroom, and marital intimacy, taking care to dress modestly at home whenever possible can help us hold on to the presence of angels in our lives.

ʿ*Aṭr*, or delicious smelling oils, candles, incense, and perfume, makes our home smell beautiful and increases the presence of angels.

ACTIVITY: ANGEL MAGNET

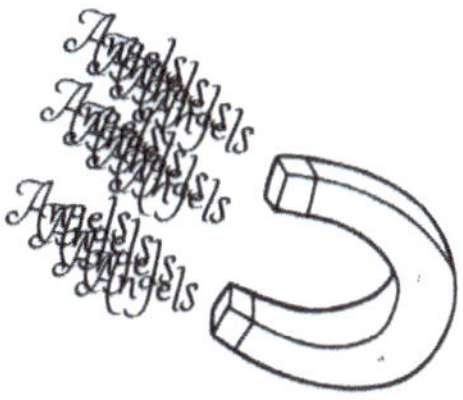

What is the magnetic force of your home?
Rate your home on a scale from 1 to 10.

Scale for Cleanliness

1 = Something to the tune of filled kitty litter box; diapers strewn around; accidents left to dry; bloodied clothes mixed in with other laundry; vomit wiped up but tissues left in garbage container, which is inside the house.
10 = All surfaces free of any trace of filth, removed by pouring water in free flow in accordance with the rulings of *fiqh*; any used diapers or menstrual pads taken out to an outdoor garbage can daily; dirty tissues and toilet paper disposed of appropriately.

Scale for Modesty

1 = Adults shouting "Don't look!" and streaking from bathroom to bedroom after showers; short shorts and underclothes worn around the house as clothing.
10 = Avoiding nakedness even in the shower; dressing and undressing modestly; covering the head while reading Quran; general modesty in dress.

Scale for Pleasant Scents

1 = Raw garlic and onion pervasive; sour and off smells; old garbage; bad pet smells; rancid food.
10 = Musk; clean and clear perfume; maybe faint citrus or floral scents.

1 Scent 10

1 Modesty 10

1 Cleanliness 10

A Note about the Angels

Iblīs, or Lucifer, is not a fallen angel but rather a jinn who disobeyed God. Jinn are another creation of God, and like humans, they have free will.

It is important to note here that in the Islamic understanding of the unseen world, good and evil are not at war. Good is in charge, and evil has only the ability to influence. This flies in the face of most Western literature and film. As Muslims, we recognize evil and certainly work to avoid it and eradicate it as much as possible, but we are also grounded in the clarity that God and goodness is greater than Shaīṭān and evil. It is not a fight. Evil only has the power we give it by listening to its suggestions and acting upon them.

Prophets and Messengers

When we say that we believe in prophets and messengers, we are bearing witness to a unique class of people. We are admitting that there were people chosen to carry God's message and that they were chosen because of unique characteristics. It is important to understand that they were elevated above the rest of their people due to their special qualities. We do not equate ourselves with prophets and messengers. Indeed, the most pious and faithful people of today still fall far short of the elevated nature of prophets.

In Arabic, prophets and messengers are not the same. The Arabic word for prophet is *nabī*, and the Arabic word for messenger is *rasūl*. A *nabī* is one who receives revelation from God, and a *rasūl* is one who receives revelation that must be communicated to humanity (as in the case of a sacred book, for example). Not all prophets are messengers, but all messengers are prophets.

Prophets were fully truthful, telling the truth even if it seemed to go against their own selves. Hence, Noah told his people that he was building an ark even though they were in the desert, and Prophet Muhammad told the Meccans about *isrā'* and *mi'rāj* (his miraculous night journey to Jerusalem and ascension to the heavens), though they mocked him and refused to believe him.

Prophets and messengers were given a trust. One of their qualities was that they would fulfill their trust and complete the job. For most, their people did not believe, but they still fulfilled the trust and relayed God's message. It was not a trust of success, but a trust of offering their people the opportunity to believe and live an ethical life.

Michael Hart, in his book *The 100: A Ranking of the Most Influential Persons in History*,[71] says that Prophet Muhammad ﷺ was a genius. It is certainly true that our prophets and messengers had a measure of intelligence above and beyond the norm for their societies, but the word genius here is problematic. Prophet Muhammad ﷺ and all other prophets were more than simply genius. Prophets are above the limitations of genius, in that they are chosen, purified, and helped.

Prophets are also people. They eat, drink, walk in the marketplace, marry, and go to war. But they do all of these things with the utmost goodness and elevated purpose, setting an example for the rest of us.

There are some qualities we would never see in a prophet or messenger. They would never betray anyone or conceal the truth. A prophet would also never be foolish or dull.

Prophets perform miracles. These miracles are facilitated and gifted to them by God. Jesus ﵇ cured the blind and brought the dead to life. Moses ﵇ parted the Red Sea. Their miracles helped their followers believe and made fulfilling the trust easier. The English language has one word for those things that are seemingly impossible but nevertheless happen: a miracle. Arabic has many words. The Arabic word *muʿjiza* refers to the unique and amazing miracles of prophets and messengers, and the Arabic word *karāma* refers to the miracles of the pious. This differentiation in terms emphasizes the importance of the unique type of miracles afforded prophets and messengers. We believe in their miracles with certianty.

Shared Prophets

Islam is an Abrahamic faith, and as such we share the stories of our prophets with our Jewish and Christian brothers and sisters, but there are some important variations in the stories. Here we will touch very briefly on some differences that are related to *ʿaqīda* and how we interpret and interact with these stories as Muslims.

Adam

Adam was the first human and the first prophet. It is important for us to note that both Adam and Ḥawa (Eve) sinned and both were forgiven. The fault does not fall more heavily on one of them than the other. In a true egalitarian relationship, each is presented in the Quran as responsible for their own actions.

Noah/Nūḥ

Noah was a messenger to his people, and when they refused to believe, Allah ordered him to build a large boat (the ark) in the middle of the desert. His people mocked him and continued to disbelieve. Then God sent a flood and destroyed those who disbelieved. Although the Quran mentions that Noah gathered animals into the ark, the The Judaeo-Christian story of two creatures of every single animal on the earth is not mentioned in the Islamic story.

Abraham/Ibrāhīm, the Friend of God

Abraham is the father of Judaism, Christianity, and Islam, and much of his story is the same in all three faith traditions. The Quranic narrative adds additional details about his life: his attempt to guide his father and his father's rejection, the city elders' attempt to burn him for his belief, God ordering the fire to be cool for him, and his building of the sacred house.

The Quran tells the story of Abraham and his son Ishmael. A divine order came to Abraham, directing him to sacrifice his son, Ishmael (in the Bible it is Isaac). Abraham called upon his son who, with great submission to and patience with the divine order, told his father to fulfill the command. And of course, at the moment of sacrifice, the Angel Gabriel brought a ram from the heavens and ordered Abraham to sacrifice it instead, as he had fulfilled God's command through his willingness to comply.[72] Prophets Abraham and Ismāʿīl later built the Kaaba together; it was the first house ever constructed solely for the worship of God.

Moses/Mūsa, the One to Whom God Spoke

The story of Moses is one of a great prophet who saved his people from the oppression of the pharaoh. The Quran tells of his struggles and challenges and his triumphs and successes. We learn that after his mother placed him in the basket and sent him down the river, she was blessed to later become his nursemaid. We learn of the great woman, Asiya, who saved him from the river and raised him in the home of his future enemy, the pharaoh. We watch as he asks for help from his brother because of his own speech impediment and see his miracles overcome the magic tricks of his day. The Quran tells us that God spoke directly to Moses, but when Moses asked to see Him, God instead revealed Himself to the mountain, which then disintegrated, having been overwhelmed with awe. Moses himself fainted.

Jesus/ʿIsa, the Word of God

Jesus ﷺ, the Son of Mary, is a very important prophet of Islam. The Quran begins his story with the birth of his mother, who was dedicated to the temple as a worshipper during a time when women and girls were not allowed into the temple at all. She grew up there under the care of her uncle, Prophet Zakariyya ﷺ, and one day, the Angel Gabriel ﷺ appeared before her to give her the good news of her pregnancy. She was unamused and insisted that it was not possible since, she said, ﴾ *No man has touched me and I am not unchaste* ﴿ (Q. 19:20). But Angel Gabriel tells her that all things are possible for God, and that it was ﴾ *a matter decreed* ﴿ (Q. 19:21). The Quran tells us of her lonely birthing of Prophet Jesus and of her return to her people, who mock and chastise her. She points to the baby in her arms, and he speaks to them, defending the honor of his mother and telling them who he is and will be. Jesus ﷺ is given the miracle of cures; he cures the blind and the leper and brings the dead to life. The Quran reminds us that this was all with the permission and power of God. The disciples of Jesus ﷺ, or his helpers, promise him loyalty, but then he is betrayed. The Quran tells us that he was not crucified but that it was made to seem to them that he was. Instead, Jesus ﷺ was raised up to the heavens where he awaits his return at the end of time.

Muhammad, the Final Messenger

Since the Christian world met the Muslim world there has been an attempt to disparage the life of Muhammad ﷺ. It was important to the power structures of the church that the Messenger of Islam not be trusted. Even Martin Luther, who borrowed from the Muslims for his reform of the Christian church, wrote bitterly about our beloved Prophet and the Muslim people. And still today, his life is cast in numerous ugly frames. If the world knew him, they would certainly enter Islam with ease and speed.

At the beginning of this discussion about belief, we mentioned that people believe in things either because of their own experiences or because of a trusted messenger. At the time that revelation came to Muhammad, the son of Abdullah ﷺ, he was called *al-amīn*, or "the trustworthy one," by the people of Mecca. They left their money and valuables in his care, and they trusted his every word. In fact, when God ordered the Prophet ﷺ to go public with His message, he gathered the people of Quraish and asked them, "If I told you that an enemy tribe was around the bend and about to arrive and attack, would you believe me?"[73] They all answered in the affirmative because he was completely trustworthy. Prior to revelation, the Quraish were rebuilding the Kaaba (after some damage that needed repair) and were at a standstill as to who would have the honor of placing the final cornerstone. When Muhammad ﷺ, not yet a prophet, entered the sacred precinct, they were thrilled and asked him to place it. In keeping with his wisdom and character, however, he laid his garment on the ground and placed the stone within, then asked all of them to lift together. Then he placed the stone in its place with his blessed hands. His people loved him and trusted him.

It was only after revelation that the Quraishi leaders, fearing a loss of power, authority, and economic control of the Kaaba, insulted and rejected our beloved Prophet ﷺ. He continued to teach and call them to the way of beauty, joy, and Truth until their persecution became overwhelming, and then he sought refuge for the fledgling group of new Muslims with the people of Medina, some of whom had recently come to him pledging their faith and help.

In Medina, in spite of a constant state of war, Prophet Muhammad ﷺ built a society of people who sought the pleasure of God, loved one another, and were generous, charitable, and strong of spirit.

The Prophet's ﷺ death brought an end to the communication of revelation between the heavens and the earth, and since he was the last and final prophet, this door will not open again until the end of time.

His message was complete and preserved for generations to come—preserved for our generation, *alḥamdulillah*!

The characteristics of Prophet Muhammad's message include the following.

- It is all-inclusive and forever. It is not missing anything, and it will be protected and applicable for all time.
- It is protected by God.
- It coincides with the *fiṭra*, or the natural inclination of the human being.
- It benefits those who adhere to it and prevents harm to them as well.
- It repels difficulty and discomfort. This is not to say that a believer will

not face difficulty or discomfort, but that the message of the Prophet ﷺ, when adhered to, repels hardship like oil repels water.

- It is flexible and encompassing. The message is for people from all walks of life and all personalities.
- It was revealed to Prophet Muhammad, the Seal (or *khātim*) of the Prophets. There will be no prophet after him.
- It replaces all that came before it. While we believe in the messages and prophets of earlier times, the laws and principles of Islam replace those that were sent before.[74]

Prophet Muhammad's message is the message of Islam, and the message of Islam is inclusive, protected, joyful, flexible, and final.

ACTIVITY: PROPHETS IN THE QURAN

Who are the Prophets mentioned in the Quran, and what do you know about them? See how much of the chart you can fill out.

	Name	Story Sentence
1	Adam ﷺ	
2		He built the ark.
3	Idris ﷺ	
4		
5		
6		
7		
8		
9		
10		
11		
12		
13		
14		
15		
16		

17		
18		
19		
20		
21		
22		
23		
24		
25	Muhammad, ﷺ	

Revelation

I (Tamara) sat on a single bed with the A. J. Arberry translation of the Quran in my lap. I had just bought it and was ready to find out what mysteries it held for me. I prayed a prayer I had long prayed before reading scripture, "God, guide me to what you want me to read today," and opened the book. It opened up to the verse in Surat al-Ahzab that most succinctly describes the spiritual equality of men and women in Islam:

> ﴾ *Verily the Muslim men and the Muslim women, the believing men and the believing women, the worshipful men and the worshipful women, the truthful men and the truthful women, the charitable men and the charitable women, the fasting men and the fasting women, the men who guard their private parts and the women who do so, and the men who remember Allah often and the women who do so—for them Allah has prepared forgiveness and a great reward.* ﴿ (Q. 33:35)

I was flabbergasted. The Quran had quenched my most desperate thirst—it had declared the absolute spiritual equality of men and women.

Revelation is not the same as any other text. It carries with it guidance, light, and help for those who seek God in its pages.

The angel of revelation is Angel Gabriel, or Jibril in Arabic. This angel has had the awesome task of bringing revelation to every prophet. Revelation can also occur as true dreams (as in the example of Abraham and Isma'il), instantaneous revelations that are written on the heart, and direct divine communication (as with Moses). Revelation is the passing of a message from God to people through an appointed messenger. With the passing of Prophet Muhammad ﷺ, nothing remains of this connection to the heavens except for true dreams.

Revelation has been important for humanity. Each book came and clarified belief and reiterated the importance of faith in God. New revelations corrected the deviations of earlier peoples and fulfilled the human need for direction and law.

The revelation of the Quran began with ﴿ *Read! in the Name of your Lord Who created* ﴾ (Q. 96:1) and then wove a multilayered and nuanced book of guidance. It was revealed in Ramadan, and the Prophet ﷺ said that "the scrolls of Ibrahim were revealed on the first eve of Ramadan, the Torah was revealed after six days had passed of Ramadan, and the Psalms after twelve days had passed. The Gospel was revealed when eighteen days had passed of Ramadan, and the Quran began [to be revealed] on the twenty-fifth of Ramadan."[75] There are other narrations that indicate that the Quran was revealed possibly on another night in the last ten days of Ramadan.

The Arabic term *Quran* originates with either the root *qa-ra-ʿa* or *qa-ra-na*. The first means "to read" and the second means "to bring together chapters, verses, and letters." The word Quran is found thirty-four times within the Quran itself.

The Quran was revealed in two stages. In the first stage, the entire Quran was sent down from the Preserved Tablet (*al-lawh al-maḥfūẓ*), which is with Allah. From there, the second stage consisted of Angel Gabriel revealing it to the Prophet ﷺ over time, by the order of God, Most High. It is said that all other revelations were revealed in one stage only, that is, all at once.

The Quran was preserved by the companions on bits of bone, parchment, and papyrus. But most importantly, it was preserved in the hearts of the believers through memorization and recitation. This preservation continues today, albeit in a smaller percentage of hearts.

The project to collect all of the Quran into a written book began during the caliphate of Abū Bakr ؓ and was formalized during the caliphate of ʿUthman ibn ʿAffan ؓ. Each page was checked and rechecked by those who had memorized the Quran during the life of the Prophet ﷺ. The preservation of the Quran has continued throughout the centuries and as such, only the Arabic Quran is considered the actual revelation. A translation into any other language is considered an explanation of the Quran—valuable, but not the literal word of God.

Many converts learn one or two short *sūra*s from the last part of the Quran and recite those in prayer for life. Feeling overwhelmed by the length of longer *sūra*s, or just by the time it would take to learn them, converts often relegate the goal of memorizing the Quran to children or heritage Muslims.

But memorizing the Quran gives our internal lives something to rely on and a place to visit when we need a reminder. And the Quran is the best of reminders.

I (Tamara) knew a group of over-fifty-year-old converts who had lived in Damascus for more than thirty years but were stuck in the few *sūra*s they had learned early in their Muslim lives. As a result, their prayers were dull and routine, without the rich and comforting nuances of a lived ritual. They began to gather together under the leadership of one of their bilingual daughters (who was also a *ḥāfiẓa* and had her *ijāza* in the recitation of the Quran) to memorize individual verses chosen for their meanings. Soon they were able to pray using these short, meaningful verses, and their presence in prayer began to improve. Their love for prayer was reignited.

The Quran is a book to be memorized. *The Crowning Venture*, by Dr. (and Ḥāfiẓa) Saadia Mian offers inspiration in the form of real women from a variety of backgrounds who have completed the memorization journey and offer practical tips and tricks to make memorizing the Quran a reality in your life. You can purchase your own copy at daybreak.rabata.org.

May you find the path to memorizing easy and fulfilling.

ACTIVITY: MEMORIZING THE QURAN

1. Choose a verse from anywhere in the Quran.
2. Read along with an audio recording several times.
3. Recite it to someone who can correct your pronunciation.
4. Listen again and practice.
5. Try to write it (even in English letters) without looking.
6. Use it in prayer.
7. Celebrate! Now choose another.

The Day of Judgment

One of the six articles of faith is belief in the Day of Judgment. Muslims believe in a day of final assessment and evaluation. A day when a lifetime of deeds, intentions, and attitudes are the basis for the sorting of humanity. Some will be rewarded with the pleasure of God and Heaven; others will be punished with God's wrath and Hellfire. On that day, all of humanity will rely on God's mercy and His promise that His mercy overrides His wrath.

The Prophet ﷺ has told us of both minor signs and major signs that indicate the approach of the final hour. Minor signs are those signs which happen in some places but not others, and not everyone is aware of them. They must all occur before the major signs begin. The major signs of the Day of Judgment will be felt by all people (though they may not identify them as signs of the end of times). Some scholars identify another category of signs called intermediate signs. These are included in the major signs by others.

A sign of the Day of Judgment is a sign of the nearing of that day and is not necessarily a negative event in and of itself. Indeed, it could be a positive thing for the world as it stands, even though it heralds the coming of the Final Day. The arrival of Prophet Muhammad ﷺ as the final messenger and Seal of the Prophets was a sign of the nearing of the Final Day, for example. Of course, his life was a blessing to humanity and a light to the world; it was also a sign of the end of times. Sahl ibn Sa'd said, "I saw the Prophet ﷺ lift two fingers and say, 'I was sent, and between me and the hour is as lies between these two.'"[76]

Once all of the minor signs have occurred, the major signs will begin. We do not have a narration that tells us the order of these major signs, but we do know that they will come quickly, one after another. 'Abdullah ibn 'Umar said that the Prophet ﷺ said, "The signs are like beads arranged on a wire; the wire breaks and they follow one another."[77]

The three significant people mentioned by our beloved Prophet regarding the Day of Judgment are the Mahdi, the Dajjal, and Jesus, the Son of Maryam.

As the world degenerates into more darkness and tribulation, the Mahdi will come to assist the struggle against darkness. He will fill the earth with justice and the rains will come, replenishing the earth with blooming plants.

The Dajjal, or Antichrist, will appear after three years of famine and drought. The Prophet ﷺ said, "Between the creation of Adam and the coming of the hour, no trial is greater than the Dajjal."[78] It will be a trial because he will have abilities and powers that other people do not have. He will claim divinity but only be a person of trickery. The Prophet ﷺ advised us to read the beginning of Surat al-Kahf as protection from him.

Prophet Jesus, the Son of Mary will return to Earth at the end of time. Some narrations say he will descend in Damascus, while others say he will descend in Jerusalem. He will gain victory over the Dajjal and rid the earth of his false influence.

The other major players during the period before the end of time are Gog and Magog (who they actually are is a matter of debate among scholars). They will attempt to destroy the earth, and nothing will serve as a weapon against them but *du'ā'*.

The Day of Judgment will occur once all of the major signs have been seen.

Divine Destiny

The sixth and final article of faith is believing in *qaḍa*ʾ and *qadar*—divine destiny, whether it seems positive or negative from our perspective.

This particular article of faith can cause confusion in a world where Calvinism and postmodern individualism have created a cultural pull between fate and free will.

In Islam, the human being lives in different realities. As human beings, we have full free will to make decisions, and it is because of this that we are held accountable for our decisions. But things also happen to us that are outside of our decision-making power. Some of these things are influenced by *duʿā*ʾ and good deeds, in that these might retain blessings for us or ward off a problem or lessen it.

There are other things that happen to us that are completely out of our control—no matter what we do, they will not change. In the case of some of these things, we do not even attempt to make *duʿā*ʾ about them because the impossibility of changing them is so obvious—like who our parents are or the color of our eyes.

For other things, our *duʿā*ʾ and our actions may impact our circumstances in a variety of unseen ways. So we are directed to do two things for every situation life hands us: do our best in all circumstances and make *duʿā*ʾ constantly.

Not knowing the outcome of our life events is part of the human being's status as ʿ*abd*, or servant of God. When we do our best and make *duʿā*ʾ, whatever happens should bring with it the feeling of relief that is *tawakkul* (trusting in Allah).

Free will begins with the will of God. He granted us choice and will hold us accountable as a result. God says in the Quran, ﴾ *We offered the trust to the Heavens and the Earth and the mountains and they refused to take it on and were very wary of it. And the human being took it on. He is indeed wrongdoing and ignorant* ﴿ (Q. 33:72). And so we learn that our free will is a trust, and we are expected to fulfill it with piety, worship, and good deeds. The beauty of this free will is that it creates love. Love can only be realized through the freedom to do and feel, to react and connect. So we were created, granted free will, and given the senses and skills necessary to discriminate right from wrong, better from best.

Shaitan enters into this space of free will because of his ability to distract us and misdirect us. But part of our free will is that we know that his promises are a lie. We have been warned and taught about his base and vengeful character.

And of course, our free will is limited. We have no control over our thoughts when we sleep, we cannot tell our lungs or skin cells to work in a certain way, and we cannot control time or how slowly or quickly we grow older. We cannot replace the physical weakness of age with the energy of youth (not even with exercise and smoothies, though they will help). All of this is part and parcel of *qaḍa'* and *qadar*.

Our free will is wrapped up in our ability to choose piety. No matter what happens to us that is outside of our control, we still have the ability to choose goodness and kindness, upright behavior, and a positive attitude. It is for this that we will be held to account on the Day of Judgment.

ACTIVITY: VALUES AND BELIEFS

In the beginning of this section we mentioned that the science of *'aqīda* is built around the idea that we act according to our core beliefs. A Muslim, then, can also see the depth of her faith and the correctness of her belief in her actions.

This activity will help you think about your core belief system.

1. Look at the values in the boxes. Think deeply about each word, paying attention to your inner dialogue around it. How important is each word to you?
2. Add any words that you feel are missing.
3. Star the ten words that are most important to you.
4. Look again. Narrow down the words to eight.
5. Do it again, and this time narrow down the words to five.

Values	Stars	Values	Stars
peace		influence	
wealth		justice	
happiness		Godliness	
success		kindness	
family		authenticity	
love		competency	
wisdom		belonging	
status		generosity	
recognition		independence	
piety		*taqwa*	
community		*tawakkul*	

Values	Stars	Values	Stars
friends		*ṣabr*	
asceticism		īmān	
truth		loyalty	

Play with each word now using the phrases below. The first one has been done for you as an example:

Word and personal definition: *Ṣabr* is patient forbearance. Acquiring *ṣabr* means persevering during hard times without complaint. It means finding joy and thankfulness when times are tough.

What I believe: Everyone can have *ṣabr*.

How I think about this word: *Ṣabr* is possible.

What I do: I practice *ṣabr* and fight bitterness within, avoiding an internal dialogue of complaining.

What is the evidence that I live the word in this way? When my grandmother asked me if it was raining outside while I was putting on my scarf, I did not lose my temper, but rather smiled and made a joke about the possibility of rain. I was able to leave without a heavy and angry heart.

Word and personal definition:

What I believe:

How I think about this word:

What I do:

What is the evidence that I live the word in this way?

Word and personal definition:

What I believe:

How I think about this word:

What I do:

What is the evidence that I live the word in this way?

Word and personal definition:

What I believe:

How I think about this word:

What I do:

What is the evidence that I live the word in this way?

Word and personal definition:

What I believe:

How I think about this word:

What I do:

What is the evidence that I live the word in this way?

Word and personal definition:

What I believe:

How I think about this word:

What I do:

What is the evidence that I live the word in this way?

Belief That Is Grounded

Declare your independence in belief. This section has laid the groundwork for the six articles of faith, but the rest is up to you. A strong faith can withstand trials and tribulations; it can hold us up when the world gets to us and can be a soft place to land when we are thrown. It can give us the wide and strong roots of the palm tree.

In order to grow your faith, see the next section for the tools of independence.

PART THREE: KNOW THE TOOLS

Over the years we have learned the essential tools of spiritual growth in the Islamic context: the Arabic language, a healthy worship life, strong teachers and sisters in faith, and (to circle back to module one) you!

Arabic Language Learning

One of my (Tamara's) Arabic teachers once said that Arabic is a richer language than English because each word has so many layers of meaning. Internally, I disagreed. *Why have a multitude of meanings when you can just have more words?* I thought to myself. But later, during a seven-year translation project, I began to understand what she meant by "rich."

Al-Jahiz (d. 253 AH), an early philosopher, said that the Arabic language is eloquent, rich, and terse. He believed that the Arabic language itself is one of the miracles of God—that the structure showed a Divine guidance and a spontaneous growth about two hundred years prior to the Prophet's ﷺ life.

The award-winning *sīra* scholar Sheikha Samira al-Zayid, says in the introduction to her book *Durus min al-Sīra* (*Lessons from the Life of the Prophet*) that one of the reasons the Arabs were able to embrace Islam fully and completely, and one of the reasons those who did not were so adamantly against Islam, was their deep and full command of the Arabic language. Believers and nonbelievers understood the implications of *lā ilāha illa Allāh, Muḥammadun rasūlullāh*. Those who believed rushed into the requirements and self-work of Islam, giving up status and long-held traditions of classism and other ugly social habits. Nonbelievers stayed far away, understanding that admitting to the presence of only one God meant they would have to worship Him and Him alone.[79]

Al-Zayid says that their skill in the Arabic language was one of five ways that the Arabs of the peninsula were prepared to receive our final and beloved Prophet ﷺ.

When my Arabic began to improve, I began to understand what my Arabic teacher had meant by nuance and multilayered meanings. In fact, it was my fascination with the Arabic language that inspired the name Rabata for the nonprofit organization we started in 2013.

I wanted to use a root word, and a verb, so that it would imply all the meanings of that same word when it was expanded in all the possible ways.

Learning Arabic

As a convert begins to build her Muslim life, this stumbling block—or ever-present elephant in the room—cannot be ignored. It is time to learn Arabic.

Tamara's Arabic Journey

I began learning Arabic like most converts: a little of this and a little of that. I started with cassette tapes and a little booklet that taught me how to read (decode) the letters. Then I took a course at the University of Minnesota the summer after my first child was born. As she grew and another arrived, I audited bits and pieces of university Arabic courses and tried to build a language base that would give me access to understanding the Quran and other Arabic texts.

It was slow going, and my ego struggled with the condescending tone of the Arabs around me—"Can you recite the Fatiha?" and "How cute!"—when I struggled to get out a sentence or two.

But time passed, and I kept at it. When I moved to Syria, I began a serious course of study and was faced with papers and exams in Arabic. The prospect of this was overwhelming, to say the least. But one day in *sīra* class, learning about Christian history (part of formalized *sīra* study is to learn about the early history of Jerusalem and the Arabian peninsula), the instructor spoke about the disciples of Jesus: "God ordered them to go forth and teach, but they refused, and so they woke up the next day speaking in the tongues of the lands they had been assigned, and they could no longer speak their own language." This was a whole new interpretation of the "speaking in tongues" of my childhood, and at the moment I was not concerned with the veracity or source of the information—instead I had an epiphany. Language was (as are all other things) in God's hands. I began to pray in the wee hours of the morning that God would teach me Arabic as He had taught the disciples of Jesus the tongues of those they were to preach to but without forgetting English.

I had already met three or four women (converts) who had forgotten how to speak fluent and educated English, and I did not want to join them. I wanted to know Arabic, and I wanted to remain a native speaker of English.

Along with the prayer, I did two things to promote my language learning. First, I began to seek out people who would speak Arabic with me because even though I lived in Syria, I was surrounded by people who spoke English all the time. My mother-in-law is American, so the entire family was used to speaking English at home, and I worked in the English department in schools, so it was policy to speak English with teachers and students. Finding people who spoke only Arabic was a challenge. My best oral instructor was Muna Nadir (and I have not changed her name here, hoping you might make *du'ā'* for her). She was in her thirties when she showed up at my house to clean it and had finished school only up to grade six. But she was bright and talkative, and I threw myself into her desire to talk. We learned from each other, and ten years later, she had memorized the Quran, entered college, and become a teacher at her local mosque. I had become fluent in Arabic, could laugh and joke, and most importantly, could attend classes in Arabic and interact with the students and teachers. I had been successfully immersed in the school of Muna and had graduated with flying colors.

The second important step I took toward language learning happened more by the Grace of God than my good plans. Before I moved to Damascus, I had attended *sīra* classes with a translator and did not have to take any exams or write any papers. When I showed up for class in Syria in 1993, all bets were off. I was informed that I would have to take the tests and write the papers in Arabic. I promptly gave myself a fever of 104°F and went to bed. After I spent three days lamenting my fate, my sister-in-law (who was and remains my mentor, partner in crime, and beloved friend) stopped by the house. She ripped off the blankets and said, "Enough! Either do the tests and do poorly or quit the whole project! You can't stay in bed forever."

I realized she was correct. I got up and decided to approach my problem strategically. I was a trained teacher with a master's degree in curriculum and instruction! Surely I could find a way to succeed (I told myself daily), and finally I set upon an idea. I would write eleven test questions, guessing what the teacher might set for us, and then answer them, memorizing both the questions and the answers. The first time I tried this (ingenious) method, I went to the test nervous (but without a fever) and lo and behold! Nine of the questions I had set for myself were on the actual test! I wrote my memorized answers and, while I was not even close to the top of the class, I was also not at the bottom. Success! I continued with this method for years, until my Arabic improved and I could attend study groups and benefit from more traditional methodologies of study.

Even now, however, I freely admit that my language skills are weaker than I wish them to be. My writing skills are poor, and my grammar is not at the level it should be considering the work I have done in Islamic sciences.

Najiyah's Arabic Journey

The first memory I have of learning Arabic was walking with my then-husband through a park. I was trying to learn the letters. He was trying to explain the difference between *sīn* and *ṣād*, *dāl* and *ḍād*, etc. I couldn't understand why it was the letters that were different, when it sounded to me like it was the vowels that came after them that were different: "aa" vs. "aw." He left much to be desired as a teacher, and I was an even worse student.

When I was finally able to audit an Arabic class at the University of Kansas, I managed to become even more confused. This was in the late eighties, when anyone who could speak Arabic and had a pulse qualified as an Arabic teacher and when the big orange book (*Elementary Modern Standard Arabic*) was about the only thing going. I had always been a language fanatic—taking French, Spanish, and German in high school—but this structure was beyond my grasp, and my burning desire to speak my husband's language, access heritage texts, and talk to my in-laws seemed to be ever more unattainable.

But then I had the opportunity to live with my in-laws in Syria for six months. My mother-in-law taught me cooking and, with the help of my brother-in-law, set me on my way to learning Arabic. Thereafter, every time we visited, I learned more. Later, when I lived in Syria for two years, I became pretty fluent in spoken colloquial Syrian Arabic. That left me able to talk to anyone but unable to read or write or understand the classical Arabic of the Quran.

Upon my return home, I found Rabata and Ribaat. I began classes and can now read the Quran, understand much of it, and write in Arabic. I still have trouble with grammar (probably due to my initial difficult introduction to it), but I do have a successful path for studying, with qualified teachers who understand how English speakers learn Arabic best. It's incredible.

Tips and Tricks

Along the way we learned that a little Arabic goes a long way. Soon you will find yourself understanding sections of the Quran, and this will be the day your heart overflows with joy. Here are the necessary skills.

1. Knowing the letters well enough to phonetically decode the Quran (read without understanding)
2. Understanding the basic structure of Arabic (a beginner's level)
3. Being able to hear the rhythm of the Arabic language. This can be picked up by
    - taking a conversation course given by a native speaker
    - hanging around Arabic-speaking people
    - listening to Arabic TV programs
    - listening to Arabic *nashīds* (religious songs)

4. Learning to use an Arabic-English dictionary (and later an Arabic-Arabic dictionary). For this, you'll need to understand the root system of Arabic words.

The following are some methods to acquire these skills.

1. Register for an Arabic course through Ribaat. Our program was designed to get you from zero to a level where (if you wished) you could begin to study *in Arabic* within six levels. We have had great success, and if you apply yourself, you will be able to write a one-page essay by level three.

2. Use YouTube or find someone to teach you the Qaʿida Nuraniyya, an old-fashioned method for learning how to decode/read Arabic. (See activity below.)

3. Hire a tutor who has experience with Arabic as a second language. A non-native speaker will be more useful in helping you learn the structure of Arabic, and a native speaker will be most useful for you to learn conversation skills.

4. Take a university Arabic class. You can audit if you don't need the credits.

5. Register for any other Arabic program and stick with it.

ACTIVITY: READING

There are a number of YouTubers who present the Qaʿida Nuraniyya. Run a search and watch a few. Decide which you think is most useful, and tweet out the link!

My favorite was ______________________________ because ________________

____.

Now commit to completing the twenty-four or twenty-five lessons and tweet again at the end! You are most likely now a fluent decoder of the Quran!

Use the hashtags #PLTools #BestQN #ICanReadQuran! #LinaProjectActivity and tag us at @Rabata_org.

Worship

Converting to Islam touches every aspect of our lives. The spiritual experience of our new faith can begin with intense connection and beauty and then dwindle in the face of spiritual stumbling blocks. We may have hoped for a consistently rich spiritual life, but community stressors and our own shortcomings can be obstacles to achieving our dreams of deep prayer, ethereal meditative moments, and loving angelic embraces.

Some immediate issues that can hold the spiritual experience at bay include mosques with ridiculous spaces for women, prayer in a language not yet understood, and lack of a congregation you feel comfortable worshipping with.

Preconversion, many women (and men) were used to finding solace in their place of worship. Whether church, temple, or the woods, globally people gravitate to spiritual spaces at times of pain and difficulty—or weekly for sustenance in an empty world. The convert comes to the mosque expecting to find the same experience, and too often she is bitterly disappointed.

Her worship activities prior to Islam were almost fully in her native language, and much of it was personal worship. Among some groups, there is disdain for ritual, and it is looked upon as a cold and empty practice. These people may favor the personal prayer, a walk in the woods, or a hymn sung with gusto. When the convert raises her hands in her first salat, she may find that she is so busy trying to mouth the Arabic words that the concept of it being a prayer totally escapes her. She feels frustrated and confused, wanting to have a fulfilling worship experience but not sure where to turn.

Leadership in churches and synagogues is driven by people who have been through a seminary or have some training in pastoral care. Their job is to create a spiritual environment for their flock. In mosques in the Western world, leadership is often taken on by good-hearted volunteers who are not trained in the creation of community. When a convert turns to her local mosque, she may not find what she needs for spiritual sustenance.

Spaces

It is entirely possible for converts and other concerned community members to come together and insist on adequate and acceptable space for women in the mosque. We both prefer that the mosque be as it was in the time of Prophet Muhammad ﷺ, without a barrier or any sort of division between the men and the women. In this way, men and women fill the mosque as they arrive, and both men and women go to the basement (or wherever) when the main prayer hall overflows.

Alternatively, converts can create or frequent third spaces that have been created in their communities to fill the gap left by inadequate mosques. In Minnesota, Daybreak Bookshop includes a place to learn and a pop-up mosque for women's *tarāwīh* every Ramadan. Also in Minnesota, the Gemali Project is a third space under the leadership of Brother Ali (the hip-hop artist). In Birmingham, UK, the Olton Project has a lovely space for men and women to come together in fellowship and spiritual care. Other communities provide both a mosque and a third space–like environment that is nurturing and uplifting; the Rhoda Institute/Sanad Collective in Ottawa is an example of such a space.

Converts can and should be advocates for their own spiritual space needs.

Worship Practices

There are three types of prayer in Islam; each is nourishing in its own way. Salat is the ritual prayer, *duʿāʾ* is supplication (talking to God), and *dhikr* is meditative work on the heart. All of these work together to build an inner life of spirituality.

Salat

The first months of learning salat can be dry because of the difficulty in remembering the Fatiha and the movements—"How many times do I stand up?" Later, salat can remain a less than spiritual experience as the convert resorts to the few *sūras* she memorized in the first six months of her Islamic life. Overcoming these feelings requires focus, concentration, and effort.

Understanding what you are reciting helps, and so memorizing short but very meaningful verses will open up the recesses of your mind in prayer.

Creating an environment for prayer is another way to increase spiritual fulfillment in your prayer. Set up a prayer space at home, even if it's just a corner. Fill it with a lovely candle, a thick and comfortable prayer mat, and easy access to your Quran, favorite books, and prayer beads. I (Tamara) have a number of favorite prayer mats. Each evokes a different feeling of nostalgia for me. I have a white mat that was a post-hajj gift from one of my teachers. When I pray on it, I am reminded of her and strive to pray as I have seen her praying—with great seriousness, concentration, and focus. I also have a soft-plush purple carpet. It is so soft it feels like it embraces me with care and kindness every time I fall into *sujūd*. This carpet was a post-hajj gift to me as well, and when I pray on it, I remember to make *duʿāʾ* for the lovely young woman who gave it to me. Find a beautiful prayer mat or have one made. Rabata had quilted mats made in 2013, and it was a beautiful melding of American culture and Islamic prayer. You can find what sparks spiritual nostalgia in you and create new traditions that will fill you with longing to stand and pray for years to come.

A third method of finding peace in prayer is to pray at the beginning of the time. We find that the first fifteen to twenty minutes make a difference in the feeling of connection. So if you can, jump up and pray right after the *adhān* calls; it will help you in building your inner spiritual life.

Duʿāʾ

Often translated as "supplication" or "invocation," *duʿāʾ* simply means talking to God. It is internally or externally pleading for forgiveness, expressing thanks, complaining about our difficulties, and asking for our wants and needs. This is the prayer most familiar to the Westerner and—for reasons unbeknownst to us—the mode of prayer most often dropped from one's repertoire of worship activities after conversion.

God says in the Quran, ﴾ *Indeed I am near. I respond to the invocation (duʿāʾ) of the supplicant when he calls upon Me* ﴿ (Q. 2:186). And the Prophet ﷺ said, "*Duʿāʾ* is the essence of worship"[80] and also "*Duʿāʾ* is worship."[81] It is said that Salah al-Din al-Ayyubi was told that the Crusaders' ships were sailing toward them with reinforcements, and so he went to the masjid and spent the night in prayer and *duʿāʾ*, begging God for help. The next morning, deeply concerned about the danger on the horizon, he asked another pious man to pray about the ships, and he responded, "Verily the tears of the night have drowned the ships." And soon afterward they received the news that indeed, the ships had sunk.

Duʿāʾ, calling on God, is important and real, and it is powerful. *Duʿāʾ* is not a ritual. It is in any language and at any time, silent or out loud, alone or in a group. Creating an inner prayer life will help to build the foundation of faith so necessary for converts.

There is a terribly sexist joke that used to be passed around in Syria—we share it here because it makes an important point about prayer. A young man asked his friend for help in finding a wife. "My only requirement," he said, "is that she does not nag. I have no other conditions." So his friend looked and looked and finally, defeated, returned to him and said, "I have failed you, I could not find a woman who does not nag. I have, however, found a woman who nags every other day." Thinking that he would have respite 50% of the time, the man decided to offer marriage to the every-other-day-nagging woman. She accepted, and after their wedding, she set to nagging. The man was patient because he said to himself, "Tomorrow will be nag-free." The next morning, the man woke up to the joyful thought that today was the nag-free day! As he opened his eyes and gazed upon his wife, she smiled and said, "Tomorrow I nag! Tomorrow I nag! Tomorrow I nag! Tomorrow I nag! Tomorrow I nag!"

This joke is usually met with belly laughs, and while we find it obnoxious in its original message, we do think it makes an important spiritual point—no one likes a nag except for God. He loves for us to call to Him, to beseech Him. God loves to hear our voice at night and in the day, seeking forgiveness for our errors and asking for our needs.

Making *Duʿāʾ* Together

We have a Ramadan tradition at Rabata where we work on reading *khitma*s (complete readings of the Quran) collectively and then come together for a group *duʿāʾ*. We start the *duʿāʾ* by reciting the very last *sūra*s of the Quran together, and then we make a general *duʿāʾ*. Then we take *duʿāʾ* requests and we collectively pray for each other. It is incredibly powerful, and we have been told again and again of prayers that were answered. One year, a young woman with brain cancer asked for prayers, and the next year she came back cancer-free and with a new baby! Another woman asked for prayers for her eyesight (she had eye cancer), and she said that immediately after the prayer, the spots in her vision were gone. *Duʿāʾ* is strong. Another woman who was about to have in vitro fertilization asked for our prayers, and we prayed that she would have three children. The fertilization was successful and resulted in four embryos. One died, and she gave birth to three beautiful babies. The power of *duʿāʾ* is real.

I (Tamara) once met a woman in her eighties with ten successful and religious children. At the time, I was struggling to raise my three, and I asked her, "What's your secret?" She began by telling me about the books she'd read, but I kept probing. Finally, she brought me into her bedroom and showed me the prayer carpet that was wedged in the thin space between her oversized bed and the wall. "Do you see this carpet?" I nodded. "My husband would take care of the children after Fajr, and I would settle here and make *duʿāʾ* for each of them individually. Fifteen minutes a child!" I was calculating fifteen minutes times ten children when she continued. Shaking her head, she said, "I was so worried about my eldest daughter Nada. She didn't like to iron or do any type of housework. How would she marry?" I had no idea where this conversation was going, but my American self thought, maybe she could find a guy who liked to iron? She continued, "I used to pray for her every day that she would find a groom with two servants!" She looked at me and said, "And you know, when Talal came to ask for her hand, he said to her, 'Before you say yes, you need to know that my single aunts have spent their lives caring for me, and they will live with us.' One cooked while the other cleaned, and my daughter was able to marry!" The power of *du'ā'* is no joke.

Du'ā' can be made at any time and any place. It does not need *wuḍū'* or a special formula. We have records of the *du'ā's* of the Prophet ﷺ, the early companions, and some of our pious predecessors, and many of these are breathtakingly beautiful. They can serve as beautiful beginnings to long, heartfelt *du'ā's* of our own, or can serve as complete *du'ā's* (even just the translation!) at times when your own words fail you or feel insubstantial. Or you can forgo them altogether and just pray your heart out in your own words.

In order to build your spiritual life, make a habit of talking to God and praying for yourself, your children, your family, your work, your health, and your life. Nothing is too small or insignificant, and nothing is too big or complicated for God.

Dhikr

The third type of prayer in Islam is *dhikr*. This is a meditative practice meant to train the heart and mind to be in a state of remembrance at all times. It is done in Arabic and is a repetition of phrases of praise or simply one of the names of God. The Quran mentions *dhikr* often, and the sunna speaks of the value of various phrases of praise, but *dhikr* is fluid, without a specific time, amount, or state of being. Hence, there are a number of ways to remember God.

﴾ *Then remember Me, I will remember you; Be grateful to Me and reject not Faith.* ﴿ (Q. 2:152)

﴾ *And Remember your Lord much, and praise (Him) in the evening and the morning.* ﴿ (Q. 3:41)

﴾ *And remember your Lord within yourself humbly and with awe, and with low voice, at morning and in the evening, and be not of the neglectful.* ﴿ (Q. 7:205)

﴾ *Those who have believed and whose hearts are assured by the remembrance of Allah. Unquestionably, by the remembrance of Allah hearts are assured.* ﴿ (Q. 13:28)

There are many phrases of praise, repentance, and glorification. The choice between one phrase or another is usually dictated by the needs of the seeker or the occasion of the gathering. I (Tamara) have often recommended that people suffering from a waning faith repeat *lā ilāha illa Allāh* numerous times a day in order to reroot their faith deeply within. Imam al-Ghazali and other scholars recommend repeating specific names of God to remedy individual problems of greed, illness, and other spiritual and physical ailments.[82] And for centuries, scholars have recommended various forms of sending prayers, greetings, and blessings upon Prophet Muhammad ﷺ. There are many books available today in English and Arabic that can feed a hungry soul with the nourishment of recommended phrases of *dhikr*.

Three simple and often recommended phrases of *dhikr* follow.

1. *Astaghfirullah*, meaning "I seek forgiveness from God." This is a phrase of repentance and is recommended as a daily litany. The Prophet ﷺ himself would repeat it one hundred times a day.

2. *Allahumma ṣalli wa sallim ʿala sayyidina Muḥammad*, meaning "O God, laud and greet our venerated Muhammad." The Quran tells us that ﴾ *Allah and His angels send blessings on the Prophet: O you who believe! Send your blessings on him, and salute him with all respect* ﴿ (Q. 33:56).

3. *Lā ilāha illa Allāh*, meaning "Naught is divine but God" but more traditionally translated as "There is no god but God." The Prophet ﷺ said, "The best *dhikr* is *lā ilāha illa Allāh*, and the best *duʿāʾ* is *alḥamdulillah*."

4. Silent or audible repetition of God's name "Allah"

5. The ninety-nine names of God

Bringing the three types of prayer together, salat, *duʿāʾ*, and *dhikr*, will build a rich inner life of spirituality. Together these three types of prayer will fortify the new convert as she moves forward in faith.

Teachers and Sisters

The act of conversion is a giant step on the road of spiritual growth and upbringing, and in an attempt to continue on the path, converts look to spiritual leadership for guidance. Out of habit, we tend to look to the leader of the local masjid—the imam. Our mind naturally equates the imam with the pastoral care of pastors, ministers, priests, and rabbis. But since Islam does not have an official clergy, this is not necessarily a valid assumption. Historically, spiritual leadership was sought from those teachers who specialized in spiritual upbringing. Allah ﷻ says in the Quran ﴾ *Ask the people of dhikr if you have understanding* ﴿ (Q. 16:43), and certainly we are used to relying on experts in all matters of our lives. There is an Arabic proverb that says, "The one who learns grammar from books alters rhetoric, and the one who learns *fiqh* (jurisprudence) from books muddles rulings, and the one who learns medicine from books kills the sleeping." While awkward in English, it rhymes in Arabic and makes an important point—every area of our lives has experts, including our spiritual life, and when we ignore them, it is to our own peril. Reading a series of books will not be sufficient for us to grow in faith. We need a mentor, a teacher, an upbringer, someone who will help us look forward on our path. We also need friends who will gently nudge us, as we also encourage them, to be our best selves. We need people to help us on the path to God.

Our beloved Prophet ﷺ was our teacher, our upbringer, the lamp that lit the way of Truth, and an example of living the Quran. His inheritors are those who continue his work. Ibn Masʿud said that sitting with ʿUmar ibn al-Khattab had a greater effect on his inner state than a year of worship.

If you are able to find a personal teacher, one who advises you and cares for you, one who helps you in matters of faith and life, you are very blessed. Do go to a teacher with your eyes fully open, however. We do not have blind obedience in Islam, rather we have "seeing obedience." Do not be fooled by someone who is still struggling with his or her base self. Ibn Rajab al-Hanbali discusses the difference between scholars of inner knowledge and scholars of outer knowledge in his book *The Heirs of the Prophets* and reminds us that "one who knows the commandments of Allah does not necessarily know Allah experientially. Such are the possessors of outer knowledge, who have no inkling of inner knowledge; they neither fear Allah nor possess humility. They were deemed blameworthy by the righteous forebears."[83] He continues and differentiates between worldly scholars and righteous scholars—the first being corrupt and causing harm to the *umma*, and the second being the inheritors of the Prophet ﷺ. A virtuous scholar, one who you might choose as a spiritual leader, combines inner and outer knowledge. They are the best of humankind after the prophets. ʿAli ؑ says of people, "People are three groups: righteous scholars, students of sacred knowledge, and the riffraff."[84] As converts, it is most important that we stay away from the riffraff.

Building a spiritual life will be easier with a guide along the way, but remember that we have our share of worldly scholars today just as we had in the past— perhaps even more - and not all people in leadership are spiritual leaders. So as you interact with your local imam, realize he may be struggling just like you. This is wiser than to put your faith in an imam who you assume has made his way further along the path (he's an imam after all, right?) only to be shocked at his lack of humility or wisdom.

You can often find humility, wisdom, and community in the elders. Look for a grandmother who gets up for *tahajjud* or has served her family for years, or find an elder aunt who spends her nights with the Quran. Seek out the secret people—those who bring light and blessing but are only known amongst the angels.

If you do find someone whom you consider taking on as a formal spiritual guide, consider the following lists of questions before making a full commitment.

Question	Answer (should be yes)
Do they practice what they preach?	
Are they interested in your personal achievement?	
Do they push you toward your family?	
Do they try to make you strong and independent?	
Do they bring the vibrancy of Islam to your reality?	
Do they praise you and fault you in a healthy manner?	
Do they allow you to question?	
Do they live Islam in all aspects of their lives?	
Do they give a live talk from their heart that responds to the issues of your heart?	
Do they have a regular *tahajjud* and worship schedule?	
Do they have a teacher guiding them?	

Questions	Answer (should be no)
Do they latch on to you and act possessive of you?	
Do they flirt with you or suggest marriage (secret or second)?	
Do they have any un-Islamic behaviors?	
Do they waste time?	
Do they use students' time, money, and effort for personal gain?	
Are they ignorant of inner knowledge?	

You!

Converts often expect to find an almost utopian group of Muslims awaiting them—people of honesty, openness, and light. And instead they discover that

Muslims are a hodgepodge of very great people and the downright rotten, just like the rest of the world.

As converts navigate a new world of manners and etiquette, we can count on the good sense that brought us to Islam to help us determine which new habits to take on and which old habits to discard.

How we behave and respect ourselves is a good place to begin. When we take care of our personal and individual behaviors, we build a solid foundation of faith and begin to reach out to build a community of kind and peaceful people.

Developing a Mature Faith

Jennifer Crooker

Many things bring people to Islam: Some come to Islam after years of study, and some after learning only a few key items about our faith. Some come to Islam through books, college classes, personal relationships with Muslims (including boyfriends/husbands), or even travel to Muslim-majority countries.

The parts of Islam that first "speak" to people are unique to each individual and where they are in life—some of us are first drawn to the idea of pure monotheism, some to the ritual of salah, some to the practice of hijab, some to the ideas of racial egalitarianism and social justice found in Islam, some to the idea of a rule-governed life, some to the unchanged nature of the Quran. Here is an important reality to understand: *Often, what brought us to Islam will not be the thing that sustains us in Islam.*

Here's an analogy: When we travel to a beautiful place, we might ride in a car, train, or airplane. The experience of travel is undoubtedly part of the memory and experience of our trip, but the core purpose of our trip is to witness beautiful mountains, oceans, forests, and waterfalls. Perhaps we will also visit unique towns, learn to communicate in new languages, or eat delicious food.

The situations, people, and ideals that bring us to Islam are the means of transportation that bring us to the beautiful destination of Islam. The excitement and meaning of that trip will never be forgotten. It was beautiful. It will always be a part of us. But the destination has so much more to offer. If a person, community, culture, or country helped us get to this destination, then we must learn to stand on our own as Muslims, and experience the deep joy, love, and growth Islam can bring us as independent individuals. This also means looking deep inside ourselves to see our own shortcomings and those of others and understanding where we need to exert more effort on improving ourselves. Spiritual development is a lifelong process. We can work to be change-makers of our own souls and in our wider world.

If you are a convert of any number of years, you may have spent time in thoughtful decision-making, or you may have jumped at spontaneous intuition. Either way, you know you can trust yourself. Review module one, and stay aware of your internal compass, your beautiful brain, and your healthy heart.

Your Internal Compass

Your mind and heart brought you to this path; they can help you walk on it. One of the most dangerous stumbling blocks on the path to God is to do something that feels intuitively wrong—even if everyone tells you it is right. We have all heard stories of converts who married the first dude with a Muslim name who asked, only to end up miserable, because they were told "he's a Muslim, and half of your faith is marriage." We will discuss this at length in module three, but it is worth saying here as well: do not, under any circumstance, marry someone in Islam that you would not marry outside of Islam. If you would not have accepted a deadbeat joker before you converted, don't accept him now because he claims Islam on his passport. Many immigrant men suffer from some form of Postcolonial Stress Disorder. The historical reasons for this are irrelevant here, but women from their cultures have learned how to manage and love them in ways that are beautiful and sometimes funny. Do not assume that this will be easy for you. We knew of one Arab woman whose husband was anti-religion, so when she wanted to go to learn Quran, she would say, "I'm going out to get bread." Three hours later, she would return with bread, and her husband would say, "What took so long?" and she would laugh, act dumb, and say, "Oh, the time flies, chatting and whatnot." In this way she kept the peace, made him feel strong, and fulfilled her religious obligation to learn the Quran. However, for Western women, it can feel insulting to have to manipulate a man in order to meet the basic goals of your life. See more in module three.

Your Beautiful Brain

Don't marry the wrong man, and don't trust every site on Google for your Islamic know-how. In 2012, I (Tamara) was preparing a presentation for the Rabata Ramadan Tour and I needed to type a hadith in Arabic and English. Feeling lazy, I decided to see if Google had typed it already so that I could simply cut and paste. I ran a quick search and voilà! I found it. I cut and pasted the Arabic and went back to grab the English. As I highlighted the text to copy it, I read the translation and froze. The translation had an addition that was not in the original and was disturbingly misogynistic. The hadith in question is the story of Salman al-Farisi ﷺ visiting Abū Darda' ﷺ. At the time, Abū Darda' had taken to some maddening habits, like not eating or sleeping. The Arabic version of the hadith tells us that Salman went to visit Abū Darda' ﷺ, whose wife opened the door. Here is where the translation took a ludicrous turn. In this particular translation, "Abū Darda's wife opened the door in a disheveled state (in a way that a wife should never look for her husband)." The original uses an adjective which can be translated as "frazzled," but also as "shabby" or "disheveled." But the portion in parentheses is an additional piece of text that does not appear in the hadith at all. I was flabbergasted. This was a clear insertion of personal views about the role of women in a relationship that was not present in the hadith at all. Quite the opposite, I see her coming to the door in the frazzled *psychological* state (represented to be sure in her physical state as well) of a woman dealing with a man who has stepped away from being a husband. We are shown so beautifully and gently the role a man has in his family life and how his antics affect his wife's state of being. And we can all relate. Even Hollywood relates to this idea—we are inundated with men in the movies who hit a midlife crisis and go off gallivanting to the distress of the women they love. But of course, Abū Darda' was not gallivanting. He was a tremendously spiritual man who was digging deeply into his ascetic practices of fasting and praying. When Salman ﷺ came to visit, Abū Darda's wife was close to the end of her rope. But the translator that I had happened upon had warped this hadith and turned it into a treatise about women dressing up for their husbands. I was irate.

My mother used to tell me "Paper takes any ink," and as a young person I used that to look critically at the black marks on the pages of many books. Today we must remember that Google will take any type—just because someone said it does not mean it is true. There are sites on Google that will give you the willies about Islam. Some are set up by Islamophobes and others by extremist Muslim groups. My search for a hadith to cut and paste showed me an irresponsible translation. Google is a wonderful resource, but it is not a substitute for a pious teacher.

We became Muslim in the years before the internet. We could not look up a YouTube video about how to pray or ask a search engine about marriage rights and responsibilities. We had a few books, and to be honest, we found them unpalatable, so our resources were mighty thin. I (Tamara) found human beings to help me and eventually found my way without having any access to the internet while it was growing. Whereas I (Najiyah) fell prey to a lot of the misogyny, literalism, and harshness that ran rampant on the net in its early days. It took me decades to find human beings who would quench my thirst for real knowledge and spiritual upbringing. But today the net is The Resource. We recognize this, and so we say to you—bring yourself to that research. Use your intellect and common sense. If it feels wrong, it probably is. Find sites that are reliable and avoid sites that trial your faith. Take care of yourself when you walk the dangerous alleys of the internet. See Appendix B for some sites we recommend.

Your Healthy Heart

A third stumbling block that a convert can trip over if she does not use her mind and heart is the trap of law. Do not come to Islam as though it is a game with a rule book. It is not football with yellow flags and red flags, and our sheikhs are not refereeing in our game of life. Islam is a religion of over a billion people. It is flexible and gentle. The social rules are malleable and work to help us live a good life in peace, to keep our families together, to be able to worship God, our Merciful Creator. We will not change people's behavior by throwing a hadith at them or asking an imam to speak to them about the *fiqh* of a matter. Which is not to say that Islam is without rulings—quite the opposite. Sharia is a large body of rulings, opinions, laws, and debates. It is in its vastness that we can build a healthy spiritual life.

Begin to learn the rules of personal worship and spiritual growth. Think well of God and expect His mercy and help. Use all your faculties of problem-solving when faced with relationship difficulties and struggles in life rather than seeking a law to solve your troubles. Laws are there as a last resort, when all of our efforts with *taqwa*, gentleness, and kindness have failed. And we are not guaranteed that we can control another person's behavior with a law or a hadith. Our power lies in making our own choices.

In one township in New York, you can report your neighbor for poor grass-cutting skills, and they will be fined $1,000; for repeats, the fine may reach $10,000. That is the law. But if you report your neighbor, you won't have much neighborliness. So when do you decide to report your neighbor? You report them when their lawn becomes more important than the relationship. In Islam, we have ethics surrounding treatment of neighbors, and we also have laws and rights. Sharia is a body of laws meant to uphold a healthy society. Be careful of becoming addicted to finding the "right" law and the "right" answer. Avoid the stumbling block caused by leaving your mind and heart behind. Focus on knowing God and growing in faith. Find teachers who can take you by the hand and walk with you on this beautiful path.

Independence!

Declare your independence by strengthening your Muslimese so that words used every day have deep meaning for you, reviewing and consolidating the pillars of *ʿaqīda*, and filling your toolbox with Arabic, worship, good companions along the road, and your very own self. Now that you are a strong Muslim, with deep roots in the soil, a strong trunk and lovely fronds—let's learn how to grow fruit by learning how to manage all of our (now even more) complicated relationships.[85]

MODULE THREE

TEND YOUR TIES

3

MUSICAL WEBS

When we go through any transition in life, we may wind up lonely for a time. Moving to a new area leaves us lost. A divorce may separate us from not just our spouse but their family as well and perhaps an entire group of friends. Even going from elementary to secondary school landed us in an entirely new pool of people and potential activities. The opportunity to join new clubs and make new friends felt, at the beginning, like more of a challenge than a blessing. But it's a challenge we rose to. Our classes helped us meet new people, we joined this or that activity, and eventually we found our tribe. But as adults, cultivating new relationships is more difficult than it was when we were young, and when you throw in the added wrench of the many different cultures in mosques, it can look nigh on impossible. But we can learn to balance our treasured ties and find new connections as well. It just takes a more concerted effort.

It's often said that we are what we eat, but even more so, we are who we know. Our lives are lived within a web of relationships that begins with our parents and expands outward to include siblings, extended family, friends, teachers, coworkers, and acquaintances.

When we become Muslim, our web can expand and become more lovely and intricate. But at the same time, some threads can be tested. So we embark upon the adventure of tending new threads and old ones, both of which may need some extra nurturing. In the end, inshallah, our webs will be larger and more supportive.

PART ONE: PARENTS, FAMILY, AND OTHER PEOPLE WHO DIDN'T BUY A TICKET TO YOUR CONVERSION

Parents

The Quran doesn't say be good to your *Muslim* parents. The *ṣaḥāba* converted at a time when many of their parents were on the opposite side of an ongoing war, yet they interacted kindly with them. Islam doesn't ask us to ignore our parents, judge them, or cut ties with them. Allah will reward us for being friendly and gracious with our parents of other faiths (or no faith), even if we have to turn the volume down on Islamophobic News program to do so. They may not reciprocate at the moment, but oftentimes the more kindnesses we dole out, the more their hearts will soften.

Our families have spent a lifetime (ours) watching us form into the person we are—someone they think they know well, someone who reflects their culture, beliefs, and values. Most parents take it for granted that we will continue to reflect those qualities; they do not even consider the possibility of us taking a drastically different path. They know their children might identify with a different political party or be more or less permissive parents than they were, but it's assumed that we will eat the same foods, celebrate the same holidays, and worship (or not) in the same way they have always done. So when a child converts to a different faith, it feels like a family's bedrock of culture and values is being called into question, and they're suddenly faced with a stranger in their own dear child's skin. For many, it is not just experienced as loss but as rejection. And if one's parents are, for example, devout Christians, it is even worse, because it is not just about lifestyle choices but about salvation.

Some parents handle this exceptionally well, welcoming their child's new faith journey and seeking to support her however they can. But many parents experience a child's religious conversion as a trauma to one degree or another. They may argue, cry, or withdraw. They may cut off ties completely. They may insult the new path and seek to belittle it. They may pretend it doesn't exist. This can cut deeply for the new convert, who wishes nothing more than to bring her family to the same joy she has found. As you can imagine (or have experienced), this puts a new convert and her parents at cross-purposes.

Push Reset on Your Relationship

I (Najiyah) have a very clear memory of myself at about sixteen informing my dad that I didn't have to respect him because respect was earned. Oh yes, I was a big proponent of people earning their respect. Other people, that is. I myself could be as lazy and rebellious as I wanted and expect to be treated as an adult.

The truth, of course, is that treating others, especially our parents, with respect is a sign of the maturity I was so desperately grasping for. Little did I know, all I needed to navigate those waters was Islam!

Allah has provided us with a beautiful system for nurturing and even repairing family ties. One of the most important tenants of Islam is *bir al-wālidain*, or devotion to one's parents. It is step one in Operation: Push Reset. Allah says in Surat al-Isra᾿:

﴿ *And your Lord has decreed that you worship none but Him. And that you be dutiful to your parents. If one of them or both of them attain old age in your life, say not to them a word of disrespect, nor shout at them, but address them in terms of honor.* ﴾ (Q. 17:23)

وَقَضَىٰ رَبُّكَ أَلَّا تَعْبُدُوٓا إِلَّآ إِيَّاهُ وَبِٱلْوَٰلِدَيْنِ إِحْسَٰنًا ۚ إِمَّا يَبْلُغَنَّ عِندَكَ ٱلْكِبَرَ أَحَدُهُمَآ أَوْ
كِلَاهُمَا فَلَا تَقُل لَّهُمَآ أُفٍّ وَلَا تَنْهَرْهُمَا وَقُل لَّهُمَا قَوْلًا كَرِيمًا ﴿٢٣﴾

﴿ *And lower unto them the wing of submission and humility through mercy, and say: "My Lord! Bestow on them Your Mercy as they did bring me up when I was small."* ﴾ (Q. 17:24)

وَٱخْفِضْ لَهُمَا جَنَاحَ ٱلذُّلِّ مِنَ ٱلرَّحْمَةِ وَقُل رَّبِّ ٱرْحَمْهُمَا كَمَا رَبَّيَانِى صَغِيرًا ﴿٢٤﴾

This translation reads "say not to them a word of disrespect," but the actual word used in the Quran is "uff"—"Say not unto them even uff." God asks us to be very careful of the words we use with our parents, and to avoid even *noises* of disrespect, even in times of frustration or hurt. Think of all the times your parents have asked you to do something or told you the same old story *yet again*, and you've muttered under your breath (usually while rolling your eyes) "ufffff!" (or any other collection of letters that indicates annoyance). This is the degree to which God wants us to be good to our parents—to the degree that we don't even mutter "uff" or sigh in annoyance. We are to speak gently to them, spend money on them, honor them, and obey them in matters that don't contradict Islam.

To be a good Muslim means, in part, to be a good son or daughter and a good family member. It means being the one to reach out, the one to take care, the one to overlook.

Notice that this verse talks about our parents reaching old age—which means that it's addressing us *as adults*. As children, of course we respect our parents, but we can't slack off just because we have grown up and think we know better than they do. This is particularly hard in these times because technology has progressed so fast that the way the world works is different from how it worked when our parents were growing up. So it becomes tempting to think that since we understand communications and the internet better than they do, we understand everything better. But this is a trick. It's a trick that the children of immigrants can easily fall into as well. When parents from back home sometimes don't speak English well or understand how things work in the West, there may be a lot of "uffing" going on. But the truth is that even if our parents aren't best friends with Siri® or Alexa®, they have been where we are emotionally and intellectually, and they have learned things from their experiences that we haven't had the opportunity to learn yet, about people and relationships and behavior and its consequences. We call this wisdom, and knowing how to use newest social media app doesn't earn us any. So we have to remember to revere our parents.

Diseases that Affect our Family and Other Relationship Ties

Convertitis and Clingosis

There is a condition that new converts are particularly susceptible to, which can subvert even one's best intentions with parents and family. It is commonly referred to as convertitis, a term coined by Timothy Winter (Sheikh Abdal Hakim Murad). Symptoms of this dread disease include unbridled zeal, rabid proselytizing, and overt condescension. Victims often look down their noses and spout newly learned *āyah*s and hadiths, informing all and sundry of how they could do things better. Severe cases may include extreme judgmentalism and even bashing parents over the head with theological arguments.

Parents and family, on the other hand, may be suffering from converititis's mirror malady, clingosis, which can cause a convert's friends and family to adhere blindly to their own traditions and culture. Signs of clingosis include elevating the faith of origin; bitter digs at manifestations of the new religion, such as prayer or hijab; and religious discussion avoidance. Acute cases may result in kicking out or even disowning the new convert.

The good news is that both maladies can be treated. The reality is, though, that much of the treatment may have to be undergone by the convert alone, at least at first. Below are some prescriptions that have proven effective in battling these two conditions.

Treatments	
Convertitis	**Clingosis**
Deep Dose of Humility (five times daily) At each salat, bring to mind your parents' good qualities and characteristics.	**Hearing Tunnel** This device is one that the convert installs between her two ears, so that snide remarks and biting comments travel easily in one ear and out the other. Very useful in preventing the further progression of clingosis.
Injection of Patience Although you may be bubbling over with things you want to share, remember that your family may not be ready to hear them. Give your family time to adjust, and be kind to them during that process, even if they are not kind to you.	**Daily Deeds** This prescription is for daily acts of kindness that soften family members' hearts. Bring cookies, offer to stop at the store, fix the leaky faucet, or even just call them every day. Not many people can hold on to their anger in the face of such an onslaught of kindness.
Heaping Shovelfuls of Forbearance Some family members may cut you off. Some may sit together and laugh at you or insult you, even when you're sitting right there! Some may turn into social media scourges, venting vile ideas they are not able to say to your face. Allah (swt) teaches us in the Quran to respond to people of ignorance with peace ﴿ . . . *when the ignorant address them they respond with "Peace".* ﴾ (Q. 25:63) So meet their sharp tongues with a calm and polite response.	**Well-Timed Gift Capsules** We learn from the Prophet ﷺ that gifts soften hearts.[86] And miraculously, they soften the heart of both the giver and the receiver! So find small things you know your family members would like—even intangible things like babysitting time—and make *du'ā'* that their hearts melt.

Treatments	
Convertitis	**Clingosis**
Intravenous *Du'ā'* Some people feel as if *du'ā'* is a last resort in life. They only fall back on it if they can't change things physically. But the opposite is true. *Du'ā'* is the most powerful tool a believer possesses. Make good use of it. There is a lovely *du'ā'* for one's parents in Appendix C.	**Dietary Supplement of *Dhikr*** There is nothing lovelier than eating food you know someone made especially for you, unless it's eating food made for you that has been blessed with recitations of *lā ilāha illa Allāh* or blessings upon the Prophet ﷺ! Invite your family over or bake them sweets that you have recited *dhikr* over.
Intense *Bir al-Wālidain* Therapy There is a prayer that Imam al Ghazali recommended[87] recommend adding to your Friday eve worship routine (Thursday night). It consists of two *raka'as* with the following prescribed *sūras*: First *raka'a*: Surat al-Fatiha and fifteen Ayat al-Kursi Second *raka'a*: Surat al-Fatiha and fifteen Surat al-Ikhlas After the salat: twenty-five *ṣalāwāt* Intend the reward for this salat to go to your parents.	**Memorable Infusions** Create fun events that parents will remember: a movie night with you and the children, a special dinner where you cook the food of their childhoods, a road trip together, a day in the park, or a canoe trip down a local river. Any occasion you think of doing on your own, invite them to join you.

Tamara's Parents

I was living away from home when I became a Muslim, so I had a full six weeks of practicing my newfound faith and new style of dress before the first postconversion meetups with my parents. They are divorced, so it was a one-at-a-time challenge.

The first time my father saw me in hijab was also the first time I met his new lady friend, who would later become the mother of three more brothers. So I suppose we were both a little nervous. When I came up to the table he said, "What? Are you going to be one of those Moslems now?" and I—who had already been practicing Islam for six weeks—said, "I'm thinking about it." To my utter astonishment he said, "Well, you should, it's the most logical religion."

My mother, on the other hand, avoided the topic for ages. When she finally got up the gumption to say something, she tried to negotiate me out of my hijab by promising to quit smoking if I would stop wearing it. I really had nothing to say to that, so we silently agreed to stop bringing it up.

Now, so many years later, they are both huge supports in my life. I live next door to my mom and near to my dad. They cheer me on, listen to my stories of stress and challenge, and support our work at Rabata with their donations.

Najiyah's Parents

I lived far from my parents when I converted, so after a visit home, I left them a letter explaining my conversion. They took it about how I had expected—they were utterly devastated. And it didn't help that the letter was more than a smidge condescending (convertitis rearing its ugly head). Things were initially very strained, and my parents remained in active grief and anger for a long time. Things were made more difficult because I had fallen under the influence of some harsh people who insisted that parents could not be visited during Christmastime and that children's birthdays could not be celebrated at all. So that further alienated them. But slowly, things became more normal. Eventually my mom, God bless her, would babysit my kids while I was speaking about Islam at a church. She even said she was proud of all that I did for my faith. That is when I knew she had been able to make some peace with my decision. Recently, my mom was in the hospital, and when I told her I was sorry but I needed to step out to pray Zuhr, she said, "Yes, go pray. Pray hard for me, please."

When my mom eventually passed away, she asked us all if she was dying. No one answered so I said, "Mom, the angels are all surrounding you, protecting you, covering you with their wings." And she said, "I knew they were there because I saw <she made a hand gesture like when you flick water off your fingers onto someone>. I'm ready for them." And then at the moment of her death I prayed out loud, "Oh Allah, please accept Mom into Your mercy and protect us without her. Please help us live the way she taught us to live." None of this would have been possible 32 years ago when I converted.

"All this to say that there are as many kinds of reactions to conversion as there are families. So make take your IV du'a and keep up your injections of patience."

Extra Tools for the Relationship Trade

Of course writing the prescription is easy. Translating these treatments into reality is often much more difficult. Here are three things to remember that may ease your task of tending ties.

> I (Tamara) witnessed the mother of an adult convert come to Islam, and after she bore witness to her belief, she cried and apologized to her son for her anger and poor behavior when he became a Muslim. He cried, too. There is hope.

Authentic Interactions

Pretending you haven't become Muslim or acting like you don't wear hijab will not help you build a solid relationship with your family in the long run. Much of what has already been said in this section is really about bringing your authentic self to relationships. It is easier to sustain an authentic relationship, even when it is difficult, than to create a fake one and have to carry it along under all its heavy pretenses. Of course, that does not mean that you should shove your Islam down your family's throat. No one likes anything that's shoved in their face. Bring your Islam to them with extra kindness and care, and give them the time and emotional space to experience whatever reaction they have, while you remain kind, caring, and authentic.

Vulnerability

Vulnerability is often defined as holding space for others while keeping yourself in the arena with both courage and empathy. It's about being who you are with strength and good intentions while allowing others to experience their own emotions and be who they are without caving in to their desires for you.

Triangular Thinking

Instead of thinking about how horrible your family member is for saying X or Y, or how there is just no way you can deal with them for one more second, let alone get them to respect Islam, think in triangles. If you consider that God stands between you and every other human being, then you can think about your behavior as you would prefer God to see it, instead of just reacting. Similarly, you can remember that their behavior is seen by God as well and know that God will reward you for keeping ties of kinship, even (especially) when your feelings are hurt. And lastly, you will be comforted knowing that you're doing your best, and the mind-changing is God's department.

Resources for Adult Survivors of Abuse

- National Association of Adult Survivors of Child Abuse - http://www.naasca.org
- Child Welfare Information Gateway: Organizations for Adult Survivors of Abuse - https://www.childwelfare.gov
- Stop It Now! Resources and Support for Adults Who Experienced Sexual Abuse as Children - https://www.stopitnow.org
- National Association for People Abused in Childhood - https://napac.org.uk
- Co-dependents Anonymous (CODA) - https://coda.org/

Tying Ties with One Hand

There may be a period of time when a convert must maintain the ties of kinship single-handedly, as her family members retreat and take time to adjust.

Jayne's mother and father were visiting for Thanksgiving. They lived four hours away, so it was a treat to see them, even though it was awkward as they all danced around the topic of Jayne's recent conversion to Islam, talking instead about the university's new basketball coach and the ice storm they'd just had.

The turkey was tempting everyone with its succulent aroma when there was a knock at the door. It was the international student Jayne and her husband had invited to spend the otherwise lonely day with them.

Jayne's husband welcomed the young man as Jayne went into the bedroom to retrieve her scarf. When she saw her daughter emerge with her head covered, Jayne's mom was apoplectic. She began gathering her things, preparing to leave. As she regained her ability to speak, she informed Jayne that she would never be able to stand seeing her in her scarf. "That means we'll never be able to go anywhere in public," Jayne replied. It was her turn to be aghast.

"I don't care. I can't stand it," her mother insisted before she left, abandoning the turkey in its hour of service.

Emma's parents told her, "It would have been easier for us if you had died. At least we would be assured of your place in heaven."

Maria's mother stopped speaking to her, refused to meet her grandchildren, and forbade her husband from speaking to his daughter. He would sneak out to have coffee with Maria, while her mother remained aloof.

Theresa's mother told her when she complained of having to layer clothes because there were no summer dresses available with long sleeves, "Well, you shouldn't have such stupid rules then."

Stories are plentiful. Converts whose parents forbid them to pray in their house, converts hiding their fasting, young women taking off their scarves as soon as they enter the driveway of their parents' house. But these situations open the door for the new Muslim to show her family the kindness that is real Islam. And that's some of the most effective mind-changing medicine available.

If your family is overtly hostile, begin with the prescriptions for convertitis. This way, you strengthen and soften yourself as you prepare to reach out to your family. Deep doses of humility and intravenous *duʿāʾ* are perfect places to start. And a month or so of intense *bir al-wālidain* therapy will serve as a springboard to your clingosis treatments. As you establish the convertitis treatments as habits, also try sending snail mail notes, cards, or gifts (these can be as simple as a photo of your kids). Then work your way up. The idea is to put your family on project level. Make a special place in your heart for this new dynamic and a special time in your schedule for tending those ties.

Special Cases: Overcoming Dysfunction

Converts aren't immune to the circumstances and situations that plague the rest of society, and indeed it is sometimes those who are hurting desperately who are the most open to Allah's guidance. And although it isn't instantaneous, Islam does offer ways forward into the healing of oneself and one's relationships.

Situations where family has been dysfunctional for whatever reason are challenging, and old dynamics complicate the tending of ties. The residual effects of a difficult childhood or strained relationships don't just evaporate when we say our *shahāda*. So it is imperative that a convert deal with her own trauma and potentially destructive coping mechanisms. And if solitary reflection isn't enough, she should unashamedly seek professional assistance. Once her own issues are being dealt with and her physical safety isn't at risk, she can double down and get creative with her *bir al-wālidain.*

A person who has extreme challenges in her relationships with her family will have to come up with clever ways to support her parents. I (Najiyah) have a friend named Carla who was an angelic daughter to her mother, who suffered from paranoid schizophrenia. Carla couldn't care for her mom directly because every time she or her brother reached out, their mom became convinced they were part of a conspiracy to kill her. So Carla struck a workable balance, helping her mother by supplementing her rent payments and following how she was doing by keeping in touch with neighbors. At the end of her mother's life, she was able to be there and hold her hand and make *duʿāʾ* for her because she had kept that communication open with her neighbors.

Not Alone

If you find yourself trying to be devoted to a parent who has harmed or is actively harming you, take heart. You're in good company. Remember, the *ṣaḥāba* were converts too.

Saʿad ibn Abi Waqqas was one of the very first believers in Mecca. His mother, Hamna bint Abū Sufyan ibn al-Ḥārith, was appalled. How could her son leave the religion of his ancestors? She swore that she would not speak to him until he abandoned his new faith. When that didn't work, she tried to manipulate him with the very faith she was rejecting, "You claim that your God orders you to obey your parents. I am your mother, and I command you to abandon your religion or else I will neither eat nor drink until my death. You will then be dishonored among your people and called 'his mother's murderer.'" He tried to tell her not

Resources for Family Members of the Mentally Ill

- National Alliance on Mental Illness - https://www.nami.org
- American Psychological Association -https://www.apa.org
- PsychCentral - https://psychcentral.com
- Institute for Social Policy and Understanding - https://www.ispu.org
- Substance Abuse and Mental Health Services Administration - https://www.samhsa.gov

to starve herself, that he could not and would not leave his new faith, but she insisted. After three days, she fell faint, and when she regained consciousness (no doubt expecting her son to acquiesce), Sa'ad reiterated that nothing would make him leave Islam. Even seeing her thirsty, hungry, and unconscious did not cause him to waver.[88] Eventually, his mother gave up trying to manipulate him into disbelief. God says in the Quran, ﴾ *And We have enjoined upon humanity goodness to parents. But if they endeavor to make you associate with Me that of which you have no knowledge, do not obey them. To Me is your return, and I will inform you about what you used to do* ﴿ (Q. 29:8).

We do not have a record of what became of Sa'ad's mother, but we do know what became of Sa'ad. He became one of the closest companions to the Prophet ﷺ and is one of those given the good news of Paradise—a category of companions whose place in heaven was announced. The twenty million Muslims of China credit Sa'ad with bringing Islam to them. No doubt both his kindness to his mother and his firm refusal to return to disbelief contributed to the blessings of his later life.

Mus'ab ibn 'Umair also struggled with his mother. When he became a Muslim, he kept it secret, afraid his mother, Khunnas bint Malik, might find out. She was known to be a staunch believer in the religion of her ancestors. But one day, someone saw him leave Dar al-Arqam, the place where the Muslims met in secret, and that person ran and told Mus'ab's mother. She was furious. Mus'ab was just a teenager and had been pampered his whole life. His mother thought that if she stripped him of everything she had given him, he would relent. She imprisoned him in the house, chained him in the darkest room, starved him, and left him in isolation. Even in this condition, and even though he was so young, he held on to his faith. One day, he broke free of the chains, snuck away from the guards she had set to keep him imprisoned, and escaped to Abyssinia with the other Muslims who had been able to make the trip. Later, he would be sent as the Prophet's ﷺ first ambassador to Medina. He survived his mother's terrible treatment and helped build the nascent Muslim community.[89]

During the *hijra,* Um Salama left Mecca intending to travel to Medina with her husband and son, only to be overtaken by their relatives. They took her young son from her, claiming that family privilege gave them the right to keep him back. She tried to prevent them from taking him, fighting for her new faith and the right to raise her child in the light of Islam, but the child's relatives pulled on him until the toddler's shoulder was dislocated. Then the family of Abū Salama took the child and refused to allow him to go to Medina. Um Salama became a captive of her own tribe and the child a captive of Abū Salama's tribe. It was an entire year before a family member took pity on her and she was allowed to go to Medina with her son. Um Salama would later become one of the Mothers of the Believers when, after her husband died, she married the Prophet ﷺ.[90]

Salman al-Farisi was the son of a priest of Magianism. When he first saw the light of guidance, it was in the hearts of some early Christians. When his father saw that he was interested in another religion, he imprisoned him. Salman was able to escape and follow the Christians to their land, where he would live with one bishop after another, until the last one told him that there were no more priests alive who believed as he did and that the time had arrived for a new prophet to appear. Salman found himself in Medina as a slave and later became one of the members of the Prophet's ﷺ household.[91]

All of these companions endured great emotional and physical pain at the hands of their parents and relatives because of their faith. Much of what they endured would be defined by us today as abuse (at the very least). But they remained steadfast, honest, and kind. And with the right support and copious amounts of the medicines prescribed for convertitis and clingosis, you can too.

Family Gatherings, Holidays, and Other Stuff about Getting Together

Grueling Gatherings

With family comes gatherings. Whether it's Christmas dinner, a funeral, or a graduation, there will be many events that call for close contact with one's extended family. Sometimes even the joyful occasions can be difficult for converts, though, because they involve being in the midst of people who not only don't understand your new path or the reasons you chose it but also may be curious, disparaging, or downright belligerent. This is not to mention the sometimes challenging nostalgic feelings that may accompany holidays and other family gatherings. There's your brother Morgan, who wants to know what the Quran says about abortion; your cousin Josh, whom you overhear asking his dad what your problem is; and good ol' Uncle Patrick with the Islamophobic bumper stickers, who feels it's his solemnly sworn duty to inform you of how evil Islam is, as evidenced by "the news" and a few broken, mistranslated verses from the "Koran" that he heard parroted by his favorite radio host.

These situations can be tricky, but a few rules of thumb can help create a smoother experience.

1. Keep yourself busy, either in the kitchen or with cleanup duty or parking the cars—anything that will allow you to contribute something positive while minimizing potentially combustible situations.
2. Serve, serve, serve with a bright, open smile. Bring people another cup

of tea, pass around the pie, bring your grandma a pillow to put behind her back. Make yourself the person who takes care of others, and they will hesitate to badmouth you. Most of them, anyway. There are some people you could be kind to all day long without it making an iota of difference. That's OK. Keep serving. It's not about how they act; it's about who you are. It's about loving for the sake of Allah, even when it's a challenge. It's about strengthening your relationship with Allah by serving His creation, even when that creation is scowling back at you.

3. If someone is verbally abusing you, remove yourself from their physical company. But the occasional snide remark can be overlooked.
4. Remember, you don't have to stay at family gatherings from the cooking until the last car pulls out. There's something to be said for just putting in an appearance. You can drop by to offer your congratulations and give your gift, sit for one piece of cake, and then gush that you wish them the best and look forward to being together again soon. Done. Fifteen to thirty minutes is usually enough, unless your immediate family members are the hosts.
5. Keep your sense of humor honed and at the ready.

ACTIVITY: ANTICIPATE POSSIBLE ISSUES

- Imagine scenarios where you might need to avoid alcohol at a family gathering, and brainstorm ways to do that.
- What is your family's communication style? How does that affect your ability to communicate your needs? For them to hear your needs?
- Role-play a visit to your mother. Now do the same but bring along a friend. Does the role-play change at all? Would it be helpful to bring a friend when you visit family?

Holidays

Of course most of the family gatherings people attend are celebrations of one type or another. Finding a balance between one's family and one's new faith in this regard can be a huge issue for new Muslims. Christmas or Rosh Hashanah, for example, are especially difficult since they often carry so much nostalgia for both a convert and her parents, and since people in the Muslim community may advise her to simply shun these celebrations altogether.

But joining one's family while they celebrate this or that holiday is not the same as celebrating these holidays ourselves. By attending our family's Christmas brunch, we are not claiming that it is a holiday to us. We are simply recognizing a regional tradition and, more importantly, recognizing the importance of our family's traditions, and thus their hearts.

When weighing whether or not to attend family gatherings at holiday time, remember that not all holidays are created equal. When looking at a holiday, we have to decide where it stands in relation to our core beliefs (*ʿaqīda*) in order to decide whether we will join our families when they celebrate it or not.

Below is a list of holidays and ways of thinking about them that may help converts in deciding how to proceed.

Holiday: New Year's Day - January 1

Description: Marks the beginning of the Gregorian calendar. Often celebrated with alcohol and dancing.

Things to Consider: This is Islamically neutral. There's nothing wrong with marking the beginning of the year, but celebration methods may need to be modified.

Ideas: Invite family over for board games, maybe fall down in *sujūd* (prostration) at midnight.

Holiday: Valentine's Day - February 14

Description: Originally the Roman celebration Lupercalia, the Church appropriated this to commemorate Saint Valentine. Now it is a celebration of (mostly romantic) love.

Things to Consider: Love is a perfectly healthy emotion, and we can celebrate its many halal incarnations.

Ideas: Some Muslims have repurposed Valentine's Day as a day to focus on love for the Prophet ﷺ. (See letterstothebeloved.com.)

If your family does something on Valentine's Day, you could join them, focusing your love on your children, parents, or spouse.

Holiday: Easter - the first spring Sunday

Description: Commemorates the Christian belief in the (crucifixion and) resurrection of Prophet ʿIsa ؑ.

Things to Consider: Trinitarian Christianity is based on the belief that Jesus (as both God and man) had to be sacrificed in order for God to be able to forgive our sins. Unlike Christmas, which celebrates Prophet ʿIsa's birth and is something

that is not incompatible with Islam, Easter is theologically incompatible with *tawhīd*, and we need to be thoughtful about this in our decision-making.
Ideas: We don't encourage participation.

Holiday: April Fools' Day - April 1
Description: This holiday has its roots in Europe, where a day was set aside for pranks and tomfoolery
Things to Consider: Any prank that harms or embarrasses someone is not permitted in Islam. Lying is also not permitted.
Ideas: We don't encourage participation.

Holiday: Mother's Day - the second Sunday in May
Description: An almost universal holiday to revere and appreciate moms. This is celebrated in much of the world in March but in the US in May.
Things to Consider: Appreciating Mom is always on point Islamically. Setting aside a specific day to do it ensures that everyone acknowledges Mom together and she feels honored in a special way.
Ideas: Traditional ways of celebrating Mother's Day abound – from making Mom breakfast in bed to taking her out to brunch to bringing her flowers. Whatever way you normally honor your mother is wonderful – or you can make an even more concerted effort to make the day special for her, since Islam honors mothers so much.

Holiday: Memorial Day - the last Monday in May
Description: This day is set aside to remember those who have died serving in the armed forces. This commemoration has spread to all those in one's family who have passed on. Many families camp or picnic.
Things to Consider: Remembering those who have gone before us is a commendable act in Islam. Remember also that there are many Muslim women and men in the armed forces around the world.
Ideas: We could use this as a reminder of our own mortality and an encouragement to strengthen our relationship with Allah.

Holiday: Independence Day - July 4 (in the US)
Description: Celebration of a country's founding or gaining of independence. Communities gather to picnic and watch fireworks displays.
Things to Consider: Loyalty to the country you were raised in is part of religion (even as you recognize the mistakes in its history).
Ideas: This is a great day to spend time with family and enjoy fun activities.

Holiday: Halloween - October 31

Description: Pagan in origin and Christianized in the Middle Ages by being merged with All Saints' Day, this holiday is celebrated in the States by getting ghoulish and dressing up in costumes. Children go trick or treating.

Things to Consider: This holiday, like almost all Christian holidays, has a pagan origin. The Celts celebrated it as Samhain, which was their new year. They believed that the lines between the seen and unseen world were blurred on that day. Romans adapted it into Feralia, their equivalent of Memorial Day. In the eighth century, Pope Gregory III moved All Martyrs' Day from May 13 to November 1 and redefined it to include all saints; most believe this was done to replace the pagan practice with a church observance. The next day was dubbed All Souls' Day and celebrated all who had passed. It was still celebrated with bonfires and dressing up, but became (and still is) a major Catholic time of remembrance and praying for the dead. In the eighteenth and nineteenth centuries, immigrants brought various Halloween customs to America, and in the early twentieth century, there was a concerted effort to remove "the superstitious and religious overtones" from Halloween, in addition to the pranks it had been known for. It became for most a night of dressing up, attending parties, and trick or treating with kids.

As Muslims, we always want to avoid occult-leaning practices or activities. We don't pull pranks, believe in ghosts, or glorify evil characters. Children participating in parades at school, however, can be considered differently.

Ideas: There is nothing inherently wrong with dressing up, or even going door-to-door for candy (Kuwaitis and some other cultures do this in Ramadan). Parents need to make decisions based on their children's ages when they entered Islam, their temperaments, and their individual situations.

Holiday: Thanksgiving - the third Thursday in November in the US. In Canada, it falls in October.

Description: A traditional day of thanks, commonly believed to have been first celebrated by a group of pilgrims after surviving their first year. The story goes that they celebrated the harvest with the First Nations people who had helped them grow and reap it.

Things to Consider: This is a prime holiday for family get-togethers. In the US, Thanksgiving and Christmas are often the only times in the year when an entire family may gather. Giving thanks is a very Islamic practice, as is spending time with family.

Ideas: Invite the family to your house, so as to avoid alcohol and pork products. Offer to say grace if your family concludes it with "in Jesus's name." Enjoy the parade, the football, and the nice fall weather, and be fully present with your family.

Holiday: Christmas Day - December 25
Description: Commemorates the birth of Prophet ʿIsa 🌿, whom Trinitarian Christians believe to be the son of God and/or God Himself.
Things to Consider: Muslims believe in the virgin birth of Prophet ʿIsa 🌿, and though we know it didn't occur in the winter (as do Christians), and we don't believe Prophet ʿIsa 🌿 is God incarnate, we do believe in his miraculous birth and life. Also, keep in mind that this holiday is often extremely important to our societies and families. Refusing to partake in these family gatherings could result in lasting damage to relationships.
Ideas: We can bring our own beliefs to their celebrations and please our parents by joining in their joy as part of tending our ties.

Winter

The winter holidays are often the most challenging in the calendar for Western converts. Many families plan their entire winter break around the holidays, and Thanksgiving, Christmas, and Hanukkah are times of great community and familial good cheer. Long-standing traditions, such as cookie and pie baking, eggnog drinking, and hall decking, serve as tent stakes of family togetherness. These are often, in our families' points of view, the ties that bind.

A daughter or son who sheds their heritage faith is hard enough for parents to swallow; a child who then refuses to participate in family traditions of love and togetherness alienates them to an extremely painful degree (trust us on this).

A prominent twentieth century Egyptian scholar writes that "Maintaining ties, giving gifts, making visits, and congratulating non-Muslims are acts of goodness. God has enjoined us to say good things to everyone without exception."[92] The Prophet 🌿 sent gifts to people of other faiths and accepted gifts from them as well. There is no harm in participating in kind acts between family members. God knows your heart. You are not replacing your new holidays with your old ones, rather you are doing your best to be good to your family.

There are some who claim it is haram even to greet people of other faiths on their holidays, but these advisors are missing several vital pieces of information.

The first is that Christians and Jews belong to a unique category, that of People of the Book, and are addressed as such in the Quran. It is such a different category that we are allowed to eat their meat, whereas we are forbidden from eating the meat of polytheists. Even if your family actually are pagans or atheists, remember that the Prophet ﷺ once sent 500 dinars to the polytheists of Mecca during a drought. He sent money as a gift to help his kin.[93] Kindness brings guidance much quicker than harshness.

With this in mind, we must remember that in all things there is a weighing of the potential good or harm that stands to be done. To say "Merry Christmas" or to attend the annual cookie-baking afternoon with your family does not violate any Islamic precept, because it's neither a confirmation of a belief system nor a celebration of that holiday. As noted above, we believe in Prophet ʿIsa ﷺ and his miraculous birth, and there is no harm in baking cookies. On the other hand, to shun these celebrations or rudely ignore your family's good wishes can result in aggrieving them greatly, and this is the opposite of tending one's ties.

Of course, if your family's eggnog is the spiked kind or if you're invited to midnight mass, then these are different situations. But giving and receiving gifts and otherwise honoring your family and remaining in their bosom during the holidays is a wonderful way to show them that your new faith fills you with love and joy and holds them in a place of respect and high esteem. You can then invite them to your ʿEid celebrations as well.

A Spoonful of Patience

Occasionally while spending time with family, there may be little incidents that make you feel uncomfortable. Use your creativity to overcome these and find new ways to bring happiness to everyone. Stacie's family had a habit of holding hands while saying grace at large family dinners, and the prayers usually ended with "in Jesus's name we pray, amen." So Stacie asked that her thirteen-year-old son be given the honor of saying grace (she had prepped him ahead of time). Her family was thrilled, and this simple solution allowed her son to feel special and her family to see that Islam is not a "strange" or "foreign" religion. She solved her problem with grace and love and avoided harshness and drama.

Love usually overcomes hate, and patience wins against abrupt reactions. These are traits all parents would like to see in their children, and when they see that Islam has nurtured them in you, they will hopefully take off their Islamophobic-colored glasses and see more clearly.

Holidays at Home—Kids Included

The above discussion centers around celebrating your family's holidays with them. In a Muslim household, Christmas is not generally celebrated in any way, for all the reasons we can recite forwards and backwards. But there can be exceptions to this, depending on your children's ages and stages when you converted.

If you have children who are elementary age or older and who would miss Christmas enough to resent Islam if it were to be, in their eyes, suddenly snatched away, having a Christmas tree and exchanging gifts while they make the transition may be the healthiest way to go. Suddenly not having Christmas is hard enough for one who has made the decision that she believes in Islam; imagine what it would feel like to an eleven-year-old who doesn't really get this new adventure to begin with. It's not sinful to leave the rug underneath them while they adjust (and put a tree on top of it). A person who converts when her children are young can arrange her entire household culture around Islam and its holidays and celebrations and be perfectly fine. But if your children are sixteen and twelve when you convert, for example, you have to go about things differently.

Each person will have things that are extremely important to her and others she cares less about. Alicia, a convert in Minnesota, converted when her oldest was sixteen. Her children were used to Christmas and big family events. Alicia didn't take those celebrations away from her children but rather added Islamic celebrations into the mix. This willingness to respect her children's feelings and experiences enabled her to demand that her children respect her new faith, even though they didn't necessarily agree with her decision or understand her hijab. Alicia found that creating a two-way street made the road smoother for all.

Birthdays

Muslims run the gamut regarding birthdays. Some claim that they are haram to acknowledge, much less celebrate, and others are willing to spend thousands of dollars on children's birthdays to keep up with the Ahmads. So what is the ruling around birthdays? As we've seen with so many other things, birthdays are about what we intend and how we behave. Again, remembering non-Muslim family members' birthdays is important to them, and thus it is an important part of tending those ties. Birthdays offer a chance to make people feel loved, and this goes a long way toward beautifying their attitudes toward both you and Islam.

As for ourselves and our nuclear families, birthdays are a great time to reflect on the year that has passed and to hold ourselves accountable for striving toward our goals. Below are some ways that Muslim families have adapted birthday celebrations for themselves or their children to reflect their Islamic practice.

Managing Our Muslim Holidays

As people who grew up in the West, we naturally have loads of nostalgia around the dominant holidays of our childhood culture. When I lived far from my family, I got homesick every summer because I was missing the big Independence Day barbecue. But we don't have to spend a lifetime pining for the old days—we can create new traditions that we will begin to feel nostalgia for. And more importantly, our children will look back on our traditions with the same feelings of fondness and love that we have for our favorite holidays. If we treat Ramadan, *Eid al-Fitr*, and *Eid al-Adha* with the same sense of joy and togetherness, our children will feel that special, tender emotion when they come around each year. We can also find other days in the Islamic calendar to commemorate and build traditions around, such as ʿAshuraʾ, the Prophet's birth month, Rajab, and Shaban.

Ramadan

Make Ramadan unique and special, beginning with anticipation of the month. Here are some ways to celebrate:

1. Sight the moon. Even if your community calculates the month, you can take the children out to look for the moon.
2. Plan a special first *suḥūr* that you will then repeat annually.
3. Create an angel-filled home environment.
4. Let children attempt fasting. Honor your children's efforts to join in the spiritual season, even if they only manage to fast for an hour or part of a day.
5. Divide Ramadan into three parts. Ramadan is traditionally divided into three ten-day periods: the Days of Mercy, the Days of Forgiveness, and the Days of Freedom from Hellfire. Mark the beginning of each period with a special family *duʿāʾ*.
6. Commemorate important dates. The Battle of Badr took place on the 17th of Ramadan, Fatḥ Mecca took place on the 21st of Ramadan, and the Night of Power (the night the first verses of the Quran were revealed) is looked for on the odd nights in the last third of Ramadan. This is a good time to pray extra prayers and make lots of *duʿāʾ* for and with your family.

Create this nostalgia whether or not you have children. Your heart is important, too, and taking care of it by building attachments to new holidays is a crucial part of spiritual growth.

Fun Nostalgia-Building Activities for Ramadan
Create a Ramadan calendar. Each day in Ramadan, allow your children to open a little pocket or cubby and get a small gift, like a sweet, a sticker, or a small decoration to hang. As children get older, you can attach a task to the gift: "Fast until noon and open a prize," or "Pray Maghrib with the family and open a gift."
Make traditional *suḥūr* treats and fast-breaking delicacies. I (Tamara) lived for years in Syria and treated my family to a taste of home with made-from-scratch cinnamon rolls on the first morning of Ramadan, while Najiyah's grown children still look forward to Ramadan-only pizza bites for *suḥūr* on the first day.
Decorate. Make Ramadan festive and lend it its own atmosphere and traditions! Many converts decorate with lanterns. Julia, a convert in Michigan, adds one lantern to her collection every year. Now that her children are older, they buy one for her every Ramadan, and the place is alight with a soft glow that makes its own atmosphere.
Craft. All the crafts that we did as children can be modified for our own children for use as Ramadan activities. Remember construction paper chains? Make one with your children and add a chain every day. Or take away a chain every day. Or just make long ones and decorate the house with them.
Get in the moon mood. Ramadan decorations often involve crescent moons. Make paper plate moons, buy moon-shaped knickknacks, or get moon-shaped wall stencils. Add some pretty stars to fancy it up.

Eid al-Fitr

One of the great things about Islamic holidays is that they commemorate accomplishments. Eid al-Fitr celebrates the individual accomplishment of fasting the month of Ramadan. Unlike the holidays of our youth, we often come to this holiday exhausted and glad to eat in the light of day—and possibly without the energy to do much else. Be careful of holding yourself to a standard of celebration that you cannot maintain. Be gentle with yourself and remember that there are three days of this Eid. What you don't do on day one can be done on days two or three. Invite your parents, neighbors, colleagues, and friends to your celebrations, but maybe do that on the third day or the first weekend after Eid.

1. Prophetic Way - Fasting on one's birthday is a great way to express gratefulness to Allah.
2. Birthdays in Reverse - Some families have the birthday person buy gifts for the rest of the family or for their mom specifically. This teaches gratitude and the joy of giving.
3. Year in Review - Birthday celebrations in some families include a look back at what one has learned in the past year and setting goals for the year to come. These can be written in a birthday journal that's written in every year.
4. Birthday Classics - Traditional birthday celebrations, especially for children, don't include any forbidden activities. Combining these with any of the above, or your own ideas is one way to balance the celebrations.

In many cultures, this holiday traditionally involves lots of baking and visiting. Each culture has its own Eid treats, and as a convert you have the glorious power of deciding which of your favorite treats will be your family's traditional Eid go-tos. Perhaps your German grandmother's *Pfeffernüsse* cookies, or your Puerto Rican *tembleque*, or maybe a smooth, sweet date milkshake will be among your first-day treats. In many Muslim countries, traditional treats are served to guests, who come calling in large numbers on each day of Eid. When I (Najiyah) lived in Syria, the three days of ʿEid were dedicated to different activities. Day one was to visit and honor the matriarchs and patriarchs, day two was for visiting aunts and uncles, and day three was for teachers, neighbors, and friends. Back home in the States, day one for our family was for eating brunch after the prayer at Cracker Barrel and then taking a long nap. Days two and three were either camping trips or, as the kids got older, were often swallowed up into regular life, since everyone still had work or school the next day. But Cracker Barrel was nonnegotiable.

Some communities host activities for their members. Many mosques provide a catered or potluck brunch for their congregants after the ʿEid prayer. Other communities provide carnivals for the kids or sponsor trips to the arcade or the skating rink.

Many Muslim cultures give out money to children on the first day of Eid, and this can feel foreign to those of us raised in the West. But there's no reason for our family members to have to abandon their traditions from home. In Elizabeth's family, her husband gives the kids money and takes them to the toy store, while Elizabeth wraps gifts for them that they open on Eid evening. This way, everyone's customs are uplifted and enjoyed. Think of it as a bonus!

It is sunna for everyone in the family to wear new clothes on Eid. Farah buys new clothes for her children in the weeks before Ramadan so that on Eid, when they wake, they have entirely new outfits laid out. From dresses and tights and shoes to belts and ties. If that's too much for the family budget, one new thing will do, even if it's socks. Even clothes we already own can be made spiffy with a quick ironing and a flower or one of Mom's brooches pinned on.

Eid al-Adha

Eid al-Adha is special in that part of its celebration is to slaughter a lamb or other animal. For families who do this, a trip to the farm to choose a lamb can be part of the festivities. This provides a good opportunity for children to see the circle of life and appreciate the sacrifice of Prophet Ibrahim (a). My (Najiyah's) son-in-law Abdurrahman, a second-generation Syrian-American, fondly remembers his Eid trips to the farm in Oklahoma.

> I remember the warm rays of the sun gently beaming down on my cheeks while my father chose a lamb to slaughter. After agreeing on a price with the shepherd, we took the lamb and walked through the beautiful lush field with it, stroking and caressing its wooly back. I remember him saying "assalamu alaikum" to the lamb, and I wondered, *do sheep speak Arabic?* He then had me do the same. He fed it a handful of freshly picked green grass with his bare hands, then filled a bowl with water and quenched its thirst. I remember the supplications he recited, asking God to accept his sacrifice and to bless him, his family, and all Muslims across the world on this blessed 'Eid day. I remember the calm clearly experienced by both us and the lamb. My father laid the animal down onto the soft grass facing the *qibla*, gently covering its eyes with its floppy ears and, while reciting "bismillah, Allahu akbar," he performed a clean swipe with a very sharp blade, severing the carotid arteries. The animal maintained is composure and calm demeanor throughout the process, as if even it had known exactly what was occurring, and had understood the meaning of its sacrifice. His flesh would go on to feed the needy and the family of the man who slaughtered him. Even as a young child, this seemed completely natural and innocuous to me. The lesson I take now as an adult, having performed this sacrifice multiple times myself, is the importance of continuing this holy ritual, and by doing so, honoring the sacrifice of Prophet Abraham (a) and commemorating the tradition of Prophet Muhammad ﷺ.

These memories are now being passed on to my granddaughter, as Abdurrahman and my daughter Jenan continue this Eid al-Adha tradition.

Below are some Eid ideas previous Project Lina attendees have suggested, along with space for you to write your own.

	Ideas from Project Lina Work-shops	My Ideas
Food	1. Traditional regional food one day and traditional international food the next	
	2. Dishes from all over the Muslim world, honoring the people from all the different communities who are completing the rites of hajj	
Decorations	1. White and green twinkle lights	
	2. Lanterns	
Smells	1. Special incense	
	2. Cinnamon rolls in the oven	
	3. Scented candles	
Clothes	1. New nightgowns/pajamas for ʿEid night	
	2. New clothes	
Activities	1. A sheep piñata	
	2. A family movie	
	3. Gifts that "appear" in the morn-ing but aren't opened until after the prayer	
Community and family	1. A sisters' get-together to make holiday sweets (pies, cookies, sweets from other cultures)	
	2. Visits to the elderly or those who might feel lonely during ʿEid days	
	3. Invitations to family members of other faiths to your celebrations or visits to them in your ʿEid clothes	

Ashura, which falls on the 10th of Muharram, was originally commemorated (and still is) in the Jewish faith as Yom Kippur (The Day of Atonement). It was honored also by the Prophet ﷺ when he saw the Jews of Medina fasting on it. It is recommended that Muslims fast both the 9th and 10th or the 10th and 11th.

This day has a bit of a different meaning for Shiʿi Muslims than for Sunni Muslims. Shiʿis mourn the martyrdom of Ḥussain (the son of ʿAlī ؓ and the grandson of the Prophet ﷺ) and display their grief with sad processions and sometimes self flagellation. In Syria, Bosnia, and other places, a special sweet bean pudding that is served only at this time of year is sold from pushcarts and made up in festive family kitchens. Converts can commemorate this day by choosing a favorite restaurant or heirloom dish to break their fast with and carry that tradition forward every year. Duas for forgiveness are also a blessed way to spend this day, especially in the quarter hour before breaking fast.

Mawlid al Nabi

The Prophet's ﷺ birthday is not celebrated on one special day; it is beautifully celebrated as a season of remembrance, praise, and love. The entire month of his birth is a time when Muslims gather in homes and mosques to hear poetry about his life and his attributes ﷺ and share sweets like Jordan almonds with their guests, especially the children. In Egypt children get a special candy made of caramelized nuts and coconut. The girls receive a doll and the boys receive a toy man on a horse. In Lebanon the boy scouts march in the streets and people gather in homes for remembrance parties. A reciter is invited to regale guests with poetry praising the Prophet ﷺ, and the hosting family spends an afternoon sitting around the table making little pouches of candied almonds and other sweets to be passed out to the guests as they depart. Chinese Muslims have traditionally held festivals where children put on programs and painting and calligraphy contests are held.

Converts can make the Mawlid al Nabi fun, especially for their children, by finding creative ways to gift them candy or other treats. By getting together to make dhikr or hear poetry, or by enlivening the house with hand-crafted decorations and twinkly lights. Joining the Rabata mawlid observance by adding your salawat (prayers of blessings and peace on the Prophet ﷺ) to those of sisters all over the globe is also a great way to feel the warmth and guidance of our Beloved ﷺ.

PART TWO: FRIENDS

"Miss Barry was a kindred spirit after all," Anne confided to Marilla, "You wouldn't think so to look at her, but she is. . . Kindred spirits are not so scarce as I used to think. It's splendid to find out there are so many of them in the world." -LM Montgomery, Anne of Green Gables

Tamara's Friend Story

When I (Tamara) was four years old, I had a naughty little friend who fed me an entire bottle of Flintstones vitamins. At eleven years old, my best friend and I dressed exactly alike and went to downtown St. Paul to ride the elevators in turns trying to confuse the bank workers. At sixteen, I would drive two of my friends to a local restaurant and we would skip class in order to eat whole wheat pancakes. I also had friends that I prayed with and have more than one embarrassing memory of praying loudly in restaurants and accosting people, calling on them to be "saved by Jesus." Friends are the stuff of memories, adventure, hilarity, and fun.

I became a Muslim in my first year of university. Yet to meet new friends, and now distant from my old, it was a lonely time. Hence my first real effort as a sparkling new Muslim young woman was to find some friends.

It was a struggle. The pickings were limited and I was used to having a gaggle of friends. Slowly, I met Muslim women. In fact, if I am honest, searching out new friends was probably one of my most important adulting activities of those young years. For the first time in my life I was not in the middle of dozens of people who looked like me, believed like me, ate like me, and lived like me. I had to go out and find some women who could walk with me on my newly chosen journey of faith.

My new convert friend, for example, had an educational and economic background that was so vastly different from mine that she was the first person I had ever met from either demographic. She was also ten years older than I was and already had two children in tow. My Malaysian friends ate food that made my eyes water, spoke in gentle tones, and moved with grace. I ate mashed potatoes, spoke loudly, and moved more like a bull in a china shop. I met some more new convert friends. One was Mexican-American and the other was from a small town in Minnesota. Then another friend came to town, older than me but young at heart. We became bosom buddies and would dream together about the future of Muslim education.

I grew as a person because I needed to find new friends, but what of my old friends? We fell out of touch. These were the days before social media connections, and my high school friends were all over the United States pursuing vastly different activities. It would be twenty years before I heard news of anyone, only to hear of a death, and thirty years before I met up with any friend of my younger years. I have mixed feelings about this and certainly wish I had done a better job of staying in touch. But those years were tumultuous and intense. I had all I could do to walk forward as a new Muslim, finish university, tend my family ties, get married, have children, and continue my Islamic education.

Throughout the years I have laughed till I cried with friends, found myself in deep grief because of friends, and relied on friends to drag me up and out of my personal trials. Today I am who I am because of the friends who stand next to me, pushing me and holding me accountable and the friends who live in every corner of the world praying for me and loving me, reminding me that a sisterhood of faith does indeed run deeper than oceans and wider than great savannahs. May Allah preserve them and grant everyone reading these words wonderful friends who uplift and love them as the companions uplifted and loved one another.

Najiyah's Friend Story

When I became Muslim I was alone, friend-wise. I had acquaintances from work, but hadn't lived in my college town long and so hadn't met anyone who was "my kind of weird," as they say. But as soon as I took my shahada, Allah sent me Layla. Layla was an old hand at being a convert. Her boys were four and two, and she had even been to Iran and met her in-laws. I was in awe of her.

Layla taught me how to pin my scarf, how to shop for hijabable clothes, how to cook rice. Her younger son was named Muhsin, and she used to say, "No way, Mo-sain!" and laugh. She was delicate and devout and I owe her so much, for she guided me through what would otherwise have been a jarring and rocky transition.

Soon it was time for me to move, and although it wasn't far, I was sad to leave Layla. But Allah rescued me again with Christine and Hannah. These two turned out to be kindred spirits and remain so to this day. Hilarious and down-to-earth, compassionate and loyal, these are the kinds of friends who are always there for you, even in silence. No matter how much time has gone by, you can pick up right where you left off. We keep each other grounded and accountable with virtual hugs when necessary and a good smack when that's what's called for.

Several of my friends from high school look askance at me now or don't look at me at all, with one intent on enlightening me about my impending damnation every chance she gets. But the ones I do maintain friendships with are wonderful.

Old friends serve as both touchstones and envoys. They share your past and can stand by you in the present. My high school friends fiercely stand up for Muslims when allyship is needed. Hearts of gold and arms ready to welcome you anytime, the friends who stay past your conversion are true gems. May Allah bless our friends, new and old, and bless us through them. If you haven't found yours yet, keep making du'a for friends and keep putting yourself out there in caring ways.

Friends in the Sira

The Arabian peninsula previous to the revelation was a place of tribal bonds and alliances. During the Meccan stage of the dawah, we see some of the closest companions abused and oppressed because of their lack of social status. We might recognize close relationships between Abū Bakr and the first six men who came to Islam at his hand. Perhaps they had been good friends for years and their friendship was finally brought to a unique beauty through Islam. We also see the loss of friends. There came a day when men of Quraysh, including 'Utba b. Rabi'a, abused Abū Bakr to such a degree that his face became bruised and bloodied so that you could not distinguish his nose from his face. When his clan heard of this they rushed to his defense (his clan would have included many disbelievers, who rushed to his defense not out of loyalty to his new faith, but because it was a society built on these types of ties).[94] But previous to Islam we can assume that Abū Bakr was friends with the likes of 'Utba ibn Rabi'a and Walīd ibn al Mughīra (another of the polytheists who abused the Muslims). Abū Bakr and all the Meccan Muslims lost friends and allies when they embraced Islam. We do not read about this in the *sīra* books because what they *gained* was the story of the day. They gained the love of the Prophet, revelation, Islam, and a great and glorious future.

The Medinan period brought about a change in relationships. One of the first things that the Prophet did upon entering Medina was to create bonds of brotherhood between the Muhājirīn - Muslims from Mecca, and the Ansar - Muslims from Medina. He was redefining friendship. He pulled them out of their tribal alliances and taught them what friendship based on faith could be. Friendship stories abound in the accounts of Medina. When 'Abdullāh ibn Rawāḥa became a Muslim, one of his first thoughts was his good friend, and still polytheist, Abū al Darda' (may God be ever pleased with them both). He hatched a plan and put it into action. ʿAbdullāh stood hiding outside Abū al Darda'’s home waiting for him to anoint his idol, cover it, and bid it farewell. ʿAbdullāh ﷺ then went quietly and quickly into his home and entered the room where the idol sat. He smashed it with his axe. ʿAbdullāh ibn Rawāḥa ﷺ did not do this out of excess zeal against idolatry but out of deep love for his brother and a belief that his plan would work. Abū al Darda'’s wife was mortified and sat in tears next to the idol until he returned. She told him that his friend had snuck in and done this terrible deed. Abū al Darda' was immediately furious and then just as suddenly dumbfounded. He quickly realized that had the idol had power it would have defended itself. The light of truth began to enter his heart. ʿAbdullāh ibn Rawāḥa's plan had worked. He found his friend in front of him asking to go together to the blessed Prophet ﷺ so that he might declare his faith in front of both of them.

After Abū al Darda' became Muslim, the Prophet ﷺ assigned him a new friend, or brother, in the path: Salmān al Fārisī. They grew in friendship. One of the first scenes of their relationship is of Salmān rebuking Abū al Darda' for too much fasting, praying, and self-denial. Later, in a letter, we see how their relationship had grown as we read Abū al Darda'’s words of care and love, giving Salmān advice to take advantage of his health and free time before his death, to care deeply for orphans, not to be extravagant, and other beautifully rich words of advice that speak to a deep relationship of spiritual friendship.

We are offered a window into the friendship between Abū al Darda' and ʿUmar ibn al Khaṭṭāb when the latter visits him in Damascus and they sit together, crying over the years without the Prophet ﷺ and wondering at what they had done during those years.

Throughout the stories of Medina we find stories of concern, care, and companionship. We find narrations of friendship.

It is this friendship that we hope to emulate as we set out on the path of friend finding.

Change and Growth

When one changes something as significant as her faith, it can throw her social circles for a loop. Likewise when one embraces Islam, the activities of some of her old friends may be revealed as self-destructive.

If you are a person whose previous relationships were built on pubs, parties, drinking, and dancing, you may find that those friendships are just not deep enough to survive your lifestyle change. If your friends were Bible study buddies, they may be angry at you for changing your religion. Perhaps your friends were local pals you read books, watched movies, and ate dinner with. If you did not share your process of faith development, they may feel confused by what they see as your sudden change.

For many of these friends, you may be the first and only Muslim they have ever met and, as such, you become their gauge for Muslim behavior. They may come to you with pointed and accusatory questions, or simply ask you "Are you happy?"

There is an Arabic proverb that claims, "One who lives with a people for forty days becomes like them" and this is a pretty good rule of thumb to use when evaluating friendships. Before worrying about which of your friends will stick around, you may want to ask which of them you are inviting to the party of your new life.

The old friends who truly fit a rigorous definition of friendship will be able to survive the storms of change. As Ralph Waldo Emerson, an early 19th century American philosopher, has said, "I do not wish to treat friendships daintily, but with roughest courage. When they are real, they are not glass threads or frost work, but the solidest thing we know."[95] For Emerson real friendship needs truthfulness. We should be able to uncover our thoughts and feelings and show our true selves. His second element of solid friendship is tenderness. The interaction of real friends is not based on circumstance but on love, humbleness, and long patience. We find Emerson's rules of friendship to be reflective of Islamic thinking. To strive to be authentic humble believers and to be of the *ṣadiqīn* (the truthful) while acting in mercy (*raḥma*), love, and understanding is the epitome of what it means to be a sister in Islam.

When Islam comes into our lives, it clears out cobwebs and helps us to reevaluate and rethink the course we want to take going forward. It is an opportunity to decide whom to befriend and whom to casually know.

Many converts find themselves in a sort of limbo as far as friends go. Old friends may not be able to handle the change, or the convert may realize that the relationship or its activities were never healthy and decide to leave them behind. There is no need to feel guilty about this. We choose our friends and we need to surround ourselves with those who nourish us and help us forward, not those who drag us down or cause us pain.

New Friends

I (Tamara) sat in my international economics class and beamed as a ḥijābī sister walked in. I was all of three weeks into Islam and desperately in need of female companionship. "Assalam alaikum," I gushed. She was an extremely shy Malaysian gal who had never met a convert before. She looked at my get-up - headscarf with a fedora cap, pants, boots, and a Mexican poncho - and asked herself (she later confessed), "Is she a Muslim?" But she responded in a barely audible voice

"Wa alaikum assalam." As far as I was concerned, I had a new best friend.

The Prophet ﷺ said, "A person follows the religion of his friend, so each one should consider whom he makes his friend."[96]

I had identified my new friend by her identity as a Muslim, and truly Allah blessed me in this friendship.

New acquaintances may be from different cultures or speak different languages, and this can make forming friendships feel less natural. Add to this the fact that forming the quick, close friendships of youth becomes more difficult as one ages, and you've got a recipe for potential loneliness.

So how do you make friends if they do not just walk into your economics class? How do you bridge language and cultural differences? Here are some tips especially designed for you!

Tips to Make New Muslim Friends

1. **The Muslims you know might know your potential new friends.** Attend gatherings that include more than your regular circle of people. Look for local events, find one person you know even vaguely, and ask if she would like to attend with you. Having another person there will help you meet others at the event. Who was there when you became a Muslim? Call them up and invite them for tea. They may know other new Muslims or older Muslims who are also in need of friendship.

2. **Stop looking for people who look like you and start looking for people who think like you.** Not every Muslim practices Islam in the same way. Listen carefully to sisters around you and online and find those who like to celebrate the parts of life that bring you joy. No need to force a friendship with someone who likes to bake bread if you like to hike. If a new friend is constantly criticizing your practice of religion (as opposed to uplifting you and helping you forward), she may be better as a once-in-a-while acquaintance. Check your prejudices, racism, ageism, ableism, and any other barrier that may be keeping you away from new and wonderful friends you may not be meeting because you haven't included them in your vision of friendship.

3. **Choose to be vulnerable instead of a "Pretend Perfect Muslim**." We recommend Brené Brown's books for plenty of discussion about vulnerability, its benefits, and how to achieve it. Suffice it to say that it is exhausting pretending to be the perfect Muslim and it builds zero real relationships. Take off the mask and wrap a soft piece of velvet around your heart. Be ready for disappointments and be ready to make some of the best friends of your

entire life.

4. **Make the time to be a friend.** No sense complaining about your lack of friendships if the reason you do not have friends is that you do not return messages, emails, phone calls, or visits. You need to put in effort to keep in touch in this age of social media interactions. If your friend spends a lot of time on one social media app and you have shied away from it because you are overwhelmed by all the notifications, maybe it is time to learn how to use it to keep your friendships alive. (PS - Turn off notifications).

5. **Start something.** Start an online book club that meets once a month online and once a quarter in person. Join or start a *ḥalaqa* (learning circle). Begin a weekly bread baking get-together. Play with your children in a monthly playgroup. If you cannot think of anything to start, then find events near you and sign up. In my (Tamara's) first year back in Minnesota after my twenty years away, I signed up for a crochet class. I did not meet any new friends, but I practiced my meeting skills and learned how to make a scarf. I also started a halaqa in my house, applied for a job in a local masjid, and offered to teach *tajwīd* on Tuesday mornings. All of these efforts were meant to help me meet people. They did not all work as I had hoped they would. But over time I began to meet my own kindred spirits and now have some lovely and wonderful sister-friends right here in Minnesota.

6. **Join something**. It could be that your future friend is busy volunteering at a local nonprofit organization. Find a cause that is meaningful to you and get ready to meet people who share your passion for refugees, the environment, or the local masjid community.

7. **Move.** Kristine spent fifteen years in a toxic community with a lot of misogyny and little traditional knowledge. She eventually realized, through a visit to another state, that healthy communities did exist and she was able to move to one. "I'm so thankful that I've found a place where I'm valued and can learn," she reports. In big cities you may just have to switch mosques to get away from an unhealthy community. If you cannot move and you do not have a healthy Muslim community in your area, then rely on the possibilities of digital religion and online communities to help you find lifelong friends.

How to be a Friend

Friendship in Islam is a sacred bond of sisterhood and brotherhood. Indeed Allah ﷻ says, ﴾ *The believing men and the believing women are friends one and another.*

They call to good and proscribe evil. They establish prayer, pay zakat, and obey God and His Messenger. It is they who Allah will show mercy. Surely God is Almighty, Wise. ﴾ (Q. 9:71)

The Prophet ﷺ further explains, "The believer to the believer is just like a building. Its parts support each other."[97]

How does this manifest? During the time of the Prophet ﷺ ʿUmar ibn al Khaṭṭāb demonstrated true qualities of friendship that we need to both offer and be able to receive from our friends.

ʿUmar ؓ demonstrated how to be supportive, respectful, thoughtful, generous, and how to stick around when the going gets tough.

ʿUmar and ʿAyyash

In order to understand the unique qualities of friendship demonstrated by ʿUmar ibn al Khaṭṭāb in this story of intrigue and drama, we have to first understand the climate they lived in.

It was a time of great animosity between the nascent group of believers and the powers that were, especially the leaders of Quraysh. The people of hate were burning with anger and would find any opportunity to hurt, harm, abuse, insult, mock, oppress, and tear down the young Muslim community. It was in this precarious and dangerous time that the Prophet ﷺ gave the Muslims permission to leave Mecca and travel to Medina. This only infuriated the disbelievers. They attempted to hunt down, grab, and imprison any Muslim attempting to leave Mecca. The situation was so treacherous that most of the Muslims escaped Mecca in secret.

ʿUmar ibn al Khaṭṭāb, in his bravery and strength, was the only Muslim to leave in front of their eyes and clearly declare his intentions. "May the face be foul of such as desire that his mother be bereaved of him and his child be left an orphan and his wife a widow, and if there be such a one, let him meet me behind this valley."[98] No one was brave enough to follow him, and he left Mecca. His plan was to meet two other companions, but only one got away: ʿAyyash ibn Abū Rabiʿa. The pair traveled the long, hard road to Medina. It may have been that they were accompanied by others, as well. But ʿUmar's friendship had yet to show itself. When they arrived at the outskirts of Medina - they were almost there! - ʿAyyash's relative, Abū Jahl ibn Hishām, along with his brother, al Harith ibn Hisham, caught up to them.

They wanted to take ʿAyyash back to Mecca and had a number of trumped up reasons to convince him. ʿUmar was not fooled and immediately began to attempt to shore up ʿAyyash's waning resolve. They told him his mother needed him - ʿUmar said that his mother would be fine. ʿAyyash began to think about the money he had left behind in Mecca, and ʿUmar offered him half of all his money. Then when it became apparent that ʿAyyash would return with Abū Jahl and Hisham, ʿUmar, understanding the ramifications of this decision, offered him his camel saying, "If you insist, then take my camel. It is well-bred and docile: do not dismount it. If you suspect your people of trickery, escape upon it."[99]

ʿUmar had done his very best to protect ʿAyyash. He did this without ugly judgement calls or personal sensitivities. He did not call him names or insult him. He just kept offering support.

ʿAyyash took the camel but was eventually convinced to dismount it. He was then captured and imprisoned in Mecca.

I often wonder how ʿUmar felt about this. He lost his camel. His friend was completely overcome by the sweet-talk of the enemy and taken. ʿUmar had no idea if he was still a believer or not, but he never gave up on him. When the verses of acceptance and forgiveness were revealed regarding those who were imprisoned by family in Mecca, he wrote them for his friend and sent the verses to him hoping for his heart to be relieved by their beauty.

ʿAyyash made every wrong decision, but ʿUmar stayed steadfast. He offered advice, financial support, property, and continued hope. May we be and may we have such friends.

ACTIVITY: CHECK YOUR FRIEND SKILLS

1. I initiate contact between me and my friend by texting, phoning, emailing, asking for a coffee date, etc...

   ☐ never ☐ rarely ☐ sometimes ☐ often ☐ always

2. I create a supportive atmosphere, making a point of being cheerful, encouraging, and positive.

   ☐ never ☐ rarely ☐ sometimes ☐ often ☐ always

3. I plan special events to do together (her birthday/an Eid event, etc.)

   ☐ never ☐ rarely ☐ sometimes ☐ often ☐ always

4. I stand up for my friend with other people, do not gossip about her business, and support her if people are not treating her well.

   ☐ never ☐ rarely ☐ sometimes ☐ often ☐ always

5. I focus on my friend's problems, offer empathy, understanding, support, kindness, comfort, and help when I can.

   never rarely sometimes often always

6. I show up when needed - for babysitting, when she needs help moving house, when she is ill, etc.

   never rarely sometimes often always

7. I give gifts that are meaningful to my friend and remember occasions that are significant to her.

   never rarely sometimes often always

8. I compliment my friend. I praise her for the classes she takes and the effort she puts into spiritual and religious growth.

   never rarely sometimes often always

9. I help my friend feel better after unpleasant interactions and life's dramas and traumas.

   never rarely sometimes often always

10. I make a point of being punctual for appointments with my friend, keeping promises, and remembering commitments.

    never rarely sometimes often always

11. I am a safe space for my friend. I keep her secrets.

    never rarely sometimes often always

Managing Acquaintances: Classmates and Coworkers

If a convert is studying or works when she becomes Muslim, and especially if she puts on hijab right away, this can make for some awkward encounters. Some coworkers will be curious and interested while others may give the side-eye or be downright hostile. A good way to reassure people that you are the same old you is to smile and be friendly. Don't hide or avoid them. Maybe a dish of chocolates on your desk inviting people to stop by and say hi (and maybe "Hey what's with the headscarf?") would help to break the ice on that first day at work or school as a visible Muslim.

Sometimes a smile is not enough. Helen was fired from her job as a receptionist when she began wearing hijab. "Take it off or leave," her supervisor told her. So she left and went straight to the Equal Employment Opportunities Commission. She later sued her employer and won a financial settlement, as well as a provision that required the company to post its new non-discrimination policies publicly. Not every country will have the same laws, however France, for example, has laws in place intentionally meant to stop the wearing of hijab in public workplaces.

Ideally, when in the process of becoming Muslim, we should give consideration and planning to the people in our lives who are neither friend nor family, but are part of power structures that may affect us positively or negatively. In reality, acquaintances should not have so much influence over our personal life decisions, but they are often in positions where they can.

If you believe that you may be at risk of losing your job at any time on your convert journey, begin to quietly look for a better job with a better, more accepting policy in place. Take careful steps, always relying on Allah for guidance and help.

It may be that your coworkers and your boss will surprise you with full acceptance and joyful support , so remember to keep an open heart when you debut your new faith. If things go south, however, here are some Muslim organizations in the USA that work for workplace justice:

1. The Council on American-Islamic Relations: CAIR has chapters all over the USA so check their website for a chapter near you: cair.com

2. KARAMAH: Muslim Women Lawyers for Human Rights is available for legal assistance. They support Muslim women involved in lawsuits by contacting the lawyer, teaching them about the legal precedents involved, and answering any questions the legal team may be unclear about: Karamah.org

A Final Note on Friendship

Rabata has worked hard to create communities where women can live in the shelter of one another. We have online WhatsApp communities, local chapters, and other forms of digital sisterhood. Our Facebook convert women's group has been dubbed the safest place for women converts on the net. The page is called Muslim Women Convert Circle: Rabata.org and it is a community of *only* converts. The volunteer admins (also converts) work hard to keep it free of men, non-converts, and anyone just seeking to find an audience for their products. It is a place for questions, support, and a whole lot of women ready to support and embrace you.

PART THREE: WED WISELY

Finding a Suitor

When a person becomes Muslim, very often they are bombarded with an avalanche of must-dos and must-don'ts. And, too often, one of the classic must-dos is to get married. "Get married!" you may hear from every corner of the masjid. "Marriage is half of faith!" Those doing the instructing believe that the act of getting married *itself* is so important that it completes half of one's faith. It's possible that this is also convenient for the people at the mosque, for if the convert is paired off with a husband or wife (usually a born-Muslim), their Islamic education can be considered taken care of.

In actuality, though, a new convert who marries immediately, especially if she's a woman, puts herself in a precarious position. She's entering a marriage to a person with radically different ideas and expectations, whose concept of Islam she probably can't identify or judge, and who may very well believe that he now has control over aspects of her life that she considers her own personal domain. Or worse. In majority Muslim countries, women are not as easily taken advantage of. They have the backing of their fathers or other male family members when suitors come calling. In many cultures, it's the mothers, grandmothers, and aunties who usually suggest potential matches or a woman may meet a man at college or work, but either way, when the rubber meets the road, her suitor knows that he must meet certain standards and behave in certain ways if he is to win the hand of his intended. He knows that her father will check out his background by asking around about him and his family, meet with his own father to hammer out a fair (probably tilted toward the wife's interest) dowry, and generally ensure that his daughter isn't walking into a situation where she won't be cared for. And his protection doesn't end when the wedding reception is over. A man's new father-in-law will usually be there to keep the husband in line if that should ever become necessary.

To Western ears, this may sound condescending or patriarchal. But these ties of community provide a scaffolding upon which men know they must rest in order to maintain their position in society, in their family, and in the eyes of their peers. This accountability is a positive force, for it is human nature to sometimes slack off when there's no structure to your social life and no one looking who will encourage upright behavior with both love and authority. Men reared in a society where these checks and balances formed part and parcel of community life are sometimes more likely to bend to their *nafs* in marital matters when living outside of that cultural scaffold. In fact, some men actually prey upon convert women *because* they don't know their rights. These men prefer to teach their wives a version of "Islam" that serves their egos. They weaponize Islam as a means of control and unjustly keep their wives ignorant of their rights.

Muslim immigrant men who find themselves single in a new country and are likely to harbor very different expectations of marriage and communication than the women they meet, and indeed very different values about relationships between members of opposite genders. They may even have hidden agendas. So women have to be careful not to let infatuation run away with them or allow themselves to be pushed into marrying someone before they feel ready.

Beware of These Red Flags

There are several different types of unhealthy situations convert brides may find themselves in. Here are a few to look out for.

The Green Card Seeker

Although there are many, many men who come to a Western country and fall in love with a citizen there, desiring both a green card *and* a loving wife and family, there are also some men who come to a Western country expressly to marry a citizen and make a bid for a green card. The wife is nothing more than a means to an end. These marriages are particularly difficult because the husband may look down on his wife and may even have a "real" wife back home. The unsuspecting new wife will have difficulty pleasing her husband and not understand that she is not doing anything wrong, but that her husband married her under false pretenses. This is difficult to suss out once the deed is done, for how does one prove that another's intentions were impure?

The Man Unable or Unwilling to Support Himself

Another difficult situation women can find themselves in is being married to a man who has no money and no real prospects for making money. These kinds of men are often very attractive to new Muslims, as they may appear to be students of knowledge or imams making paltry wages. The woman wants nothing more than to marry a good Muslim man, and one who appear to care more about religion than money can seem like the perfect catch. But some men who are billed as pious are more lazy and self-righteous than genuinely humble. Women in these situations may need to either become the family financial support, or apply for government assistance. Often with growing families this situation can beome intolerable.

The Dreamer

Then there is the dreamer (or drifter) who will be perfectly comfortable making his wife earn the money while he sits home not taking care of the house or the kids. In Islam, a man is charged with the financial upkeep of his family, and while very often husbands and wives cooperate in this realm, a man who is perpetually studying or founding the next great business venture while his wife supports him (*and* takes care of the domestic duties) is creating an unhealthy dynamic. This is one of the reasons the dowry is so important. If the suitor cannot pay a dowry, a legitimate question is "will he be able to support a family?"

In some cases, a young man may not be able to support a family *now* but is a hard worker and will most likely be able to later. This is a risk that the young woman may find acceptable, and she may be happy to invest in their shared future. If her husband cherishes her and makes her happy, then there's nothing wrong with that. The poor man who loves to care for his family is better than a rich and stingy man who resents every penny that's spent or a rich man who treats his wife with contempt. But a poor man who is willing to take advantage of the government and/or his wife is no catch.

The Dictator

Some men are good providers, but their interpretation of Islam is warped so that they believe their job is to control their wives. This can cause real stress and lead to spiritual abuse. In a worst-case scenario, this kind of man may refuse to allow his wife to go out alone, may force her to dress according to his rules, or may even forbid her from interacting with male customer service agents on the phone. These women's lives can become limited to the four walls of their homes and their company limited to the children that they must raise alone, because often this kind of husband believes he is above going down into the trenches of family life. Living with this level of stress is detrimental to the physical and mental well-being of the wife—not to mention the poor children.

For this reason, careful attention should be paid to a suitor's treatment of those as arrogant person would considers beneath him (cashiers, wait staff, etc.). No matter how well a man treats his potential wife now, he'll probably treat her like those other people when he becomes angry or even disenchanted. And who wants a man who treats others poorly, anyway?

Give Me Back the Wheel

Another situation that should give a bride-to-be pause is the sense that her suitor suffers from control issues. Barbara was engaged to a man who lived in another state. He gave her an iPhone as an engagement present, and as soon as she started using it, he got unreasonably upset every time he texted and she didn't text back right away. God forbid he should call and she didn't pick up! Although Barb felt this was annoying and inappropriate, the man had many other attractive qualities, so she went ahead with the marriage. Five years later she was forced to leave him. It turned out the controlling streak was just the tip of the iceberg.

When we are at the beginning of a relationship, we tend to let things slide. We figure that we'll deal with this or that issue after we're married. Or that we're overthinking things. But take this advice from a father to his daughter during her engagement: if you're not having the time of your life, don't marry him.

The Good Guy

Even if a potential suitor is an all-around great guy, a new convert has a more important relationship to focus on at first: her relationship with Allah. She needs time to learn the basics of Islam, find balance in her new identity, and decide what her practice will look like and which groups of Muslim men are most likely to have members with similar practices. If she is to marry a born-Muslim, she needs to get familiar with different cultures and think about which ones she could most easily adapt to, rather than being thrown into a random culture based on whichever guy happens to be single at the mosque. We recommend that new Muslims (men and women) take between one and five years to become solid, confident Muslims before they think about marriage. Women especially should be leery of jumping into marriage, as a woman may be linking herself up with a man she doesn't know and who may believe he has the right to take control of her life.

True Colors

An important thing to remember when considering how to interpret a red flag is this: often the behaviors that sneak through when a person is ostensibly on their best behavior, such as during the engagement period, are magnified greatly when the shine wears off and you meet the real person. So be sure to be observant during your courtship and engagement. Observe how your suitor treats your parents and the children in the family. Observe how he treats servers in restaurants and what comments he may make about people of other ethnicities or economic classes. All these are windows into a person's true self. You don't want to marry someone who made your heart go pitter-patter when you were engaged; you want to marry someone who has true *taqwa* and Islamic ethics. Someone who treats others, including the future you, with respect and deference because it's the right thing to do, not just because he feels like doing so in the moment. So in short, remove your rose-colored glasses and stay focused.

Other Things to Consider

The Educational Equation

Some couples can get along wonderfully if one has a doctorate and the other only finished high school, but most often people relate best to others with similar educational experiences. In a lopsided educational equation, the person who is less educated may begin to feel insecure about their intellectual prowess and, especially if it's the husband, this can take the form of controlling behavior. Conversely, the person who is more educated can sometimes become arrogant and look down on their spouse. Both of these situations, which may happen simultaneously, are recipes for contention and consternation.

Rules of Thumb for Getting Married

Establish your own Islamic education and points of view before you get married. Become a strong, confident woman who brings that confidence to her marriage. Learn to distinguish between different interpretations of Islam, and look for a husband among those whose practice best fits your own.

Engage a *walī*. If your father isn't suitable for whatever reason, find a friend's husband or a trusted community leader. Be frank with him about what you are looking for in a husband and ask him to vet suitors carefully. The *walī* can go to bat for your marriage gift and ask difficult and sensitive questions that you may feel uncomfortable asking.

Ask Questions. Ask your suitor lots of questions. And we don't mean "What's your favorite color?" or "How many brothers and sisters do you have?" We don't even mean, "What would you do if your wife wanted to work?" These questions are easy to answer with what a person thinks you want to hear. Instead, ask open-ended, sidelong questions that will get you more authentic answers if you're able to do a bit of careful listening. For example, questions like "What was the last thing you bought?" "Tell me about your mom," or "Describe your country to me" allow you to listen to the content *and tone* of the answer and draw your own conclusions. Was the last thing he bought a used VCR player? Start planning for how to get money out of him for the kids' shoes right now. Was it a subwoofer for his car? Get ready to take a backseat to his hobbies, and ask a few more questions about his priorities. Does he consider his mom to be the best homemaker in the world? If so, be ready to compete with that image. Does he talk about his country with longing? Time to update your passport. These questions may sound harsh, but they aren't designed just to suss out his faults. Wanting to live back home isn't a fault, for example, but these questions are to help you find out what his priorities are so you can see if yours and his match. See Appendix A for Andrea's list of questions to ask a potential spouse.

Don't marry a loser! If the man in front of you is someone you wouldn't marry if you weren't Muslim, don't marry him just because you *are* Muslim! And don't marry a man with no prospects or who offers you a pittance of a dowry because you feel it's the more pious thing to do. The Prophet ﷺ said, "If one comes to you with both good character and good religion, then marry him." (Bukhari) Note that this includes both good manners and good religion. So if you meet a man who prays but is condescending or rude, he has not fulfilled the requirements of the Prophet ﷺ. And don't feel pressured by others to marry the first guy who comes along! Even if the pickings are slim in your area, it's far better to be a single woman—even if you have kids—than to be in a difficult or abusive marriage.

Keeping Up with the Joneses

Wedding wisely also includes looking at your economic expectations. People have money styles, just as they have learning styles and communication styles. Of course, having enough money to cover basic expenses should be a prerequisite to marriage. The old song lyrics about loving someone despite not having any money is a dangerous lie wrapped up in frilly, romantic paper. So much so that the singer who sang the song *and* the songwriter who wrote it eventually got divorced! A person who is accustomed to being able to freely spend whatever they like on whatever they like isn't usually a good match for someone who's either less well-off or well-off but a dedicated saver. And a dedicated saver will struggle with a spouse who is looser with the purse strings.

Attitudes about money can often reflect attitudes about other matters, as can be the case where a stay-at-home mom finds her work devalued when her husband takes her efforts for granted and, on top of that, believes that the $200 a month he gives her for household expenses is a generous "allowance." On the other hand, some wives devalue their husband's work and worth by spending frivolously on themselves and looking at their husband as a cash cow. When I (Najiyah) taught English at a university in Syria, I once assigned an essay where each student was to imagine that they woke up one morning to find that they had changed into the opposite gender. What they wrote was very telling. Several of the young men wrote with glee about being able to freely spend someone else's money.

It's no joke that the thing married couples fight about most is money, so thinking objectively about spending habits before marriage is a good way to make sure you are covering all your bases. Again, the goal is to find a respectful balance where each uplifts the other.

Dreams

Close your eyes for a moment and envision yourself in five years. In ten. Envision your lifestyle. What do you imagine your days will be filled with? Will you still be in school in five years? Will you be working in ten? Will you be homeschooling your kids? Going to bookstores on the weekends? Camping every weekend? Will you be cooking every day? What kind of house will you be living in? An apartment in the bustling city or a quaint farmhouse in a small town? Write down what you dream of.

Now have your potential partner imagine the same. How does he see your life in five years? In ten? Do the same for his life—both of you independently imagine his life in five and ten years and write it down. Do you envision the same sort of lifestyle? Do you agree on urban vs. suburban vs. rural living? Do you envision him driving the family to visit your mom every weekend, even though his law firm will require him to be working most weekends during that time? Does he envision you cooking biryani every night, even though you've only eaten it twice?

If you carry out this exercise and then compare your visions and speak frankly about the places you're willing to compromise and the things that are non-negotiable, you will be more assured that you're both on the same page as far as lifestyle is concerned.

Place both visions of your life in five and ten years on a continuum. Do the same for your shared visions of his life. Remember that in this exercise there is no value judgment on either end of the different spectrums. Both ends of the spectrums can be positive, depending on the temperaments and expectations of the spouses. But prospective partners who answer with vastly different visions will need to negotiate a few things before moving forward.

Beware of the suitor who sees a life where both spouses work, but the wife takes care of the nighttime feedings, the diaper changes, the sick-kid duty, the chores, the after-school activities, and the weekend recreation. This is a common unhealthy setup in many households. Beware also of the wife (or of being the wife) who thinks her husband will be both supporting a large gaggle of kids on his income alone *and* driving them to soccer practice. If one spouse has an outside job, it's not reasonable to expect them to have an enormous amount of time to spend doing family chores on weeknights.

On Intercultural Marriages

One challenge faced by those in intercultural marriages is that of expectations. A woman raised in the West probably has expectations of being consulted and working in cooperation, of enjoying hobbies and activities together. But men from many non-Western countries may see marriage in very different ways.

Likewise, an immigrant who seeks to marry an American needs to be aware of the cultural consequences that will come with that decision. One Syrian man wanted to marry an American. When asked why, he replied that he had twins and knew that Americans had a reputation for being very kind to their stepchildren. That's a great reason for seeking out an American, but when asked if he realized that marrying an American meant she might also, for example, want to give gifts on ʿEid instead of money, or wear skirts and jackets, or cook American food, he demurred. Surely she wouldn't do those things! She was *Muslim* now! Of course, none of the aforementioned things are un-Islamic, but they run counter to Syrian culture. This brother couldn't imagine his new wife doing them because, to him, being Muslim meant being Syrian.

That's the thing about culture. It's not just food and clothes and music. Culture runs deep. And it makes it difficult to see some things as simply different rather than wrong. So when considering entering a culturally mixed marriage, it's important to really examine your own culture and that of your intended. Discuss cultural differences rather than waiting for them to ambush you, and really prepare your own heart for open communication and some meaningful compromise.

Nitty Gritty

Marriage License

As we discussed in the upcoming section on the *mahr*, (marriage gift) the provisions of Islamic marriage are designed to protect the vulnerable and ensure that everyone's rights and responsibilities are upheld. One way convert women lose the benefit of those protections is by marrying without a civil marriage license. That is, marrying "Islamically" only. In majority Muslim countries, you would be hard-pressed to find a family that would allow their daughter to marry without the benefit of a civil license. Privilege of identity as a wife and protection from the unscrupulous are two important facets of marriage, and a marriage license provides both.

Getting married with a civil marriage license is part of living in a community, and believe it or not, it protects a woman's Islamic rights. In the West, it guarantees that one spouse can be covered under the other spouse's health insurance, ensures that both parents have access to children's medical and school records, and can even form the basis for one spouse being allowed to visit the other in the hospital ICU. These are important protections. It even allows the couple to join the YMCA as a family, which requires proof of marriage! So if your potential spouse balks at a state marriage license—for whatever reason—count that as a red flag.

Contract Conflicts

Likewise, the Islamic marriage contract contains protections for the woman. Unlike civil marriage certificates, which are a way to record that a legal marriage has taken place, an Islamic marriage contract is an actual contract between the two parties, into which either partner can put whatever provisions they like.

By far, the most common provision women consider adding to their contracts today is that their husband not marry a second wife.

Polygyny is, of course, halal and in some situations a very reasonable and even mutually beneficial arrangement. However, a woman who prefers not to engage in polygyny isn't making it haram for her suitor; she is simply saying that it is something *she* does not wish to participate in. Her potential husband is free to move on and marry someone else if having multiple wives is important to him. Should a couple marry with this provision, it is still not making polygyny haram for the husband—it simply means that should he decide to take another wife, it would result in an automatic dissolution of the first marriage (or the possibility that his first wife will have the option to divorce him, depending on the wording in their contract). So even if it is in the contract, she is not forbidding him from doing it, just forbidding him from doing it if he wishes to remain married to her. If a man shies away from this or any other contractual condition that is important to you, it is wise to think twice before tying the knot.

But people change, right? What if a woman, after ten years of marriage, decides she could use some extra time to herself and is no longer opposed to polygyny? In that case, she can always relinquish that stipulation.

You've Decided and Now It Is Time for the *Mahr*, or the Marriage Gift

The word *mahr* is often translated as "dowry," which is unfortunate because it carries considerable Old World cultural baggage. Rather than being a "bride price" that goes to the bride's father like a dowry, the *mahr* is a beautiful gesture of commitment from the new husband to his wife exclusively, and for her it is part of a system of financial independence.

Many converts feel shy about the *mahr* because they feel guilty asking for money. In Western culture it seems crass to combine marriage and money. There are converts who have married men for a dowry of Quran (an agreement that the husband will teach his wife a *sūra*), for a costume jewelry wedding band, or even for a dollar. These women felt, from the goodness of their hearts, that it was more pious to accept a lesser *mahr*. They weren't "all about the money."

But setting an appropriate *mahr* is not immodest or somehow less pious. Allah created this system. God designed Islam to protect everyone and maintain everyone's rights. Receiving a marriage gift allows a woman a measure of independence in her marriage. She has money starting out. She can invest it, save it, or spend it, and whatever she chooses to do, it lends seriousness to this new relationship. The husband understands that he is committing to a family and to the financial burden of that family. The *mahr* solidifies the marriage in the mind of the Muslim husband and makes him take his new role seriously. Adhering to Allah's system is a gesture of piety whether it feels comfortable or not. If you think about it, deciding you don't want a *mahr* is tantamount to declaring that you know better than Allah, or you are more pious than the companions. Of course, that's not what a woman's intention is when she forgoes her *mahr*, but requiring one is a way of stressing the importance of the Islamic system of protecting women's financial health.

A woman's *mahr* can be divided into an immediate gift and a deferred gift. In this case, she receives the immediate gift upon the marriage and the deferred gift in the eventuality that her husband divorces her or at any time she requests it, depending on how their marriage contract is written. Tala used her marriage gift to purchase a taxi cab and hire a driver. Soon the taxi was doing so well she was able to buy more taxis. She became a downright taxi maven! And eventually took her whole familty to hajj one of her sayings: A well-invested *mahr* can provide for a woman for years to come.

Weddings

Different cultures obviously have different marriage customs, but it may surprise a new convert that even the Islamic parts of a marriage can be done at different times and carry different meanings in different cultures.

Here in the States, for example, couples may have just one event: contract signing, marriage ceremony, and reception, all at once. Some even include a hybrid celebration where Western-style vows are exchanged. Arab couples will often marry in two stages: they will sign the contract but still live apart, this being considered almost like an engagement period. They can go out together and be alone together because, technically, they are married already. But they don't live together until their actual wedding party is held some months (or even years) later. Desi families have multiphase wedding parties that last a week or more. Each event has its own timing and meaning and is attended by an expanding group of people, until the final wedding party, which usually includes family, friends, and acquaintances.

One of the perks of being a convert is that you can pick and choose from many traditions to create the style of wedding you'd like to have. Perhaps you marry a man from a particular culture, and his traditions mean a lot to him. You can still add your own flairs to the wedding, so it beautifully combines your two cultures.

After the Wedding: Raising Muslim Children (When You Weren't Raised Muslim)

Raising Muslim children—especially in an intercultural context—provides an opportunity to form new norms and forge one's own path. This pioneering spirit isn't without its share of roads to be cleared and rivers to be forged, but on the whole, converts are more prepared for the task than they sometimes feel.

Every parent has to learn to trust themselves; converts just have the added dimension of teaching Islam as they learn it. But the truth is that you were capable enough to live your life up until Islam and capable enough to make the decision to become Muslim—and you're capable enough to raise your children. Don't let panic or frustration outshout your healthy heart. Heed that healthy heart and find a path that is one of moderation, consistency, and joy. Here are some ways to navigate the journey.

1. **Keep your eyes on the *akhira*!** When setting out to raise our kids, we need to stay focused and maintain the importance of our children's Islamic education and activities. We all abhor the idea of neglecting a child's *dunyā* (worldly life and needs), and we would never leave our children filthy or neglect to feed them. But sometimes, out of the goodness of our hearts, we neglect their *akhira*. Perhaps our child has a test, so we feel sorry for him and let him sleep past *fajr*. Or maybe she doesn't speak Arabic, and we let her grow up without putting her in Quran classes because it's too hard and takes so much time. These are pitfalls to be avoided if we are to raise Muslim children who will inshallah grow up to prioritize their faith in a natural, joyful way.

2. **Set and seek a good example!** Of course we all want to set a good example for our kids, but we also need to seek good examples for ourselves. Often, a new Muslim doesn't know which way to turn for solid information and a caring mentor. A good Muslim friend is someone who reminds you of Allah. That doesn't mean that they walk up to you every day and say, "Hey, don't forget Allah!" It means that just the sight of them reminds you of Allah and how much you want to please Him, because of the way they live their own life and interact with you. (And they also aren't afraid to give you the "Hey, don't forget Allah" nudge when you need it. Which we all do sometimes.) It's a great blessing to find these kinds of friends in real life, but if there aren't many Muslims where you live or you have trouble finding someone you really click with, online friends can help fill the gap. Rabata provides many avenues for sheltering in a sisterhood full of friends who remind each other of Allah every day. That said, remember to get out in your community as well and serve people there. This will be the best way to meet friends who can support you when you need a real shoulder or a partner in crime and a virtual one just won't do.

New Habits for New Muslim Homes
Removing shoes before entering the home is a common habit in many countries, including Japan, Finland, and Germany. Muslims remove their shoes before entering the home because we pray on the floors and don't want filth from outside trekked inside. (There's been a push on social media to convince everyone to remove their shoes, as science is catching up with how unhygienic it is to wear outdoor shoes in the house.)
Waking children for *Fajr*. Although it is easier and much more peaceful to let young kids sleep, once they are the age of about seven, it is definitely time to begin waking them for *Fajr*. This habit will stand both you and them in good stead in the coming years. It allows children to see their parents in a worshipful time of day that is quiet and relatively stress- and bustle-free. There is no cooking or homework or lawn mowing to interfere with parents' undivided attention, and this can be cultivated into a time to have open communication.
Reading Quran or having a **family *ḥalaqa*** after *Fajr* or *Maghrib*. This is another habit that fosters togetherness and communication. Before going off for the day, a moment is taken to learn together. It can be something done every day, three times a week, or just on the weekends. The point is to be consistent and make it a time the kids look forward to. Perhaps they get a special treat after the morning lesson or get to go run errands with Dad afterward.
Washing with water after using the restroom is definitely one of those habits that shocks Westerners. But once it's established, no one can imagine going back to just toilet paper. Make washing easy for your children by having a bidet or keeping squirt bottles next to the toilet. (Small dishwashing liquid bottles work, or you can order peri bottles from Amazon for next to nothing.) Pro tip: Train them to check before they go to make sure the bottle isn't empty.
Teaching children to make *wuḍū*' is another habit that Muslim parents teach. Kids often don't like to make *wuḍū*', so here again, incentives may be in order make it easy as well by providing the right tools: kids sized bathroom slippers, a handy hand towel, and a stool to reach the sink. (And make sure there's a nice, thirsty bathroom rug for wet little feet.)

3. **Habits!** Every culture has habits that it inculcates into its children. We teach our kids to brush their teeth, to make their beds (if we're good), and to clean the house before the grandparents come to visit. They know they are supposed to remember their backpacks, behave in school, and speak politely to their friends' parents. To these, we now add some Islamic habits that will set the tone in our homes and help our kids live their faith out loud.

4. **Skills and Tools!** New Muslims bring noble and admirable Islamic qualities to our new lives as Muslims. Like Bani al-Azd, we have the skills and tools to be both constructive members of Muslim society and Muslim parents. Every culture brings added value to the Muslim community. Between parents and our culture has taught us to be disciplined, have a good work ethic, care for others, keep our homes clean, and be frugal. We have learned from our parents not to be litterbugs, to mind our own business, to eat our vegetables, and to make guests feel welcome. We know better than to gossip about people or cheat or steal or interrupt others or be selfish. We have garnered from our American culture many, many Islamic qualities. If we add the habits above to the previously existing arrows in our parenting quiver, we will raise faithful, well-adjusted children inshallah.

ACTIVITY: INTERVIEWS

Interview your in-laws or a community member about their childhood traditions. This will give you ideas for creating your own traditions and a foundation for understanding others' styles of celebrating. Here are some questions you could ask.

1. What was your favorite holiday growing up?
2. How did you celebrate the two ʿEids?
3. Did the celebrations change as you got older? Were they different for children and adults?
4. Did you celebrate with the same traditions when your own children grew up?
5. How would you like to celebrate with your grandchildren?

THE PROJECT LINA WORKSHOP

The Project Lina workshop developed over a period of twenty years of working with people. Converts come in all shapes and sizes, from all types of backgrounds and circumstances, and all sorts of milieus and personalities. Their differences are many, but their shared experiences are also plentiful. Over the years, we noticed that converts had certain shared experiences that often led to bitterness and a heavy heart. At one point, a close friend of mine (Tamara's) walked away from Islam, and I was devastated. I spent many days and nights wondering what I could have done to help her. As I woke from my state of grief, I realized there were many more women dealing with issues that were unique to the convert woman (and perhaps the man, but I did not know). I set out to provide some sort of program that would be a place for Muslim convert women to be open and honest with one another—a safe space for us to talk about what ails us and seek a remedy.

The workshop includes the three educational modules represented here, intentional shared food that represents the culture of the attendees, and entertainment.

CONCLUSION

Converts occupy a unique and valuable place in the Muslim community. We are the bridges not only between cultures but also between generations. By knowing ourselves, declaring our independence, and tending our ties, we will become comfortable in our own skins and comfortable contributing to the health of our communities. As Karla (Evans) Kovacik puts it in her article "As American as Apple Pie: US Female Converts to Islam": "I am a 'real American,' I am a 'real Muslim,' I am ready to have the conversation. You bring the vanilla ice cream—I'll bring the apple pie."[100]

The Long and Winding Road

Becoming a Muslim isn't an event. It's not like someone points a magic wand at you—"Wingardium Muslimosaaah"—and you're a Muslim, with all the knowledge and comfort that that implies. Rather, even for heritage Muslims, it's a process. A continual process of modifying the old, honing the new, and taking one step after another closer to Allah. It involves days where you feel comfortable and included and days where you struggle. But it is definitely possible to be yourself and be Muslim. It's possible to know Islam well enough to find your way without being shoved onto someone else's path. And it is possible to tend or repair existing relationships and cultivate healthy new ones. But it's a lot harder alone. So reach out, stay positive, and be gentle with yourself. Practice balance, bring your whole self along, and work on constructive communication. Start studying your new faith as soon as possible, create a strong foundation, and declare your independence. Love your family, look for new friends, and tend all your ties. These steps will help you become strong and tall with deep roots, a trunk flexible enough to withstand the strongest storms, and showers of fruitful blessings for everyone around you. Just like a *līna*.

Modules

Module One: Know Yourself. One of the difficulties that many Muslim convert women face is the uniting of their preconversion selves with their postconversion selves. Because we lack a childhood in Islam, we must work hard to establish a strong identity as Muslims. This module covers issues that impact our identity, such as birth names and Muslim names, personality types, and how to deeply understand ourselves so that we can grow spiritually. It concludes with a section on cultures—or how to hang on to our original culture while building a Muslim culture in our homes and hearts.

Module Two: Declare Independence. It is imperative that converts gain the knowledge and skills necessary to be able to rely on our own intuition and to know, when making faith decisions, how to live our lives. Since Islam is both a daily practice and a spiritual path, the ability to make such decisions is often dependent upon a measure of Arabic, an understanding of the sources of our faith, and a strong knowledge base in *ʿaqīda* (creed). This module discusses some basic liturgical vocabulary, quickly covers the six parts of *ʿaqīda*, and offers tools for growth.

Module Three: Tend Your Ties. Relationships are complicated. Becoming a Muslim complicates our relationships further. It can also enrich our relationships as we grow in love and service. Our relationships with our parents, siblings, old friends, and new friends need new tools to help ensure their success. Cross-cultural marriages bring their challenges, and raising children in Islam when you were not raised a Muslim is its own type of adventure. Module three investigates Islamic modes of tending our ties and provides tips and tricks for improving our relationships with our family and friends.

Intentional Food

The shared meal that ends each Project Lina workshop attempts to uphold the participants' cultural traditions around holiday dinners. When we have held the workshop in North America, we have shared both turkey with all the trimmings and a full-on barbecue. In Malaysia we shared food of the Chinese New Year, and in Great Britain, a traditional English roast dinner. This is food that is nostalgic for convert women in one way or another, and to eat it at the mosque or at a place where Muslims have gathered is to bring together our two worlds.

Entertainment

Another part of the workshop is entertainment. Humorous skits and plays, songs, poetry readings, and even a comedy act are all part of creating a memorable event.

Bring Project Lina to your town!

Email scheduling@rabata.org, and we will work together to make it happen!

A

Appendix A

QUESTIONS FOR A POTENTIAL SUITOR

Andrea Cluck*

(1986 – 2020)

Note: *Not all of these questions are applicable to everyone; tailor the list to meet your own needs. Some potential answers are deal breakers, but what constitutes a deal breaker may differ from person to person. Some questions will naturally come up in conversation, whereas others will need to be asked outright. Please ask for this information gradually; don't whip out a form for your poor suitor to fill out on your first meeting! May Allah grant us all loving, righteous spouses with whom to work mutually toward Jannah!*

His Background

- What is your marital status?
- How long have you lived in (insert country here)?
- What race(s) and/or ethnicity(ies) do you identify as?
- What is your first language?
- What other languages can you speak?
- What is your citizenship status? Do you have plans to change that?

Her Background

- How do you envision life as the husband of a convert? How would life be different for you than if you had married someone from your own culture?
- Is it a problem if my parents do not want to have a relationship with you or with us as a couple?
- Would it be acceptable to you if my parents wanted a very involved relationship with you or with us?
- Would you marry a divorcée?

- Do you mind that I am currently job hunting (am a student, etc.)?

School/Work/Location

- What are your short-term and long-term career goals?
- What did you study in school?
- How do you earn your living now?
- Where do you dream of living? Are you open to relocating?

His Family

- How old are your parents?
- Where do they live? Where did they grow up?
- What do your parents do for a living?
- Do you have siblings?
- What is your relationship with them like?
- Did you grow up in a traditional (for your culture) household?
- What was your relationship with your parents like growing up?
- What is your relationship with your parents like now?
- How will your parents be involved in your marriage decision?
- Will anyone in your family live with us in the future? Do you want us to live in your parents' house?
- Do you financially support anyone in your family?
- What will my relationship with your family be like? How do you see my responsibilities toward them? Their responsibilities toward me and us?
- If for any reason my relationship with your family turns sour, what should we do?

Personality

- Are you introverted or extroverted? (Do you feel recharged around people or after spending time alone?)
- Are you more social or reserved? Do you foresee us having people over for dinner a lot or attending gatherings at other places, or would you rather be home alone?

- How much free time would you like for yourself vs. time spent with your spouse?
- Do you consider yourself an emotional person?
- Are you comfortable with abstract discussions/thoughts?
- Do you have any pet peeves?
- How would your friends describe you in one word?
- How do you display affection to loved ones? Physically (are you a hugger?)? Verbally? With gifts or actions?
- Do you plan ahead or consider yourself more spontaneous? Are you organized?
- Can we take a Myers-Briggs test or read *Just Your Type* and talk about the results together?

Communication

- Are you comfortable discussing your private thoughts and emotions with a trusted friend or family member? With your spouse?
- How do you communicate when you have a problem with someone?
- How do you act when you are angry? How do you communicate?
- How do you expect your spouse to express anger?
- How do you cope if you have had a bad day? Do you like to talk about it? Do you need alone time? Do you need a hug? Ice cream?
- What would you do if your wife has had a bad day or is complaining about something?
- As a husband, how would you undertake important decisions (consultation, unilaterally, etc.)?
- Do you express yourself better verbally or in writing?
- Do you use foul language?

Islamic Identity

- What is your religious identity (Sunni, Shi'a, etc.)?
- What are your views on Salafism?
- What are your views on Sufism? Attending Sufi gatherings?

Pillars

- How often do you pray?
- Do you eat *dhabīḥa* only whether you are at home or out?
- Do you eat things cooked in alcohol?
- Do you drink or smoke?
- Do you play cards with friends?

Īmān

- How would you describe your current level of religiosity?
- How does Islam manifest itself in your daily life?
- What are some difficulties you face in belief and practice? What do you struggle with?
- What are some of the highlights of being Muslim for you?

Islamic Education

- How religious are your parents?
- How did you learn Islam as a child?
- How do you separate Islam and culture as an adult?
- What do you do to further your Islamic education?
- What sources do you use to learn about Islam (books, websites, teachers, etc.)?
- Do you like to attend conferences such as ISNA?
- Who are your favorite English-speaking Muslim speakers or teachers?

Holidays and Cultural Traditions

- What do you like about American culture? Your home culture?
- How do you celebrate Ramadan and ʿEid? What are your traditions and expectations?
- How do you feel about American holidays (birthdays, Christmas, Easter, Halloween, Valentine's Day, St. Patrick's Day, Thanksgiving)? Do you celebrate them? Do you want your wife and/or children to celebrate them? If we are invited to my family's or a colleague's house for a mainstream or other faith holiday, how will we approach that?

- Do you celebrate Mawlid?
- Do you celebrate any other cultural holidays?

Conduct/The Opposite Sex

- Should men dress a certain way Islamically? Do you have certain standards of modesty for your own clothing?
- Would you go to a beach or a swimming pool in the West? Is it OK if your wife does so? How would we dress?
- Is it acceptable to you if your wife goes to a gym or exercise class where there are men working out?
- How would you feel if your wife decided she wanted to dress more or less conservatively?
- How do you conduct yourself around the opposite sex?
- How should your wife conduct herself around the opposite sex?
- How should your wife conduct herself around your family members?
- How should women act in public? Is this different from the way men should act?
- If your wife made an Islamic or social faux pas, how would you handle it?
- Is it possible for men and women to be "just friends?" Do you have friends of the opposite sex?
- What are your thoughts about having friends of the opposite sex? Is it alright to interact with them at work or school? At work-related social functions? At the mosque?
- Do you want to express affection in public after marriage? What is okay and not okay?
- Do you suffer from any addictions (gambling, pornography, gaming, television, etc.)?

Friends

- Who are your closest friends? What do you like to do together?
- How did you meet your closest friends?
- What will your relationship with your friends be like after marriage?
- What relationship do you want your spouse to have with your friends?
- If your friends came over, how would you entertain them? How do you expect your wife to interact (or not) with your friends?

- Would you be comfortable with your wife having her friends over? How would you interact (or not) with your wife's friends?

Gender Roles

- Why do you want to get married?
- What is the role of a wife at home? What specific duties does she have?
- What is the role of a husband at home? What specific duties does he have?
- Is it acceptable for your wife to work outside the home? Is it acceptable for her to stay home? Whose decision is this?

Logistics

- I don't have a mahram, family member, or advisor to help with this process. Do you know of a respected imam who could fill this role? If not, how can we create trust and accountability in the absence of a *walī*?
- How do you see the "Islamic dating" process in general? Phone calls, chaperones, texting, emails, in-person visits, being alone together? Dos and don'ts?
- What is your approximate timeline from getting to know someone to getting married?
- Are we talking to each other exclusively?
- Are you willing to attend premarital counseling sessions together?

Wedding Planning

- How much should our wedding cost? Who will pay for it?
- What is an appropriate dowry given our ages, financial means, and backgrounds?
- Are you willing to have conditions in our Islamic marriage contract?
- Are you willing to grant me the verbal right of divorce in my marriage contract?
- Would you marry a second wife under any circumstances? How do you feel about having stipulations regarding this in our marriage contract?
- What would you like your wedding to look like? Cultural? Western? Hybrid? Very simple?
- Will your family be involved in the wedding planning? If so, how much?

- Where will the wedding take place?

Family Planning

- Do you have any children?
- How many children would you like to have? How soon?
- How would you feel if I decided I didn't want to have any children or wanted just one? What about adoption or foster care?
- Do you believe that it is obligatory to have children?
- What is your position on birth control? Hormonal? Natural methods?
- What is your position on abortion? Would you support aborting a fetus if the doctors believed it was the only way to save your wife's life or preserve her health?

Child Rearing

- If both spouses are working, how will we handle child care (babysitter, nanny, maid, family help)?
- Should a wife stay home when the children are young?
- What role will you play in your children's lives? What will your relationship with them be like?
- How do you want to handle schooling for your children (homeschool, private, public, co-op, charter)?
- How will you approach teaching your children Arabic? Your native tongue? Do you want your children to be bilingual?
- How will you approach teaching your children Quran? Providing them with an Islamic education?

Difficult Issues

- How will you discipline your children? How will you punish them?
- If we have a daughter and she doesn't want to wear hijab, how would you handle that?
- How would you deal with a son/daughter who is in a romantic relationship? What if it were with a non-Muslim? A son/daughter who wants birth control?

- How would you deal with a son/daughter who identifies as a member of the LGBTQIA+ community?
- How would you deal with a son/daughter who wants to get married at a very young age? A son/daughter who wants to go to college far from home?
- How would we deal with differences of opinion between us and my ex-husband?
- Do you believe in the use of corporal punishment?
- Inevitably, we will have different practices or opinions on at least some issues of *fiqh* or *ʿaqīda*. How will we discuss or handle those differences, especially in regard to children?

Finances

- What do you expect from your wife financially?
- How do you wish to handle our finances together? Will we have a joint or separate bank accounts? Who is responsible for paying for what? Who will handle the budget?

Issues around Interest

- I have student loan debt. Are you alright with that? Do you prefer that I'm solely responsible, or would you be willing to pay it off together?
- Do you have any debt? How much? From what? How are you handling that? Do you expect us to pay off your debt jointly, or will you be solely responsible?
- Do you use Western-style banking? Do you have a savings account?
- What are your thoughts on Western-style home/renter's/life/car/health insurance?
- Would you buy a house or car if you were charged interest?
- What do you think of modern, "sharia compliant" financial products as they're commonly understood today, such as Islamic investments and mortgages?

Spending, Saving, Strategizing

- How do you manage your money? Do you have a budget? If so, is it really strict or general?

- What is your current salary?
- Are you comfortable with my salary/anticipated salary range?
- What are your financial goals? What do you consider a comfortable income for a married couple? For a couple with X number of children?

Hobbies

- Do you like to travel? Is it acceptable for one spouse to travel without the other? For work? For leisure?
- How do you spend your free time? Hobbies? Interests?
- Do you enjoy cooking?
- Do you like going out to eat? What if the restaurant doesn't exclusively serve halal meat or serves alcohol?
- Do you listen to music? What type of music? How would you feel if your wife listened to music?
- Are you a gamer? What kinds? How would you feel if your wife or children played video games?
- Do you watch TV/movies? What kinds? What is appropriate for your wife and children to watch?
- If your wife would prefer not to have cable TV at home, how would you feel about that?
- Is it okay to have a cat at home? Are you allergic? Feelings on other pets? How do you feel about dogs?

Health

- Are you willing to take a medical exam before marriage? (Note: In this day and age, both spouses should have STD tests before marriage and share the results with each other. Some STDs are symptomless, and they don't necessarily mean a person has been engaging in haram activities. It is possible that a previous spouse cheated without the person's knowledge.)
- Do you have any physical limitations, chronic pain, or discomfort that I should know about?
- Are you currently or have you in the past been diagnosed with a mental illness (including depression and addiction)? If so, what mental illness do you or did you suffer from? Do you have a current treatment plan? Do you have difficulty sticking to it?

- How do you support your own health and nutrition? How important is it for you to stay healthy? To eat healthy?
- Do you exercise regularly?
- How important is it that your spouse stays in shape? How would you feel if your wife gained weight due to pregnancy or illness?

Political Views/Social Outlook

- What are your views on the political situations in Syria, Egypt, Palestine?
- Do you vote in the US? Who did you vote for?
- Are you, or would you be, active in organizations such as CAIR?
- Do you prefer certain radio/TV/web news sources? Which do you dislike?

*Andrea Cluck Annaba was raised in Bernie, Missouri, a town of just under 2,000 residents near the border of Arkansas. Growing up in a predominately Caucasian, Protestant area, Andrea became interested in learning about other cultures when she started attending Truman State University in Kirksville, Missouri. She met and asked questions of the few Muslim students there, in addition to minoring in religious studies. Moved by what she learned, Andrea converted to Islam in 2005 and decided to pursue an academic career in Islamic Studies.

In 2012, Andrea completed an M.A. in religion at the University of Georgia. Her master's thesis is titled "Islamophobia in the Post-9/11 United States: Causes, Manifestations, and Solutions." While attending the University of Georgia, Andrea worked as a graduate instructor. "As an instructor, my impact was limited to those students in my class," she said. "As a librarian, I'll have a broader impact via providing resources to the entire campus."

While at UMSI, Andrea earned an SI Merit Scholarship and an ISF-University of Michigan Muslim Alumni Scholarship. She was also awarded a Foreign Language and Area Studies fellowship from the Department of Education to study Arabic at UM's Summer Language Institute where she completed the equivalent of a year's study in eight weeks.

Later, Andrea became an integral part of the Rabata organization - as a volunteer admin, an archivist, a student, convert supporter and dear friend.

Andrea joined the Ribaat Academic Institute as a student in 2012, taking over 35 courses until she returned to Allah in 2020. She was on track to complete the Islamic Studies Teacher Certification with Ribaat's first graduating cohort.

"My long-term goal is to obtain a teaching certificate through Ribaat. It's particularly important to me to be able to help converts keep a firm foothold in Islam," she said during her Student of the Month interview in 2017. "I feel more joyful and confident as a Muslim woman now, because of the practical and spiritual knowledge I have gained. The support system from my fellow classmates and teachers is so helpful too. Thank you, Ribaat, for being a part of my life!"

Rabata plans to honor Andrea's legacy as a da'iya by establishing the Andrea Scholarship Fund. Donations will be added to an endowment to cover Ribaat tuition and retreat expenses for convert women who apply to complete the Islamic Studies Teacher Certification.

Andrea's memory is cherished by her husband, Fadi Annaba, 3 step-children, and daughter Noura.

Appendix B

RESOURCES

A Few Top Hits

Books

1. *Joy Jots: Exercises for a Happy Heart*, second edition by Tamara Gray
2. *Being Muslim: A Practical Guide* by Asad Tarsin, with foreword by Hamza Yusuf

Websites

1. Rabata.org - Rabata promotes positive cultural change through creative educational experiences. We focus on helping Muslim women live their faith with joy and confidence, and focus on education, upbringing, and community building. Our website features, among many other things, links to the Ribaat women's seminary, Daybreak Press bookshop and publishing company, and free Leadership and Legacy curriculum resources. You can sign up for a worship thread, register for a retreat, or enroll your children in the Dragonflies program or hook your teen up with RabaTeens.
2. Seekersguidance.org – Traditional scholars providing access to learning for both men and women and an extensive library of fiqh questions, rulings, and discussions
3. Yaqeeninstitute.org – A collection of scholarly articles on topics such as Islam and science, politics, philosophy, etc. Yaqeen also carries lecture videos and provides other spiritual enrichment opportunities.

Places to Find Articles and blogs

1. The files section of the Muslim Women's Convert Circle Facebook Group - a project of Rabata – includes a plethora of articles on everything from the death of a non-Muslim loved one to dogs and Islam to poems and songs about the Prophet ﷺ. https://www.facebook.com/groups/MuslimWomenConvertCircle/ (MWCC is a private group so you will have to request to join.)
2. Muslim Matters is a rich resource for articles on Islam, Society, Life, Culture, and Current Affairs, written by contributors from all over. They also have podcasts.
3. Tails of Faith and Love: Sailing through the Seas of Middle Age on the Ship of Faith https://tailsoffaithandlove.com Poignant, thoughtful articles on being a Muslim, being a woman, being a person. And animals, of course.

Digital communities

1. The Muslim Women's Convert Circle is heralded by members as the safest place on the web for converts to get real and keep it real. It is a moderated Facebook group that offers deep sisterhood, nurtures an akhira-focused attitude, and explores challenging issues without inviting members to have coffee and tea with their bitter feelings.
2. Rabata regional threads

Resources for times of crisis

1. Khalil Center - A project of the Zakat Foundation, The Khalil Center offers counseling, psychiatric services, immigration evaluations, pre-marital counseling and much more. khalilcenter.com
2. Karamah Muslim Women Lawyers for Human Rights - KARAMAH is a nonprofit organization committed to promoting human rights globally, especially gender equity, religious freedom and civil rights in the United States. It pursues its mission through education, legal outreach and advocacy. karamah.org
3. CAIR: Council on American-Islamic relations - CAIR is a nonprofit, grassroots civil rights and advocacy organization. It is America's largest

Muslim civil liberties organization, with affiliate offices nationwide. cair.com

Podcasts

1. Joy Jots podcast and associated book club - available on the Telegram app.
2. ImanWire: Spirituality in a Modern Context - Podcast and articles on topics from racism to spiritually sound and inspiring financial advice. almadinainstitute.org/blog/

Appendix C

SALAT AND *DU'Ā'S* FOR PARENTS

Salat Birr Al Walidain – The Salah of Filial Piety

Very often when one is struggling with family, *ṣalāt birr al-wālidaīn* (The Prayer of Filial Piety)[101] is just what the doctor ordered. The Prophet ﷺ himself recommended this prayer when he said, "Whoever prays two *rak'as* on the eve of Friday between the sunset [*maghrib*] and nightfall [*'ishā'*] prayers in which he recites:

> "My father (may Allah Most High have mercy upon him) said, '... It is mentioned in *Sharḥ al-Sharī'ah*: "The prayer for one's parents [*ṣalat birr al-walidaīn*] is a *sunnah*, due to the saying of the Prophet (Allah bless him and grant him peace): "Whoever prays two *rak'as* on the eve of Friday between the sunset [*maghrib*] and nightfall [*'ishā'*] prayers in which he recites:

The Fatiḥa (Q. 1) once and,

- *Ayat al-Kursi* (Q. 2:255) fifteen times [i.e. in the first *rak'a*],
- *Qul huwa Allahu aḥad* (Q. 112) fifteen times in the second *rak'a*, and
- Sends benedictions upon the Prophet ﷺ twenty-five times after completion of the prayer, *and intends that the reward of this ṣalāh be for his parents*

will have fulfilled the rights of his parents and will have perfected his filial piety, even if he was undutiful towards them when they were alive. Allah Most High will bestow upon him that which He bestows upon those of great faith and the martyrs." (This has been mentioned in the abridgement of Imam al-Ghazālī's *Iḥyā' 'Ulūm al-Dīn*)

It is also recommended to recite the "Supplication of Courtesy to Parents" *du'ā' birr al-walidaīn* after the ṣalah of filial piety:

Supplication of Filial Piety

Muḥammad b. Aḥmad b. Abū-l Ḥibb al-Ḥaḍramī al-Tarīmī (d. 611 H)

Praise be to Allah, who commanded us to thank parents and to treat them well, and enjoined us to seek every opportunity to be courteous with them and to do good in their presence. He obliged us to lower the wing of mercy upon them out of exaltation and esteem, and He counseled us to show compassion towards them just as they did toward us in our infancy.

O Allah, be merciful with our parents (3 times), forgive them, and be content with them in a manner that permits Your divine pleasure for them, by virtue of which You grant them the abode of Your generosity and security, and the regions of Your pardon and forgiveness. Drench them in the subtleties of Your goodness and of Your perfect extension of beauty.

O Allah, forgive them in an all-comprehensive manner that effaces their past sins and evil. Bestow upon them a kind of mercy through which their final resting abodes are illuminated and by virtue of which they are shielded on the day of Judgement when they are resurrected.

O Allah, show compassion when they exhibit weaknesses, just as they showed much compassion to us in our times of weaknesses. Be merciful to them when they break ties with You, just as they showed immense mercy to us when we broke ties with them. Care for them just as they ardently cared for us when we were young.

O Allah, preserve the love that You poured into their hearts, the compassion that You filled their chests with, and the kindness that You occupied their limbs with. Reward them for the efforts they exerted for our sake. Recompense them for the struggles they underwent for our sake, and for the care they displayed towards us.

Let it be a recompense that exceeds what is given to those who strive to rectify and to those who are sincere in their care and concern. O Allah, be good to them over and above the good that they showered upon us, and gaze upon them with the eye of mercy just as they used to lovingly look at us.

O Allah, grant them what they omitted from the rights of Your mercy due to their preoccupation with the rights of our upbringing. Overlook their deficiencies in true service to You due to their desire for being in our service. Pardon them for the doubtful matters they indulged in for the mere purpose of earning enough

دعاء بِرِّ الْوَالِدَيْنِ

محمد بن أحمد بن ابو الحب الحضرمي التميمي

الْحَمْدُ لِلهِ الَّذِي أَمَرَنَا بِشُكْرِ الْوَالِدَيْنِ وَالإِحْسَانِ إِلَيْهِمَا، وَحَثَّنَا عَلَى اغْتِنَامِ بِرِّهِمَا، وَاصْطِنَاعِ الْمَعْرُوفِ لَدَيْهِمَا، وَنَدَبَنَا إِلَى خَفْضِ الْجَنَاحِ مِنَ الرَّحْمَةِ لَهُمَا، إِعْظَاماً وإِكْبَاراً، وَوَصَّانَا بِالتَّرَحُّمِ عَلَيْهِمَا كَمَا رَبَّيَانَا صِغَاراً.

اللَّهُمَّ فَارْحَمْ وَالِدَيْنَا (٣ مرة) وَاغْفِرْ لَهُمْ وَارْضَ عَنْهُمْ رِضىً تُحِلُّ بِهِ عَلَيْهِمْ رِضْوَانَكَ، وَتُحِلُّهُمْ بِهِ دَارَ كَرَامَتِكَ وَأَمَانَكَ، وَمَوَاطِنَ عَفْوِكَ وَغُفْرَانِكَ، وَأَدِرَّ بِهِ عَلَيْهِمْ لَطَائِفَ بِرِّكَ وَإِحْسَانِكَ.

اللَّهُمَّ اغْفِرْ لَهُمْ مَغْفِرَةً جَامِعَةً، تَمْحُوْ بِهَا سَالِفَ أَوْزَارِهِمْ، وَسَيِّئَ إِصْرَارِهِمْ، وَارْحَمْهُمْ رَحْمَةً تُنِيْرُ لَهُمْ بِهَا الْمَضْجَعَ فِيْ قُبُوْرِهِمْ، وَتُؤَمِّنُهُمْ بِهَا يَوْمَ الْفَزَعِ عِنْدَ نُشُوْرِهِمْ. اللَّهُمَّ تَحَنَّنْ عَلَى ضَعْفِهِمْ كَمَا كَانُوْا عَلَى ضَعْفِنَا مُتَحَنِّنِيْنَ، وَارْحَمِ انْقِطَاعَهُمْ إِلَيْكَ كَمَا كَانُوْا لَنَا فِيْ حَالِ انْقِطَاعِنَا إِلَيْهِمْ رَاحِمِيْنَ، وَتَعَطَّفْ عَلَيْهِمْ كَمَا كَانُوْا عَلَيْنَا فِيْ حَالِ صِغَرِنَا مُتَعَطِّفِيْنَ.

اللَّهُمَّ احْفَظْ لَهُمْ ذَلِكَ الْوُدَّ الَّذِيْ أَشْرَبْتَهُ قُلُوْبَهُمْ وَالْحَنَانَةَ الَّتِي مَلَأْتَ بِهَا صُدُوْرَهُمْ وَاللُّطْفَ الَّذِيْ شَغَلْتَ بِهَا جَوَارِحَهُمْ، وَاشْكُرْ لَهُمْ ذَلِكَ الْجِهَادَ الَّذِيْ كَانُوْا فِيْنَا مُجَاهِدِيْنَ، وَلَا تُضَيِّعَ لَهُمْ ذَلِكَ الاجْتِهَادَ الَّذِيْ كَانُوْا فِيْنَا مُجْتَهِدِيْنَ، وَجَازِهِمْ عَلَى ذَلِكَ السَّعْيِ الَّذِيْ كَانُوْا فِيْنَا سَاعِيْنَ، وَالرَّعْيِ الَّذِيْ كَانُوْا لَنَا رَاعِيْنَ، أَفْضَلَ مَا جَزَيْتَ بِهِ السُّعَاةَ الْمُصْلِحِيْنَ، وَالرُّعَاةَ النَّاصِحِيْنَ. اللَّهُمَّ بِرَّهُمْ أَضْعَافَ مَا كَانُوْا يَبَرُّوْنَنَا، وَانْظُرْ إِلَيْهِمْ بِعَيْنِ الرَّحْمَةِ كَمَا كَانُوْا يَنْظُرُوْنَنَا.

اللَّهُمَّ هَبْ لَهُمْ مَا ضَيَّعُوْا مِنْ حَقِّ رَبُوْبِيَّتِكَ بِمَا اشْتَغَلُوْا بِهِ فِيْ حَقِّ تَرْبِيَتِنَا، وَتَجَاوَزْ عَنْهُمْ مَا قَصَّرُوْا فِيْهِ مِنْ حَقِّ خِدْمَتِكَ بِمَا آثَرُوْنَا بِهِ فِيْ حَقِّ خِدْمَتِنَا، وَاعْفُ عَنْهُمْ

for us. Do not take them to account for their prejudice due to the passionate rage that overcame their hearts because of their love for us. Bear the wrongs that they committed due to the sins perpetrated on our behalf and that they sought after for our sake. Be gentle with them in a place where one withers, in a manner that far exceeds their gentleness with us whilst they were alive.

O Allah, any acts of obedience that You have guided us unto, and any good deeds that You have facilitated for us, and any acts of endearment that You have decreed for us, we beseech You, O Allah, that You grant them a portion and a fair share of it. And whatever evil we have committed, or wrongs that we have earned, or consequential misdeeds that we have burdened ourselves with, we implore You that You do not attribute our sins to them nor take them to account for any of our misdeeds. O Allah, just as You made them happy with us in life, then make them happy with us after death.

O Allah, do not allow news about us that would cause them sorrow to reach them, and do not burden them with our sins that weigh heavily upon them, and do not allow us to disgrace them in front of the army of the dead through the shameful acts that we have innovated, and the reprehensible deeds we have done. Make their spirits happy with our deeds in the assembly of souls, just as the righteous are prone to be happy with the children of righteousness. Do not gather them on the plains of exposure because of the evil sins that we commit.

O Allah, whatever recitations that we recited that You purified, or prayer that we prayed that You accepted, or charity that we expended that You made flourish, or good deeds that we performed that You were content with, we entreat You, O Allah, that You make their fair share of it greater than our share, their portion of it larger than our portion, and their lot more abundant than our lot, as You have indeed commanded us to treat them well and be thankful to them, although You are more deserving of goodness than those who do good and more right to maintain ties with than those commanded.

O Allah, make us the coolness of their eyes on the day witnesses take the stand, and allow them to hear from us the most beautiful call on the day of the call. Make them, due to us, parents who are the object of aspiration because of their progeny, until You gather us, them, and Muslims, all together, in the abode of Your generosity, and the dwelling of Your mercy, and the place of those You have befriended [awliyâ], alongside those whom You have blessed amongst the Prophets, the Veracious, the Martyrs, and the Righteous. And what magnificent company they are!

"Exalted is your Lord, the Lord of Might, far beyond their descriptions of Him. And peace be upon the Messengers. And praise be to Allah, Lord of (all) the Worlds. (37:180-182)"

مَـا ارْتَكَـبُوْا مِـنَ الشُّبُهَاتِ مِنْ أَجْـلِ مَـا اكْتَسَـبُوْا مِـنْ أَجْلِنَـا، وَلَا تُؤَاخِذْهُـمْ بِمَـا دَعَتْهُمْ إِلَيْـهِ الْحَمِيَّـةُ مِـنَ الْهَـوَى لِمَـا غَلَـبَ عَلَى قُلُوْبِهِـمْ مِـنْ مَحَبَّتِنَا، وَتَحَمَّـلْ عَنْهُـمُ الظُّلُمَـاتِ الَّتِي ارْتَكَبُوْهَـا فِيْمَـا اجْتَرَحُـوْا لَنَـا وَسَـعَوْا عَلَيْنَـا، وَالْطُـفْ بِهِـمْ فِيْ مَضَاجِـعِ الْبَـلَى لُطْفـاً يَزِيْـدُ عَلَى لُطْفِهِـمْ فِيْ أَيَّـامِ حَيَاتِهِـمْ بِنَا.

اللَّهُـمَّ وَمَـا هَدَيْتَنَـا لَهُ مِـنَ الطَّـاعَاتِ، وَيَسَّرْتَهُ لَنَا مِـنَ الْحَسَـنَاتِ، وَوَفَّقْتَنَـا لَهُ مِـنَ الْقُرُبَاتِ، فَنَسْـأَلُكَ اللَّهُـمَّ أَنْ تَجْعَـلَ لَهُـمْ مِنْهَا حَظّـاً وَنَصِيْبـاً، وَمَا اقْتَرَفْنَـاهُ مِنَ السَّـيِّئَاتِ، واكْتَسَـبْنَاهُ مِـنَ الْخَطِيْئَـاتِ، وَتَحَمَّلْنَـاهُ مِـنَ التَّبِعَـاتِ، فَـلَا تُلْحِقْهُـمْ مِنَّا بِذَلِـكَ حُوْبـاً، وَلَا تَحْمِـلْ عَلَيْهِمْ مِـنْ ذُنُوْبِنَا ذُنُوْبـاً. اللَّهُـمَّ وَكَمَـا سَرَرْتَهُـمْ بِنَـا فِيْ الْحَيَـاةِ، فَسُرَّهُمْ بِنَـا بَعْـدَ الْوَفَاةِ.

اللَّهُـمَّ وَلَا تُبَلِّغْهُـمْ مِـنْ أَخْبَارِنَـا مَـا يَسُـوْؤُهُمْ، وَلَا تُحَمِّلْهُـمْ مِـنْ أَوْزَارِنَـا مَـا يَنوْؤُهُـمْ، وَلَا تُخْزِهِـمْ بِنَـا فِيْ عَسْـكَرِ الْأَمْـوَاتِ بِمَـا نُحْدِثُ مِـنَ الْمُخْزِيَـاتِ، وَنَـأْتِيْ مِـنَ الْمُنْكَـرَاتِ، وَسُرَّ أَرْوَاحَهُـمْ بِأَعْمَالِنَـا فِيْ مُلْتَـقَى الْأَرْوَاحِ، إِذَا سُرَّ أَهْـلَ الصَّـلَاحِ بِأَبْنَـاءِ الصَّـلَاحِ، وَلَا تَقِفْهُـمْ مِنَّـا عَلَى مَوْقِـفِ افْتِضَـاحٍ، بِمَـا نَجْـتَرِحُ مِـنْ سُـوْءِ الْاجْـتِرَاحِ. اللَّهُـمَّ وَمَـا تَلَوْنَـا مِـنْ تِـلَاوَةٍ فَزَكَّيْتَهَـا، وَمَـا صَلَّيْنَـا مِـنْ صَـلَاةٍ فَتَقَبَّلْتَهَـا، وَمَـا تَصَدَّقْنَـا مِـنْ صَدَقَـةٍ فَنَمَّيْتَهَـا، وَمَـا عَمِلْنَـا مِـنْ أَعْمَـالٍ صَالِحَـةٍ فَرَضِيْتَهَـا، فَنَسْـأَلُكَ اللَّهُـمَّ أَنْ تَجْعَـلَ حَظَّهُـمْ مِنْهَـا أَكْـبَرَ مِـنْ حُظُوْظِنَـا، وَقِسْـمَهُمْ مِنْهَـا أَجْـزَلَ مِـنْ أَقْسَـامِنَا، وَسَـهْمَهُمْ مِـنْ ثَوَابِنَـا أَوْفَـرَ مِـنْ سِـهَامِنَا، فَإِنَّـكَ وَصَّيْتَنَـا بِبِرِّهِـم، وَنَدَبْتَنَـا إِلَى شُـكْرِهِمْ، وَأَنْـتَ أَوْلَى بِالْـبِرِّ مِـنَ الْبَارِّيْنَ، وَأَحَـقُّ بِالْوَصْلِ مِـنَ الْمَأْمُوْرِيْـنَ.

اللَّهُـمَّ اجْعَلْنَـا لَهُـمْ قُـرَّةَ أَعْـيُنٍ يَـوْمَ يَقُـوْمُ الْأَشْـهَادُ، وَاَسْـمِعْهُمْ مِنَّـا أَطْيَـبَ النِّـدَاءِ يَـوْمَ التَّنَـادِ، وَاجْعَلْهُـمْ بِنَـا مِـنْ أَغْبَـطِ الْآبَـاءِ بِـالْأَوْلَادِ، حَـتَّى تَجْمَعَنَـا وَإِيَّاهُـمْ وَالْمُسْلِمِيْنَ جَمِيْعـاً فِيْ دَارِ كَرَامَتِـكَ، وَمُسْـتَقَرِّ رَحْمَتِـكَ، وَمَحَـلِّ أَوْلِيَائِـكَ، مَـعَ الَّذِيْـنَ أَنْعَمْـتَ عَلَيْهِـمْ مِـنَ النَّبِيِّـيْنَ وَالصِّدِّيْقِـيْنَ وَالشُّـهَدَاءِ وَالصَّالِحِيْنَ، وَحَسُـنَ أُوْلَئِـكَ رَفِيْقـاً، ذَلِـكَ الْفَضْـلُ مِنَ اللهِ وَكَـفَى بِـاللهِ عَلِيْمـاً، سُـبْحَانَ رَبِّـكَ رَبِّ الْعِـزَّةِ عَمَّـا يَصِفُـوْنَ، وَسَـلَامٌ عَلَى الْمُرْسَـلِيْنَ، وَالْحَمْـدُ لِلّٰهِ رَبِّ الْعَالَمِـيْنَ.

(تَمَّتْ)

NOTES

1 It was after reading Gabriele Marranci's discussion of "feeling to be a Muslim" and "feelings of Muslimness" in his book, *The Anthropology of Islam* (Oxford and New York: Berg, 2008). My usage of "*feeling* Muslim" increased after reading Anne Sofie Roald's essay, "The Shaping of Scandinavian 'Islam': Converts and Gender Equal Opportunity" in the anthology *Women Embracing Islam* by Karin van Nieuwkerk (Austin, Texas: University of Texas Press, 2006). To my knowledge, Roald is the first to show a female convert to Islam stating that she does not "feel herself to be a Muslim."

2 See Lewis Rambo's incredible book, *Understanding Religious Conversion* (New Haven, CT: Yale University Press, 1995).

3 Mohammed al-Ghazzali, Al-Ghazzali *on Knowing Yourself and God*, tr. Muhammad Nur Abdus Salam (Chicago: Great Books of the Islamic World, 2010).

4 ʿAbdullah ibn ʿAbd al-ʿAziz al-ʿAqil, "ʿArif nafsaka taʿrif rabbaka" [Know Yourself and Know Your Lord], Islamway.net, August 9, 2008, https://ar.islamway.net/fatwa/22841/اعرف-نفسك-تعرف-ربك.

5 Zainab Abaid, "Dyeing Ourselves in the Color of Allah," Farhat Hashmi, https://www.farhathashmi.com/articles-section/remembrance/dyeing-ourselves/.

6 Tamara Gray, *Joy Jots*, 2nd ed. (Minnesota: Daybreak Press, 2019), 68.

7 "Marriage and Divorce Data," Centers for Disease Control and Prevention, https://www.cdc.gov/nchs/nvss/marriage-divorce.htm?CDC_AA_refVal=https%3A%2F%2Fwww.cdc.gov%2Fnchs%2Fmardiv.htm.

8 "Child Abuse Statistics & Facts," Childhelp, http://www.childhelp.org/child-abuse-statistics/.

9 Children's Bureau of the U.S. Department of Health and Human Services, "Child Maltreatment 2014," 2016, https://www.acf.hhs.gov/sites/default/files/cb/cm2014.pdf, 11.

10 "The Majority of Children Live with Two Parents, Census Bureau Reports," United States' Census Bureau, November 17, 2016, https://www.census.gov/newsroom/press-releases/2016/cb16-192.html.

11 "Child Poverty in America 2017: National Analysis," Children's Defense Fund, September 12, 2018, https://www.childrensdefense.org/wp-content/uploads/2018/09/Child-Poverty-in-America-2017-National-Fact-Sheet.pdf.

12 "Lone Parents with Dependent Children by Marital Status of Parent, by Sex, UK: 1996 to 2015," Office for National Statistics, April 26, 2016, https://www.ons.gov.uk/peoplepopulationandcommunity/birthsdeathsandmarriages/families/adhocs/005660loneparentswithdependentchildrenbymaritalstatusofparentbysexuk1996to2015.

13 "Households below Average Income: 1994/95 to 2017/18," GOV.UK, March 28, 2019, https://www.gov.uk/government/statistics/households-below-average-income-199495-to-201718.

14 Mary Pipher, Reviving *Ophelia: Saving the Selves of Adolescent Girls* (New York: Riverhead, 2005).

15 Pipher.

16 Samira al-Zayid, *A Compendium of the Sources on the Prophetic Narrative*, trans. Susan Imady, Tamara Gray, and Randa Mardini (Minnesota: Daybreak Press, 2018), 59, 86.

17 Asma Tabaa, *Stars in the Prophet's Orbit*, trans. Sawsan Tarabishy (Damascus: Publisher, 2012), 71.

18 *Musnad Aḥmad*, bk. 6, hadith 39, *ṣaḥiḥ*.

19 *Al-Ṭabaqāt al-Kubrā*, 3:155.

20 Samira Zayid, *al-Sira al-Nabawiyya* (Damascus: n.d.), 1:518–19.

21 *Ṣaḥīḥ al-Bukhārī*, no. 3374; *Ṣaḥīḥ Muslim*, no. 2378, *ṣaḥiḥ*.

22 Samira al-Zayid, *Mukhtaṣir al-Jāmiʿ fi al-Sīra al-Nabawiyya* (Damascus: n.d.).

23 Carl Jung, *Modern Man in Search of a Soul* (City: Harcourt, 1955). p. 261.

24 David Keirsey, *Please Understand Me II: Temperament, Character and Intelligence* (USA: Prometheus Nemesis Book Company, 1998).

25 Derived from Sandra Krebs Hirsh and Jane A. G. Kise, *Looking at Type and Spirituality* (Center for Applications of Psychological Type, 1997) and Sandra Krebs Hirsh and Jane A. G. Kise, *Soul Types: Finding the Spiritual Path that Is Right for You* (New York: Hyperion, 1998).

26 Samira Zayid, *al-Mufid fi Bayan ʿAqida al-Tawhid* (Damascus:, n.d.), 17.

27 Al-Zayid, *Prophetic Narrative*, 281.

28 *Ṣaḥīḥ al-Bukhārī*, no. 5997, narrated by Abū Hurayra.

29 Abdal Hakim Murad, "British and Muslim?," Masud.co.uk, http://www.masud.co.uk/ISLAM/ahm/british.htm.

30 Popular television personality and psychologist Dr. Phil McGraw is well-known for using this phrase in his books and broadcasts.

31 Code of Canon Law, #855, http://www.vatican.va/archive/ENG1104/_P2V.HTM.

32 Joe Bradford, "What's in a Name? Or Why You Don't Have To and Shouldn't Change Your Name in Islam," *Joe Bradford* (blog), January 3, 2012, https://www.joebradford.net/change-name-islam/.

33 Bradford.

34 *Sīrah Ibn Hisham*, 1:172 and Abū Naʿim, *Dalaʾil al-Nubuwwa*, 1:173.

35 *Sīrah Ibn Hisham* and Dala'il al-Nubuwwa.

36 It is said: "The Prophet ﷺ was born circumcised; in other words, his foreskin was cut away." There is a difference of opinion amongst hadith scholars about this hadith's authenticity. There are those who say it is *daʿif*, those who say it is *ṣaḥiḥ*, and others who say it is *ḥasan*. Of these is what is narrated from Anas ibn Malik that the Prophet ﷺ said, "Of the favors of my Lord upon me was that I was born circumcised and thus none saw me uncircumcised." See Abū Naʿim, *Dalaʾil al-Nubuwwa*, 1:192 and *Sharh al-Zurqani ʿala al-Muwahib*, 1:124.

37 See: Ibn al-Qayyim al-Jawziyya, *Zad al-Ma'ad*, 1:82 and al-Bayhaqi, *Dala'il al-Nubuwwa* (City: Publisher, year), 1:113.

38 Al-Zayid, *Prophetic Narrative*, 59, 86.

39 Al-Zayid, *Prophetic Narrative*, 59, 86.

40 Al-Zayid, *Prophetic Narrative*, 462.

41 A convert friend of mine had a brilliant theory about this particular attitude in Muslim countries that had been colonized and were then left to fend for their economic selves. She theorized that there was a culture of "there might not be enough for me" because, indeed, many times there had not been enough gas, heating oil, sugar, lemons, or bread. And thus, there was a cultural and society-wide anxiety about waiting your turn. After all, there was a real chance that your turn would never come.

42 Abū Qatada al-Anṣārī reported that the Messenger of God ﷺ said when asked about fasting on Mondays, "On (that day) I was born and on it Revelation came down to me." *Ṣaḥīḥ Muslim*, no. 1162.

43 For example, Ka'b ibn Zuhair, who recited beautiful lines about the Prophet ﷺ in Medina after his conversion

44 Ibn Jawzi, *Bayan al-Milad al-Nabawi*, 58.

45 Alan Watts, Goodreads, https://www.goodreads.com/quotes/122460-we-seldom-realize-for-example-that-our-most-private-thoughts.

46 Asma Tabaa, *Stars in the Prophet's Orbit*, trans. Sawsan Tarabishy (Damascus: 2012).

47 Edward William Lane, *Arabic-English Lexicon* (Cambridge: Islamic Texts Society, 2003), 1744.

48 Arabic Lexicon, s.v. "picture," by Ibn Manzur, http://arabiclexicon.hawramani.com/search/picture.

49 *Oxford American Dictionary*, s.v. "imam," computer application.

50 Halimah Krausen, correspondence with author, 2019.

51 Arabic Lexicon, s.v. "imam," by al-Manawi, http://lisaan.net/search/imam.

52 *Oxford American Dictionary*, s.v. "sheikh," computer application.

53 Arabic Lexicon, s.v. "شيخ," by Ibn Manzur, http://arabiclexicon.hawramani.com/search/شيخ.

54 Arabic Lexicon, s.v. "شيخ."

55 Arabic Lexicon, s.v. "شيخ."

56 Swathi Shanmugasundaram, "Anti-Sharia Law Bills in the United States," Southern Poverty Law Center, February 5, 2018, https://www.splcenter.org/hatewatch/2018/02/05/anti-sharia-law-bills-united-states.

57 A hadith wherein the meaning is directly from God but the phrasing is from the Prophet ﷺ.

58 *Ṣaḥīḥ al-Bukhārī*, https://sunnah.com/qudsi40/25.

59 Zakat is only *farḍ* for those who have a certain amount of savings or property.

60 "The Resolutions and Recommendations of the Ninth Annual Conference of the Assembly of Muslim Jurists on Permissible and Impermissible Foods and Medicines in Non-Muslim Lands," Assembly of Muslim Jurists of America, 2020.

61 *Sunan Nisā'i*, no. 4380, *ṣaḥiḥ*.

62 A portion of a longer hadith found in the following collections: al-Nawawi, Sunan Abū Dawud, Sunan Ibn Mājah, and others, *Ḥasan-ṣaḥīḥ*.

63 Muhammad Jurdani, *al-Jawahir al-Lulu'iyya fi Sharḥ al-Arba'in al-Nawawiyya*.

64 'Izz al-Dīn ibn 'Abd al-Salām, *Qawa'id al-Aḥkām fī Maṣāliḥ al-Anām* (1968).

65 *Ṣaḥīḥ al-Bukhāri*, *Ṣaḥīḥ Muslim*, *ṣaḥiḥ*.

66 D. H. Lawrence, *The Plumed Serpent* (New York: Alfred Knopf, 1979).

67 Al-Ḥākim, *al-Mustadrak*, *ḍa'īf*.

68 Norman Doidge, *The Brain That Changes Itself: Stories of Personal Triumph from the Frontiers of Brain Science* (New York: Viking Press, 2007).

69 *Mujma' al-Zawā'id*, narrated by Mu'adh ibn Jabal, some labeled it *ḍa'īf* and others labeled it trustworthy.

70 For example, in *Ṣaḥīḥ Muslim*, "Whoever eats onions, garlic, or leeks should not approach our mosque, for the angels are offended by whatever offends the children of Adam." And in Ibn Hisham, he recounts that the angel dispersed when Khadija (may Allah be pleased with her) bared a part of her leg (or hair). Also, there are famous hadiths that mention that angels do not enter houses with dogs (*Ṣaḥīḥ Muslim*), which is understood to be because of their *najāsah* (this hadith would be understood differently by the Malikis).

71 Michael Hart, *The 100: A Ranking of the Most Influential Persons in History* (New York: Citadel Press, 1992).

72 Quran 37:101–108.

73 Samira al-Zayid, *A Compendium of the Sources on the Prophetic Narrative*, trans. Susan Imady, Tamara Gray, and Randa Mardini (Minneapolis: Daybreak Press, 2018), 59, 86.

74 Samira Zayid, *al-Mufid fi Bayan 'Aqida al-Tawḥīd* (Damascus: n.d.).

75 *Musnad Ahmad*.

76 *Ṣaḥīḥ al-Bukhārī*, no. 6503, narrated by Sahl ibn Sa'd.

77 *Musnad Aḥmad*, narrated by 'Abdullāh ibn 'Amr.

78 *Ṣaḥīḥ Muslim*, narrated by Abi Qatada.

79 Samira al-Zayid, *Durus min al-Sira al-Nabawiyya* (Damascus: 2013).

80 *Jami' al-Tirmidhi* and al-Ṭabarānī, narrated by Anas ibn Mālik.

81 *Jami' al-Tirmidhi*, *ṣaḥiḥ*, narrated by Nu'man ibn Bashir.

82 Al-Ghazali, *The Ninety Names Beautiful Names of God* (Cambridge: Islamic Text Society, 1995).

83 Ibn Rajab al-Hanbali, *The Heirs of the Prophets*, trans. Zaid Shakir (Starlatch, 2002), 16.

84 Ibn Rajab al-Hanbali, *The Heirs of the Prophets*, 16.

85 Jennifer Crooker, "Developing a Mature Faith," *Tails of Faith and Love* (blog), December 24, 2019, https://tailsoffaithandlove.com/2019/12/24/the-convert-spirit-tails-for-converts-developing-a-mature-faith/.

86 *Jami' al-Tirmidhī*; *al-Adab al-Mufrad*, no. 594.

87 See Muḥammad b. Aḥmad b. Abū-l Ḥibb al-Ḥaḍramī al-Tarīmī, *Supplication of Courtesy to Parents*, https://www.scribd.com/doc/50677370/Supplication-of-Courtesy-to-Parents.

88 Asma Tabaa, *Stars in the Prophet's Orbit*, trans. Sawsan Tarabish (Damascus: 2012).

89 Tabaa.

90 Tabaa.

91 Tabaa.

92 Ali Gomaa, *Responding from the Tradition: One Hundred Contemporary Fatwas by the Grand Mufti of Egypt*, trans. Tarek Elgawhary and Nuri Friedlander (Louisville, KY: Fons Vitae, 2011), 58.

93 Muhammad ibn Ahmad ibn Abi Sahl Sarakhshi, *Sharh al-Siyar al-Kabir*, as quoted by Gomaa, *Responding from the Tradition*.

94 Samira al-Zayid, *A Compendium of the Sources on The Prophetic Narrative*. V1 Tr. Susan Imady, Tamara Gray, Randa Mardini. (Minnesota: Daybreak Press, 2018), 225.

95 Ralph Waldo Emerson, Essays First Series 1841 retrieved from https://archive.vcu.edu/english/engweb/transcendentalism/authors/emerson/essays/friendship.html.

96 Sunan Abū Dawud, narrated by Abū Hurayra.

97 Ibn Kathīr, 9:71.

98 Samira al-Zayid, *A Compendium of the Sources on The Prophetic Narrative*. V1 Tr. Susan Imady, Tamara Gray, Randa Mardini. (Minnesota: Daybreak Press, 2018), 325.

99 Samira al-Zayid, *A Compendium of the Sources on The Prophetic Narrative*. V1 Tr. Susan Imady, Tamara Gray, Randa Mardini. (Minnesota: Daybreak Press, 2018), 326.

100 https://usso.uk/as-american-as-apple-pie-u-s-female-converts-to-islam/

101 https://www.scribd.com/search?query=al%20ghazali%20salat%20parents.

HIGHLIGHTS

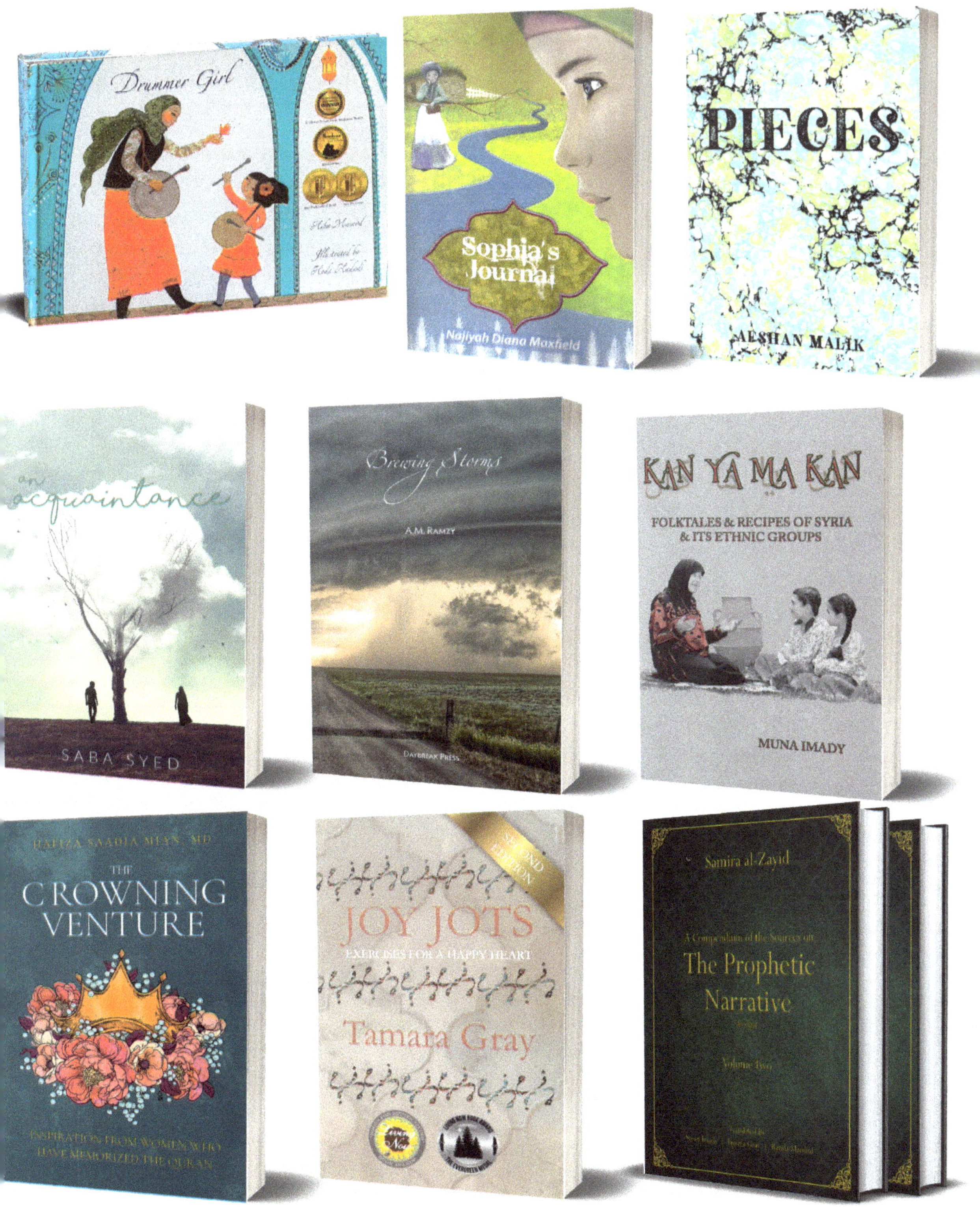

DAYBREAK PRESS

Kan Ya Ma Kan:
Folktales & Recipes of Syria & Its Ethnic Groups
by Muna Imady

978-0999299029 | Paperback | $24.99 | 408 pages

With the terrible civil war raging in Syria, one of Muna Imady's biggest fears was that her country's unique culture would suffer. In particular, she worried that the oral tradition of storytelling, and even the ancient stories themselves, would be lost. The result of her quest to preserve them is this book of folktales and traditional recipes from diverse regions of Syria, handed down through generations, painstakingly collected in numerous interviews, and charmingly retold here.

The Crowning Venture
by Saadia Mian
@saadiamian

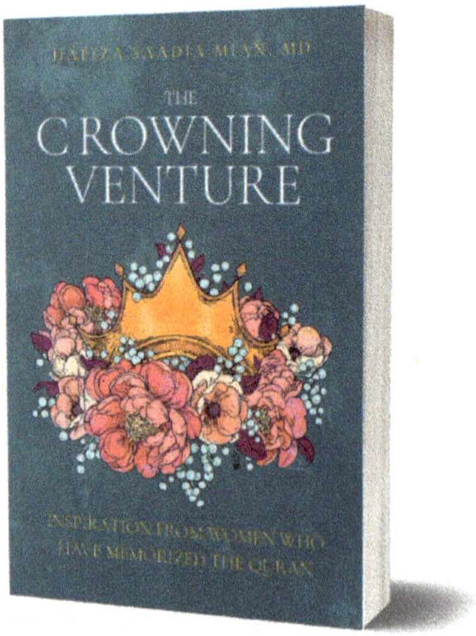

978-0999299036| Paperback | $22.99 | 156 pages

If you've ever sighed wistfully upon hearing of someone memorizing the Quran, wishing it was something you could do, too, then prepare to replace that wistfulness with determination!

Filled with inspirational stories for your heart and memorization techniques for your mind, The Crowning Venture reminds us that memorizing the Quran is not an achievement to be conquered, it's a journey to savor -A journey YOU can make.

Winner: International Book Awards - Religion, General
Finalist: Best Book Awards - Religion General and Religion Eastern
Finalist: International Book Awards - Best Cover Design Non-Fiction

Finalist: Next Generation Indie Book Awards - How-to/-Self-Help/Inspirational, Religion/Spirituality

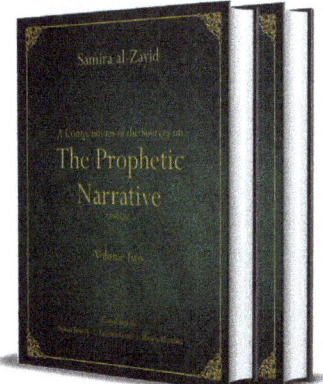

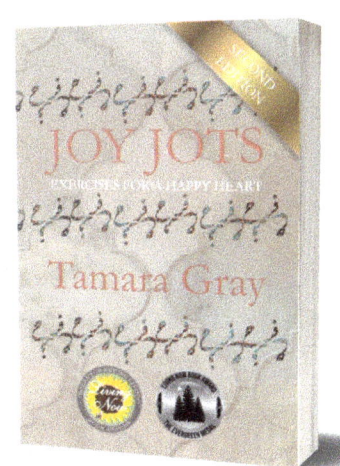

DAYBREAK PRESS

DAYBREAK PRESS

Daybreak Press publishes Muslim women writers in a variety of literary genres and academic fields, bringing to life works that cultivate positive cultural change.

rabata

Our juvenile and YA books tackle challenging issues, provide heartfelt inspiration, and serve as springboards for learning and discussion about many kinds of inclusion, breaking down walls as only literature can, and our nonfiction and academic works deepen the knowledge and enrich the lives of students and others worldwide.

Drummer Girl

by Hiba Masood
illustrated by Hoda Hodadi
@hibamasood

978-0990625971| Hardcover | $19.99 | 28 pages

Year after year, in the blessed month of Ramadan, little Najma has happily arisen to the drum beat of her neighborhood's *musaharati*. He walks through the streets of her small Turkish village, waking each family for the pre-dawn meal before the long day of fasting. Najma wants nothing more than to be a *musaharati* herself one day, but no girl has ever taken on the role. Will she have what it takes to be the drummer girl of her dreams? Find out in this inspirational story of sincerity, determination, and believing in yourself.

Gold Seal Winner in the International Book Awards. Category: Best Picture Book
Gold Seal Winner from the Moonbeam Children's Book Awards. Category: Best Illustrator
Gold Seal Winner from the Literary Classics Awards. Categories: Best Multicultural Book & Best Illustrator

Sophia's Journal
by Najiyah Diana Maxfield
@tellnajiyah

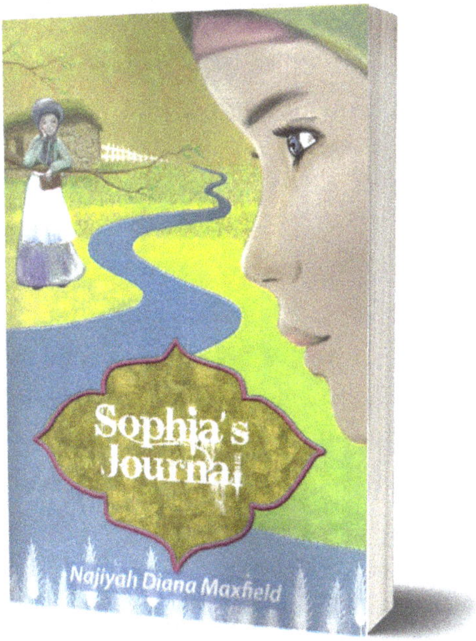

978-0990625902 | Paperback | $12.99 | 300 pages

Sophia's Journal is a fresh take on a pivotal moment in American history. After a bad fall in a river, 16-year-old Sophia suddenly finds herself in nineteenth century Kansas – Bleeding Kansas – right before the Civil War. Soon after her arrival, though, her worries turn from her own mystifying situation to the horrific ones of the slaves and native Americans she meets, and she teams up with her new friend Abby to set some things right. Filled with adventure, romance, and self-discovery, Sophia's Journal offers a glimpse into a world half-forgotten - from a vantage point like no other.

Honorable mention in the Purple Dragonfly Book Awards. Category: Young Adult Fiction

Pieces
by Afshan Malik
@afshanmalikwrites

978-0999299012| Paperback | $19.99 | 184 pages

As if track practice, yearbook meetings, and tumultuous friendships weren't enough, sisters Hannah and Noreen are catapulted into a disorienting new reality when their dad returns home from his medical mission in Syria a haunted and broken man.

All of a sudden, their once tight-knit family is falling to pieces. Little do they know, things will become a lot more crazy and unpredictable as each of them fights a different battle.

An Acquaintance
by Saba Syed (Umm Reem)
@saba_ummreem

978-0999299005| Paperback | $18.95 | 292 pages

The exciting story of a smart, driven young Muslim girl living in small town America who falls for the new guy at her high school. Family and friends misunderstand their developing relationship, and Sarah struggles to be faithful to her moral code. As rumors of misconduct crescendo throughout the school year, what will become of their mere acquaintance...or is it more?

Finalist in the International Book Awards
Category: Young Adult Fiction

Brewing Storms
by AM Ramzy
@amramzy

978-0990625926| Paperback | $9.99 | 98 pages

The stories of men as seeker and teacher abound in the pages of heritage texts and literary works, but the stories of women are rare. Brewing Storms is a collection of poems that offers a window into the spiritual path of one young woman as she navigates her way through the storms of the soul. The poems provide a deep and honest insight into the challenges of growth and spiritual development, along with moments of profound fulfillment experienced along the way.

The beauty of poetry as an art form is that it can touch readers no matter what their path or background, and it is hoped that this collection will speak to those emotions which bind us all: searching, struggle, love, and longing.

DAYBREAK PRESS

Daybreak Press is the publishing arm of Rabata, an international organization dedicated to promoting positive cultural change through creative educational experiences. Daybreak is committed to raising Muslim women's voices by publishing women authors in the genres of poetry, fiction, non-fiction, and academic works. For more information, please visit Rabata.org/Daybreak.

DAYBREAK PRESS

COLOPHON

Project Lina is set in Alegreya that was designed by Juan Pablo del Peral for Huerta Tipográfica. Its elegant qualities make it a highly readable typeface for distinctive, well designed texts. Alegreya Sans was designed by Juan Pablo del Peral for Huerta Tipográfica is used for the headers. Alegreya Sans is a humanist sans serif typeface with a calligraphic feeling that conveys a dynamic and varied rhythm. This gives a pleasant feeling to readers of long texts and stylized headers.

The Arabic font is Uthman Taha Naskh, a digital reinterpretation by the digial team at King Fahd Quran Printing Complex at Medina. It reproduces the beauty of *naskh* calligraphy by one of the masters of this style. The Quranic text used is from the King Fahd Quran Printing Complex at Medina online at: qurancomplex.gov.sa

www.ingramcontent.com/pod-product-compliance
Lightning Source LLC
Chambersburg PA
CBHW061152010526
44118CB00027B/2953
* 9 7 8 0 9 9 9 2 9 9 0 5 0 *